Ethics and Politics after Poststructuralism

D1610504

www.euppublishing.com/series/totp

Ethics and Politics
after Poststructuralism

Levinas, Derrida and Nancy

Madeleine Fagan

EDINBURGH
University Press

For Mum and Dad

Edinburgh University Press is one of the leading
university presses in the UK. We publish academic
books and journals in our selected subject areas across
the humanities and social sciences, combining cutting-
edge scholarship with high editorial and production
values to produce academic works of lasting
importance. For more information visit our website:
edinburghuniversitypress.com

© Madeleine Fagan, 2013, 2016

Edinburgh University Press Ltd
The Tun – Holyrood Road
12(2f) Jackson's Entry
Edinburgh EH8 8PJ

First published in hardback by Edinburgh University Press 2013

Typeset in 11 on 13 Sabon by
Iolaire Typesetting, Newtonmore, and
printed and bound in Great Britain by
CPI Group (UK) Ltd, Croydon CR0 4YY

A CIP record for this book is available from the British Library

ISBN 978 0 7486 8513 4 (hardback)
ISBN 978 1 4744 2050 1 (paperback)
ISBN 978 0 7486 8514 1 (webready PDF)
ISBN 978 0 7486 8516 5 (epub)

Contents

Acknowledgements

This book is based on doctoral research undertaken at the Department of International Politics, University of Wales, Aberystwyth. This was a fantastic environment in which to study: friendly, stimulating and intellectually challenging. I was extremely fortunate in having two outstanding supervisors. Jenny Edkins provided encouragement, guidance, support and inspiration; I cannot thank her enough for her patience and belief, both in me and the thesis. Hidemi Suganami offered close and careful reading of my work and provided a constant stream of challenging questions, which have improved this book's clarity and precision immeasurably. My examiners, Toni Erskine and Véronique Pin-Fat, provided support, encouragement and advice.

I would also like to express my thanks to the Department of Politics at the University of Exeter, where I found companionship and intellectual stimulation in the latter stages of the thesis and early development of the book. My thanks, in particular, to Alan Booth, Sarah Bulmer, Tim Cooper, Tim Dunne, Andy Schaap, Dan Stevens, Nicola Whyte and Colin Wight.

Most recently, I have been fortunate to join the Department of Politics and International Studies and the Institute of Advanced Study at the University of Warwick. The award of a Global Research Fellowship has enabled me to finish the manuscript and to see beyond it. Thanks to Richard Aldrich, James Brassett, Stuart Croft, Chris Hughes, Shirin Rai and Matthew Watson for their collegiality and support.

For friendship, debate, and the sharpening of ideas at crucial stages in the development of this book, I would like to thank Dan Bulley, Laura Guillaume, Emily Jackson, Tom Lundborg, Laura Routley and Maja Zehfuss.

I would also like to thank the series editors, in particular Alex Thomson, and two anonymous reviewers, who provided careful, challenging and encouraging comments, from which the book has benefited greatly. Thanks also to Rogan Collins for patient and efficient editorial assistance in preparing the final manuscript.

Most of all, my thanks go to my family, who have been brilliant. They have provided constant and unconditional emotional, financial and moral support, encouragement and understanding. Finally, Nick has been unfailingly inspirational, encouraging, engaged, patient and supportive. I cannot thank him enough.

Material from Chapter 2 appeared as an article in *Contemporary Political Theory* 8 (2009), 5–22 under the title 'The Inseparability of Ethics and Politics: Rethinking the Third in Emmanuel Levinas' and is reproduced with permission from Palgrave Macmillan.

I would like to express my gratitude to the ESRC for the research studentship that funded the original research on which this book is based.

Introduction
The Politics of Ethical Theory

The Limits of Ethical Theory

Claims about ethics underlie the most pivotal and fundamental debates in contemporary political life. From immigration to climate change, democracy promotion and humanitarian intervention to war and economic policy, political arguments often rest, explicitly or otherwise, on a conception of the good or right. This is a remarkably enduring and seductive way of organising political thought, in which ethics provides the foundation on which arguments are built, as well as the limits to the scope of what is available for argument.

These appeals to ethics in everyday life are very often justified in terms of one or a combination of many theories of ethics, which permeate current dominant understandings of the world – theories of utilitarianism, individualism, rights (of individuals or communities) and so on. Similarly, within the disciplines of Politics and International Relations (IR), appeals to ethics are most commonly employed and interrogated with reference to theories of ethics. Theories of ethics, then, do a great deal of work in contemporary political life, in terms of offering, arguing for and justifying a variety of better ways to proceed.

The broad focus of this investigation is the ways in which theories of ethics and responsibility are, and might be, used in the study of Politics and International Relations. More specifically, the book develops a distinctive analysis of, and theoretical approach to, the relationship between theories of ethics and practical political decisions. In particular, the investigation focuses on the area of so-called 'poststructuralist' approaches to ethics and the way in which these impact on the practical political realm.

The book is motivated initially by very concrete and common concerns. How might we relieve suffering? Should we intervene in the affairs of other states? How can we prevent genocide and how might we best respond to its aftermath? To whom are we responsible? What are our obligations to those both inside and outside our state boundaries? In short, what should we do? How does ethics help us to answer or resolve this question? And, most importantly, is ethics enough to provide satisfactory answers? Can ethical claims and arguments provide any basis for making better political decisions?

The core concern animating the book, then, is what ethical theories can 'do' in terms of practical politics. It seems that most often they are employed to, or have the effect of, providing a foundation from which to launch particular political moves or strategies. This is certainly how the relationship between ethics and politics is often figured in Politics and IR, where a resort to ethical theory is the dominant approach.

However, there is a problem with foundational or theoretical ethics as the basis for politics, which is demonstrated clearly by the way in which, in normal debate and conversation, ethical claims often remain contested and contestable. What is interesting is that, in everyday life, ethical theories are rarely used to back-up ethical-type claims in any consistent way. If we take this seriously, then it seems that ethical theories are not satisfactory, robust or nuanced enough for everyday life. This is not to say that ethical theories have no role in 'everyday' life, but to highlight the way that they are most often used; discussion and debate about 'ethics' occurs at the edges of ethical claims or theories, seeking out situations where they do not 'work', assembling at their limits and focusing on their fissures, fault lines or points of convergence. One clear example of the importance of limits in ethical debate is the way in which exceptional scenarios are often posited as the 'test ground' for ethical theories or positions. In this situation, the important aspects of the ethical theory at stake are to be identified and debated at its limits.

On the one hand, then, the continued invocation of theory or foundations suggests that ethical claims work in a theoretical and foundational way, while, on the other hand, the location of ethical debate at the limits of these theories suggests that something important is left uncaptured by attempts to employ ethics as a theorisable category. This everyday disjuncture points to a problem with thinking about ethics in foundational or theorisable terms.

One example of this kind of limit of theoretical approaches to ethics is the status of the claim that genocide is wrong. Many would be
uncomfortable with arguing that genocide is wrong *because* it violates
fundamental human rights or *because* all killing is wrong or *because*
of any other abstract ethical formula. Something more is going on
here, which is reflected in the very way in which we speak of, debate
and discuss these things. Something very important is missed by
attempts at explaining or looking for grounds for judgement. There
is, we might feel, something which prompts these attempts, whereby
they might be experienced as a response to an ethical impulse which
is prior to the attempts made to explain it theoretically. On the other
hand, however, it is as if we are uncomfortable about making ethical
claims without the security of ethical theories to back them up.

The limits of theoretical approaches become particularly clear, to
stay with the same example, when we then attempt to formulate a
political response to the problem. In a matter so grave, it is important
that the response and policies be right, clearly thought out and based
on secure and defensible foundations. Ethical theories make this much
easier; if genocide is wrong because it violates fundamental human
rights, then what we must do is respect these rights, further their respect
elsewhere, enshrine them in law, even protect and promote them by
use of force and so on. But this promotion of human rights might not
be an entirely satisfactory response. The defensibility of the ethical
foundations for these political decisions becomes very important when
uncomfortable actions need to be taken, force used, people killed or
alternative visions of rights quashed. The defensible foundations limit
the scope for political debate on these issues. By the time that it comes
to the political question of the use of force, for example, the ethical
debate has already been had and resolved. The exact places where
difficult, contradictory, unclear and unsecure answers need to be discussed, debated and fought out have already been both occupied and
bounded by the very foundations which prior attempts at theorising a
judgement or response have put in place.

What happens, it seems, when theoretical ethical foundations are
invoked, is that the possible space for political and ethical debate
becomes circumscribed. The issue here is not so much with the precariousness of ethical claims *per se*, but with the way in which, rather
than acknowledging this precariousness, an attempt may be made to
cover it over and instead employ the category of ethics to shift an
issue outside of the realm of contestation and debate. Ethics itself,

then, becomes depoliticised (but very political), used only for those things which are uncontested or as an attempt to move issues into an uncontested realm, rather than as the site of intense contestation, which we might otherwise think it might/ought to be. This, in turn, depoliticises the politics which rests on it.

In short, my suspicion is that theorising ethical claims or judgements is deeply problematic and that it is potentially the wrong way round to be doing things. We can look for 'solutions' in promoting ethical principles – promoting human rights may well in some or even all cases be an excellent route towards preventing genocide. But this confuses the causes of the problem with the solution. Piecemeal solutions, which call on the important political capital available to those willing to invoke ethical principles, do a great deal of work, much of which none of us would want to do away with. But as soon as this work is framed in terms of not one of many possible and imperfect solutions, but work in the service of righting the wrong that has caused the problem in the first place (which must happen once we have made the claim that genocide is wrong *because* it violates human rights, for example), then a series of problematic consequences follow. This is when opposition is marginalised or discredited (who could not be 'for' the ethical solution?), debate, discussion or dissent silenced and the possibility of the very thing we have been trying to prevent once again has the potential to emerge.

It seems, then, that at least something of the way in which ethics is used and experienced happens at the limits of theory and theorisation, and, in response to this, the approach that the book pursues is to trace the limits of theory. Perhaps ethical theory is not sufficient to the task we have set it. But perhaps this insufficiency is not a failing of particular theories, but a problem with ethics as theory as such. Recognition of the limits of theory and particularly ethical theory matters, not because the questions to which we look to ethics for the answers are unimportant, but because they are too important; because theory does not offer enough protection or because theory itself may be deeply implicated in the very wrongs which we wish to confront.

Non-foundational Ethics and Practical Politics

With this destabilisation of theoretical or foundational ethics in mind, the question of what ethics can do for politics takes on a rather different cast. Without ethics as a foundational category on which a politics might be built, the possibility of doing politics in an ethical way becomes deeply problematic. And yet, if we want to retain a commitment to an ethical politics in some shape or form, the implications of this destabilising of ethics need to be thought through very carefully. It is this task to which the book seeks to contribute by pursuing the question of what the destabilising of foundational ethics means for 'doing' practical politics. What do post-foundational accounts of ethics mean for practical politics? Is it even possible to think about politics without an appeal to foundational ethics? And, if so, what might this politics look like? Without foundational ethics, are we left, as some commentators would suggest, with a dangerous relativism, which makes any forceful ethical arguments impossible? Or might an alternative or non-foundational understanding of ethics lead to a different understanding of the role of foundations in ethical and political argument?

It is often precisely the implications of 'non-foundational' ethics for politics which so-called 'poststructuralist' accounts of the international political realm have sought to address.[1] The relationship between ethical theory and political practice emerges as a site for inquiry in a particularly pertinent and complex way, once the so-called 'critical', 'post-foundational', 'postmodern' or 'poststructuralist' destabilisation of ethics is taken into account. This inquiry has, in part, taken the form of a series of arguments which seek to put into question the theorisable or foundational nature of ethics through demonstrating both the logical contradictions and the practical and political violence perpetuated or enabled by it.

However, these 'poststructuralist' contributions to ethics in global politics are frequently accused of providing 'no answer', of being mired in a relativistic logic which renders them unable to make choices and judgements about what may be good/bad. Alternatively, they have been criticised for being inconsistent when they do provide 'an answer'. A consensus has therefore emerged within IR that poststructuralist work is fatally limited when it comes to the question of how ethics might inform politics.[2] If poststructuralism has anything to say about ethics, this is not, it is claimed, something which could be used in any practical way to provide answers to pressing ethical questions.

In the light of this rather stagnant debate, the book is prompted, in the first instance, by criticisms put to so-called 'poststructuralist' approaches, which argue that work associated with this approach cannot help us with political questions of real-world suffering, which charge it with relativism, inconsistency or blandness in its treatment of ethics and politics. In the second instance, it is driven by an element of frustration with the 'poststructuralist' literature which both prompts these charges and responds to them. Although a range of seemingly divergent responses are offered, many of these ultimately proceed along a similar path. The 'problem' is often approached by poststructuralist authors as one of identifying a (non-foundational) ethical starting point and then developing a politics from this.[3]

However, this particular response, although faithful to the terms of the question posed by the critics, seems at odds with the philosophical literature on which 'poststructuralist' approaches often draw. This leads, it seems, to an impossible bind, as noted by the critics: either poststructuralists offer ethical and political answers or starting points, which seems inconsistent with the philosophical underpinnings of the approach, or they resist doing so, in which case they are charged with relativism.

In order to look afresh at the potential and possibilities of post-foundational ethics for practical politics, the book attempts to move outside of this bind. As such, it is not an attempt to articulate a 'better' poststructuralist account of ethics on which to build a better or more progressive politics. Rather, it takes the stagnation of the current debate as an indicator that there is something missing in the questions to which its participants are attempting to respond.

The way in which challenges have been put to scholars of post-foundational ethics has meant that in order to engage in debate, poststructuralists have, in large part (although not exclusively), tried to prove their ethico-political credentials by answering the criticisms put to them in the terms in which they are raised. That is, by offering more sophisticated ethical theories (of otherness, alterity or responsiveness, for example) and demonstrating the various ways in which these might have progressive real-world political consequences; or, at least, this is how their responses have often been interpreted.

The framing of the debate in terms of theory and application, however, limits the avenues of possible engagement. The important questions of relativism or inconsistency raised by the critics frame the answers to these questions in a particular theoretical way. One possible route out of this impasse is by focusing instead on the *theoretical* nature of the foundations under contestation – that is, by exploring the assumption of ethics as primarily theoretical, at least insofar as it is useful for political practice.

The investigation undertaken here pursues this path by considering what the implications are of a post-foundational approach which problematises the theorisation of ethics. Three central questions animate the investigation. First, why might theoretically informed responses be thought of as unsatisfactory as a ground for politics? Second, why do these types of responses persist, even in the poststructuralist literature which ostensibly offers an engagement with the ungrounded nature of ethical claims? Third, what might the implications of refusing theoretically grounded or foundational accounts of ethics be for rethinking the way in which politics and ethics are related? In response to this third question, the book explores the implications of a post-foundational approach for relating ethics to practical political decisions, asks whether this leads to relativism or disengagement and what the status of political and ethical interventions might be in the light of the (anti)-theoretical, non-foundational foundations developed.

The Limits of Ethics and Politics

The book pursues these questions by recasting the theory-application approach which characterises the current debate. A theory-application route into questions of ethics and politics, which structures the responses of most parties in the existing literature, is underpinned by an assumption that ethics and politics are separate, such that one can inform or act as a foundation for the other.

It is the nature of this relationship between ethics and politics that the book takes as a starting point for developing an account of the practical political implications of post-foundational ethics. My suggestion here is that, as above, the limits of theory are an important area for investigation. The tension in 'everyday ethics' highlights the importance of what I call the practical realm, which occurs all the time at the limits of theorisation and which, I want to suggest, is worthy of further inquiry through a tracing of the limits of theory where we might find it emerging. As such, the book undertakes to trace the limits of ethical and political theory, via an analysis of the limits of the concepts themselves and their interrelation, in order to develop a 'non-theory' of the practical realm.

This book might be read as a theoretical advancement of the

argument against theoretical approaches to ethics or responsibility or, more precisely, as a theoretical exploration of the limits of such theoretical approaches. In its exploration of these limits, the book argues that it is precisely at the limits of theory that we might find ethical possibilities. The limit between ethics and politics might be thought of in the same way, because, in everyday life, it is at this particular limit that the broader limits of theoretical approaches are usually encountered. It is at limits, the book argues, that ethics and politics might happen and specifically at the limit of theorisation.

Once the problem of post-foundational ethics and practical politics is cast in terms of limits, then one thing that these post-foundational accounts might enable, I suggest, is to hold focus on the line between ethics and politics and trace its effects. Informed by this, the approach put forward here has three very broad elements.

First, the book provides an explicit examination of the limits of particular concepts, developing an ontology of ethico-politics as 'on the line' and therefore resistant to totalising closure. Through this, the book demonstrates that ethics and politics are inseparable, such that one cannot inform the other. Ethics cannot provide a foundation for politics, because no foundational answers can be secured. This means that we cannot answer, once and for all, questions such as what the best or better political system might be, whether democracy is better than other arrangements and so on. Or rather, we can, must and do answer these questions, but nothing secures our answers.

Second, the book holds a focus on lines, limits and their effects, providing a defence of the interruption of such lines as a mode of ethics and practical politics. The book presents the case for an ethico-political intervention, wherein practical politics locate the limits of theory or theorisation. The 'ethical', the book argues, should not be understood as a label; it does not mean 'good' or 'right'. Likewise, it is not an evaluation or guide. Rather, both the ethical and political are descriptions of the context in which we find ourselves; compelling and irreconcilable obligations can and do happen in a forceful way, without foundations. As such, the book proposes the need for sensitivity to the ways in which the existing order is already challenged and displaced from within, through precisely the unsecured claims made in the name of ethics.

Third, the book offers a series of insights into the separation of ethics and politics and the implications of this for practical politics. It highlights the necessity of a more politicised, practice-based rethinking of the relationship between ethics and politics. There are, I argue, ultimately no grounds for preferring an account of ethics which foregrounds aporia, nor any grounds for developing an approach to politics which draws on this – for example, approaches designed to foreground the aporetic, unlimited responsibility or a deconstructive or democratic ethos. Instead, if the problem of foundations is fully developed, all we are left with is a series of practical decisions in the realm of the ethico-political.

The book suggests a number of implications for how we might go about thinking ethics and politics in the light of the theoretical framework that is developed. The first is that relying on ethics to secure political decisions sidesteps both ethical and political responsibility. Nothing can secure practical politics, and insecurity is a condition of possibility for any ethics or politics. As such, a strategic refusal of ethics, inasmuch as it is approached as theoretical or foundational, is one way forward. This refusal might also extend, I argue, to certain 'poststructuralist' theories of ethics, which dichotomise, or are used to support a dichotomisation of, the singular/plural, immanent/transcendent and general/particular.

This refusal has the potential to enable, the book argues, a consideration of the general, abstract and particular, without privileging one element. It also opens up the possibility of rethinking ethical and political questions in terms of *response*, but specifically in terms of response to aporetic and irreconcilable demands or to the transimmanent, rather than as response to the particular, singular or transcendent.

The second, broader, implication is that we may need to think of ethics and politics as practices, rather than as theoretical things. As such, the book does not proceed to offer 'a politics' in theoretical terms, but puts forward an injunction to recognise the limits of what can be theorised and resist an overdetermination of the practical realm. Through this 'lack' of an answer, possibilities for the practices of ethics and politics are opened up. Foregrounding the importance of the 'practical' realm is one way in which sensitivity to the challenges already made by ungrounded claims might be cultivated.

The book develops this argument by recasting the question of post-foundational ethics and practical politics. In order to do this, it undertakes to re-examine a set of traditions whose interpretation and usage has become almost commonsensical. In particular, the book revisits the thinkers most often drawn on in 'poststructuralist' approaches to Politics and IR, which develop an ethical starting point on which to build politics: Emmanuel Levinas and Jacques Derrida. Both Levinas and Derrida explicitly problematise theoretical or foundational accounts of ethics, and their work has been instrumental in developing post-foundational approaches to ethics.

However, the current debate, as characterised above, has directed the ways in which these thinkers have been used or have been understood as being used by demanding that the ethical and political aspects of their work be treated as separable and related in particular ways, as well as fitting the model of what we might understand a 'theory' of ethics to be. If the reading of these thinkers has been directed by the way in which the current debate is framed, then a reassessment of their work offers the potential to reframe the debate and open up alternative avenues of investigation.

The book undertakes this reassessment in part through the work of Jean-Luc Nancy, whose work is not usually employed in conjunction with Levinas and Derrida, particularly in terms of debates on ethics. However, Nancy offers an explicit focus on lines and limits in the context of politics, which, when extended to the ethical sphere, casts a new light on the resources offered by all three thinkers, offering both an extension of, and critical counterpoint to, the more common use of Levinas and Derrida. The engagements with the three key thinkers undertaken then provides a series of different resources for approaching the problem of the relationship between ethics and 'practical' politics.

The current debate assumes that the concept of 'ethics' can, and does, undertake particular work when paired with politics – theoretical, grounding or foundational work – regardless of the type of ethics that it might be. In re-examining some key texts in the formation of a 'poststructuralist' ethics, the analysis seeks to offer a critique of the way in which 'ethics' is used in the current debate. That is, rather than focus on what ethics 'is', the analysis undertaken in the first instance centres on what the concept of ethics is employed to do, the discursive positioning of ethics in both traditional and 'poststructural' accounts and the possibilities for alternative conceptualisations of the role of ethics.

It might seem that there is an element of internal contradiction in the construction of a theoretical argument to demonstrate the limits of theory. However, the argument being made is not that there is no place for theory, but rather that its limits matter. If the limits themselves are important, as I will argue, then what is enclosed by these limits is as important to their identification, location and analysis as what exceeds them. These limits are not necessarily self-evident and require careful tracing in different contexts.

Certainly, the approach taken here will say very little in terms of policy prescriptions and concrete practical political suggestions. The intervention into the 'practical political' realm is one which attempts to carefully demonstrate its importance as such and one which is mindful of the possibility of effacing its potential by enfolding it within the theoretical realm. The 'very little', then, is not to remain silent, but is a defence of knowing when to stop. The ethico-political task that I argue for and develop throughout the book is to recognise the way in which we are situated in the ethico-political, in order that we might be able to be responsive to the incompatible, contradictory and protean demands that are made of us, without being able to offer any guidance on the content of that response.

The second potential pitfall of a defence of post-foundational approaches is, of course, the question of what foundations are drawn on here to determine that post-foundational ethics is 'better' than the foundational kind. It is important, then, to note at this point that, ultimately, the book argues that the ethico-political emerges at the limits, rather than in the absence, of foundations. Post-foundational thought is no better, because, of course, the grounds for judging 'betterness' are precisely what is put into question. Rather, my argument in this regard is that theoretical approaches are problematic, but in different ways, that we cannot escape theory, but that there is critical purchase to be gained by acknowledging and investigating the insecurity of foundations, which is a characteristic of our use and experience of 'ethical' claims, rather than constructing theory which attempts to efface this.

Map of the Book

Chapter 1 asks what assumptions inform the construction of the question of practical politics as problematic for poststructuralism. The chapter traces in brief the debate between 'poststructuralist' ethics and its critics in IR and Politics, in which poststructuralist approaches are accused of leading nowhere. Although this debate is relatively well-rehearsed by now, it is instructive, because it is the terms that are established here which, I argue, have shaped a particular type of engagement with ethics and politics in some post-structuralist work, one in which an attempt is made to explicate an ethical politics. With this in mind, Chapter 1 moves on to consider in more depth two such treatments of ethics and politics by David Campbell and Simon Critchley.

Chapter 2 focuses on the work of Emmanuel Levinas, who often provides the ethical starting point for the poststructuralist approaches discussed in Chapter 1. In this chapter, I ask whether this starting point is as clear-cut as it initially seems, whether Levinas does provide resources from which either ethical or political positions can be developed. This chapter presents a reading of Levinas' work where the figure of the Third is foregrounded, suggesting that reliance on a particular reading of Levinas in which the Third is not taken seriously enough leads to the attempt to provide an ethics which can then be used to inform politics. That is, I argue that, for Levinas, the Third represents the complication of the line between ethics and politics, rather than a secondary interruption of an originary ethics by politics.

The adoption of Levinas as a resource for the thinkers discussed in Chapter 1 is, in many ways, due to the use of his thought by Jacques Derrida. Chapter 3 investigates this relationship, asking whether Levinas can provide the ethical backbone of a deconstructive approach, as he is often taken to do. With a more explicit focus on the difficulties internal to concepts such as ethics and responsibility, Derrida's work highlights more clearly the problems involved in constructing an originary ethics. Derrida's work focuses in more detail on the nature of the relation between ethics and politics and the corresponding question of the possibility of ethics and responsibility. This chapter analyses Derrida's use of ethics and politics and their relationship to the realms of the conditional and unconditional, right and law and so on. Derrida's work also introduces the themes of aporia and hiatus, which raises the question of how we might be able to think about the concepts of ethics and politics with this in mind. How are ethics and politics connected or separated? How might they be separated or contain a gap within themselves? Is this gap or limit a problem to be overcome?

In order to examine the notion of the gap, line or limit further, Chapter 4 turns to the work of Jean-Luc Nancy. Nancy provides a resource rarely used in the literature on ethics in IR and Politics on which I focus here, but one which is useful in thinking about how the concepts of ethics and politics are related. Both Levinas and Derrida, I suggest, retain a commitment, even if only as a starting point to demonstrating their interpenetration, to thinking ethics and politics in opposition. Nancy, on the other hand, shifts the terms of the debate somewhat, focusing instead on the line or limit as the starting point. Nancy's ontology of being-with thus provides one alternative way of approaching questions of ethics and politics which allows for a move outside the framing of the debate in terms of how ethics might inform politics.

Having brought into focus the questioning of the line between ethics and politics, Chapter 5 then investigates the implications of this for the original research question. This chapter asks whether we need to appeal to an 'outside' to provide ethics or an ethical disruption, and whether there are grounds on which we can know if this disruption is the better way to proceed. Can ethics solve the questions of politics? Can a 'politics of' anything be derived from it?

The final chapter investigates the implications of an approach which refuses an answer to the problem of ethics. It asks whether this ultimately leads back to relativism and a disengagement from political decisions. It seems very difficult to break away from a notion of ethics as decidable, so a corresponding notion of politics as answerable is always present. In this instance, politics slips back into being answerable, rather than a question of practices. Re-emphasising 'practical' politics goes some way towards resisting the temptation to theorise political answers, but this move can only be made once the relationship between ethics and politics and the nature of these concepts has been re-examined. However, and perhaps more importantly, what emerges is that the decision to recognise or cover over the difficulties in providing programmes or theories are ultimately ethical and political ones. The book does not provide grounds for arguing that this uncovering or politicisation is the better way to proceed. The philosophical literature drawn on, it is argued, provides no guidance. This leads to neither relativism, nor inconsistency, but to unlimited ethical and political decisions and interventions, whether recognised as such or not, for which, in the absence of grounds, we, as singular-plural, are always responsible.

Chapter 1
Ethics, Politics, Limits

Introduction: Tracing the Limits of Theories

This chapter starts the project of tracing the limits of theory by exploring the debate around the limits of particular theories. Specifically, I suggest that an important set of arguments emerge around the accusation that post-foundational approaches to ethics encounter their limits when pushed to account for their political implications. As highlighted in the introduction, the question of foundations often becomes important in ethical thought precisely when ethics is asked to become politically useful. The question of how we might go about making ethical claims without foundational ethical theory, then, is thrown into sharp relief in debates about the relationship between ethics and politics. In fact, I will argue in this chapter that the question of the utility of non-foundational ethics for political practice has been one of the most important and influential ways in which this approach to ethics has been engaged, developed and understood. A focus on the question of political utility has meant that all parties to the debate have accepted the need to provide an account of the relationship between ethics and politics as the challenge which must be met.

My contention here is that the nature and terms of this debate reproduce a theoretical and foundational approach to ethics. As such, refiguring the ethics-politics relationship offers the possibility of thinking differently about ethics. In short, as the concept of ethics as foundational is so firmly rooted in the context of its relationship with politics, in this chapter, I propose to draw out the implications of approaching it as a product of this context. Specifically, claims about the limited 'usefulness' of post-foundational approaches are reliant on a prior assumption of the limits, in terms of conceptual separation, between ethics and politics. The separating limit is approached variously as barrier, gap or aporia, which it may or may not be possible to overcome, bridge or negotiate a passage through, and these different understandings of conceptual limit inform various responses to the question of limitations. The contours of debate around the claim that post-foundational or poststructural approaches to ethics cannot guide practical politics, as reliant on the role of multifarious but overlaid accounts of limits, provide a useful starting point for reconsideration of post-foundational ethics and politics.

The limitations of poststructuralist approaches to ethics in Politics and IR are, by now, well-rehearsed: they lead nowhere, provide no programme of progressive political action and do not tell us how to adjudicate between competing claims.[1] Post-foundational approaches, it is claimed, have nothing to say about the real world, where difficult decisions have to be made. A number of 'poststructuralist' authors have attempted to provide accounts of precisely the political import of post-foundational ethics in response to this criticism.[2] I suggest here that, in fact, these do not work; that the critics are right. At least, they are right up until the final claim – the 'real-world' problem – which is arguably the most important, since it establishes the terms on which the other criticisms make sense. The claim that post-foundational ethical theory cannot be effectively applied to the real world (of politics), and the attempts to counter this assertion by poststructuralist authors both rely on, and reproduce, a notion of ethics as theoretical, foundational and separable from politics. These are precisely the assumptions that inform the construction of the question of ethics and practical politics as problematic for poststructuralism in the first place.

The aim of this chapter is twofold: first to point to the promise of post-foundational approaches to ethics for thinking about how we might 'do' ethics without relying on foundational starting points; second, to trace the limitations of these approaches when faced with the question of the utility of this ethics in the political realm. My argument is that the reproduction of the assumption of ethics as theoretical and foundational occurs because of the nature of the separation between ethics and politics that the question of applying 'ethics', on the one hand, to 'politics', on the

other, entails.[3] This, in turn, means that the promise of poststructuralist approaches to ethics, in which its status as a theoretical
and foundational category are put into question, does not 'carry
through' when the demand is made of them to demonstrate their
political usefulness. In the literature examined here, once ethics and politics have been established as originally separate, the
overwhelming initial tendency when providing an account of how
they might then be usefully related is to posit a theoretical and
often foundational account of ethics; the problem then becomes
understood in terms of how to apply this theory to the real world.
It is, I will argue, the initial separation of ethics and politics which
underpins the tendency to recreate foundational ethics as the
dominant way of providing an account of the political utility of
ostensibly post-foundational approaches.

The purpose is not to offer a critique of poststructuralism, but to
show the ways in which, despite its strengths in terms of resisting
foundational and theoretical approaches, there is one particularly
powerful way of organising questioning, which, when engaged with,
causes this thought to run up against a limit. This is the point at
which resisting a foundational approach to ethics becomes very difficult and, as such, is instructive in terms of offering an analysis of
the very real problem of thinking through ethics and politics without
succumbing to the seduction of foundations.

The specific poststructuralist literature that I focus on in this context
can, I will argue, be characterised by a desire to offer a 'way forward'
or an account of an 'ethical politics'; a seemingly unavoidable consequence of engaging in any depth with the question of political utility,
as posed by the critics. Of course, this tendency is not representative
of all poststructuralist work which engages with themes of ethics and
politics, some of which explicitly and effectively refuses being drawn
into this particular debate and so offers alternative resources that I
revisit at the end of this chapter.[4] However, the literature focused on
in most detail here is chosen because I suggest that the difficulties
and tensions which emerge in attempting to provide a way forwards
in terms of progressive political outcomes are themselves important
contours to trace as part of the broader project of exploring the (role
of) limits in ethical theory.

These tensions highlight some important limits in terms of how
theories and theory operates, and they also open up for analysis
broader questions concerning the nature of ethics, politics and

their interrelation. I want to suggest that the deeper difficulty identified here – the relationship between ethics and politics – is, in fact, a crucially important avenue to pursue if we are to engage seriously with the question of post-foundational ethics and practical politics. In particular, I focus on the distinction between ethics and politics here, because in Chapters 2, 3 and 4, I argue that this particular line or limit maps onto a series of other hugely influential concepts in the philosophical work I examine, that the reading of ethics and politics identified here has been influential in shaping the reception of these much broader themes and that it is at these limits that the potential for making unsecured ethical or political claims emerges.

I should note at this point that, when in this chapter I refer to the separation or interrelation of ethics and politics as if they were concepts which were originally separate or separable, this is because this terminology is the organising principle underpinning much of the literature on which I focus. Part of the aim of the book is to contribute to a rethinking of this organising principle via a careful analysis of the ways in which it continues to prove seductive, even in the light of poststructuralist thought. That is, rather than simply refusing the distinction at the outset,[5] I suggest that if we are to rethink this organisation and its implications, this also requires tracing the ways it works, the places in which it operates and the effects that it has.

The chapter will proceed in three parts; first, it will offer an outline of the ways in which poststructural work calls into question foundational theoretical approaches to ethics and trace, in brief, the way that the promise and limitations of this approach has been figured in terms of its relation to politics. Second, it will trace the tensions which emerge when the challenge of making ethics 'politically useful' is taken up by poststructuralist authors and the way in which this context reproduces features of the foundational approaches that they seek to move away from. Third, it will point towards some alternative approaches which provide potential resources for thinking about ethics and politics without reproducing the limits put in place by this dominant context.

The Promise and Limitations of Post-foundational Ethics

Relational ethics

In looking for resources to think about ethics which are attentive to the problems with an approach based on universal principles and reasons suggested in the introduction, the work of Zygmunt Bauman offers a persuasive starting point. It is Bauman's work, of course, which makes the most clear and sustained case for rejecting universalist, rational ethical theory as not only insufficient to protect against, but, in fact, part of a broader way of thinking which was deeply implicated in creating the conditions of possibility in which the Holocaust could occur.[6]

The concern that a poststructuralist approach highlights here is that if our conceptions of ethics operate only in the dominant grids of rational intelligibility, then they are insufficient to an engagement with the Other who might exceed these grids.[7] Louiza Odysseos, for example, argues that within everyday conceptions of ethics, an occlusion of otherness occurs through the way in which moral norms are linked with socialisation and normalisation.[8] These are norms which fail to recognise the way in which Others are implicated in our self-constitution, meaning that we cannot 'hear' or respond to the Other.[9] Bauman's response to this problem draws on the work of Emmanuel Levinas, in common with a number of the authors discussed below. Bauman argues that ethics and morality operate in a different register altogether; indeed, to engage with them, we need to move away from rational universal codes entirely. Ethics, for Bauman, needs to be thought of as 'irrational'.[10]

Approaching the question of rationality from a deconstructive perspective, however, problematises this wholesale rejection of rational codes. The solution that is offered in terms of trying to move outside of rationality and reason is indebted to an opposi-tional framing, which is also a product of the thinking associated with Bauman's 'modernity'. As Kimberley Hutchings argues, the 'straightforward inversion of tradition' – in this case, the tradition of ethics understood as a product of reason and rationality – 'cannot in itself challenge the traditional order, but rather serves to confirm it'.[11]

A deconstructive reading of the problem of rational ethical

foundations, then, suggests that escaping from this problem by turning to what is outside the rational is not as simple as it might seem.
It may not be the case that the irrational provides an answer, but
rather one of redressing the balance as part of a strategic move. As
William Connolly argues:

> Deconstruction . . . pursues the ambiguity of rationality from within,
> striving to identify sites of rational undecidability inside perspectives that
> have been closed up in the name of reason, acknowledging its unavoid-
> able implication in the practices of rationality it seeks to disrupt. One
> way to read Derridean deconstruction is to say that it seeks to foment
> the experience of undecidability in areas where the correct decision now
> seems all too rational or obvious, doing so to render us more responsive
> to those aspects of alterity that escape current definitions of rationality,
> identity and normality.[12]

It is this destabilisation, rather than outright rejection, which, for
him, constitutes the ethical project.[13] The deconstructive ethical
task for Connolly is to emphasise that which is marginalised in any
particular code or configuration, so as to put into question whatever
might be naturalised.[14] Irrationality is not to be sought as the route
to ethics *per se*, but only insofar as it disrupts the current dominant
logic, because disruption is what enables responsiveness to alterity.

Without a firm foundation of rationality, the kind of ethical
engagement offered by poststructuralist authors looks rather different to a straightforward theory of ethics. Instead of a set of principles
by which to determine ethical action, this literature offers resources
for thinking about ethics in terms of relation. Without traditional
ethics, there is a substantial body of literature which broadly argues,
nonetheless, that, in James Der Derian's terms: 'poststructuralism
offers an ethical way of being in highly contingent, highly relativist
times'.[15]

The starting point offered here is recognition of the inescapable
relation between self and the exterior Other, so, for Der Derian, the
ethics of poststructuralism: '. . . begins with the recognition of the
need for the other, of the need for the other's recognition . . . An
ethical way of being emerges when we recognize the very *necessity* of
heterogeneity for understanding ourselves and others'.[16] Rather than
particular actions or activities being ethical, this approach offers a
way to rethink the ethical in terms of relation with the Other as

an ethical way of being.[17] An ethical mode of relation is one where the relation between the self and the Other is not covered over and where the self is thus: 'open to itself as strange and to the voice of the Other as always within it'.[18] A cultivation of this understanding of heterogeneity and exteriority makes possible a mode of relating which is open to the Other as exterior or beyond.[19]

Of course, openness to the Other does not provide an ethics in traditional terms; Judith Butler's starting point, of a disposition which entails being 'awake to what is precarious in another life', does not provide an ethics as such.[20] This ethics is not 'simply a matter of being kind to strangers'[21] and does not entail a straightforward approach of unconditional welcome to the Other.[22] Rather, it points towards the need for, in Connolly's terms: 'critical responsiveness to the claims of difference';[23] an ability to engage with the claims of Others, rather than a guideline of how to judge them. In fact, if anything, this mode of relation proposes a sensitivity to different and perhaps incompatible demands, so making much more difficult the task of judgement.

Poststructuralist work, then, very broadly speaking, attempts to offer resources for conceptualising ethics without reducing these accounts to rational theories of right and wrong. Four common elements in this attempt can be identified across work from a number of perspectives, though the four are very closely interlinked through the idea of relation: first, a sensitivity to what is excluded; second, a disposition of openness towards the Other; third, an awareness of the relational nature of the self; and fourth, ethics as disposition, rather than a theory of right and wrong.

We might also formulate these insights as offering an alternative account of limits. Relationality offers the possibility of figuring limits not (only) as points of separation, gaps and barriers to be overcome, but also in terms of interpenetration, interruption and lines of touching. The following chapters will explore these claims and their basis in Levinasian thought in more depth, but the question which emerges from the current literature to animate that exploration is whether these tentative and rather minimal claims are sufficient to make affirmative gestures. In the main, this question is taken up via analysis of the political import of these ethical resources, which critics of the approach argue is severely limited.

Relativism, inconsistency or blandness: a triple bind

The criticisms of poststructuralism are by now well-rehearsed. For the purposes of my argument, the most important is the claim that universal, rational foundations are required if we are to make convincing ethical or political arguments; in the absence of these, we are left only with a dangerous relativism.[24] As Chris Brown argues, the 'problem' with poststructuralists is that they are 'unwilling to think of ethics in terms of the requirements of justice', where justice is understood in terms of acting in accordance with impartial rules.[25] Molly Cochran goes further, suggesting that when poststructuralist authors do make ethical claims, despite their indebtedness to post-foundational philosophical thought, they end up, in fact, employing just such criteria of judgement;[26] they may not want to subscribe to an understanding of ethics in terms of justice, but end up doing so anyway. So, for Cochran, the key problem is one of inconsistency.[27]

Of course, if the analysis starts from the assumption that criteria are required, it is impossible to conceive of a political or ethical intervention which does not make reference to these criteria in some way. Thus, the logic runs, where there are judgements, there must, somewhere in the shadows, be grounds and criteria. Approaches informed by poststructuralism, then, cannot, if they are to be internally consistent, engage in ethical or political judgement. Making ethical claims without foundations is not only uncomfortable, but contradictory, illogical and illegitimate.

Accusations of relativism or inconsistency thus form one arm of the pincer movement in which critics would place poststructuralist approaches. The second is the insistence that when these approaches do offer guidance on how to go about making judgements, they do not go far enough. There is ultimately, so the critics argue, a 'lack of content' in poststructuralist ethics, insufficient guidance on how we might go about ensuring a 'better global politics'; indeed, poststructuralism leads 'nowhere'.[28] To return to Cochran, the problem is that an 'affirmative' ethics – one which might provide such guidance – does not fit with 'postmodern method'.[29]

Of course, post-foundational ethics cannot escape the bind of relativism, inconsistency or 'blandness'[30] if the starting assumption is that we need rational codes, criteria and principles in order to provide a robust, coherent and useful account of ethics. If, however, the starting point, as outlined in the introduction, is that these principles in and of themselves are at best insufficient and at worst dangerous, then the criteria by which ethical 'usefulness' might be judged look potentially rather different.

Poststructuralism and progressive politics

The question of whether poststructuralism can, in general terms, 'lead' anywhere forms the wider context in which specific claims about the possibility of 'affirmative' ethics and politics emerge in the poststructuralist literature. There is a relatively broad consensus, in agreement with the critics, that poststructuralism in general and deconstruction in particular encounters a limit when it comes to constructing alternative and progressive accounts of politics. Without foundations, constructing alternative or competing political outlooks in the same way that other theories do becomes deeply problematic. As Richard Ashley argues: 'Poststructuralism cannot claim to offer an alternative position or perspective, because there is no alternative ground upon which it might be established'.[31]

What is interesting is that amongst poststructuralist authors who are concerned with engaging with the possibility of making affirmative gestures, the dominant way of engaging with this limit in deconstruction has been to treat it as a limitation. Specifically, the limitation has been approached as the function of an underlying limit between the ethics and politics of deconstruction. The question of how ethics might have practical import is framed largely as the question of the relationship between ethics and politics. As such, the treatment of this limit as a limitation emerges most clearly when the question of progressive political outcomes is posed. Two different lines of argument emerge in response to the question of progressive political potential, but in both there is a tendency to operate on the assumption put forward by the critics – that without criteria for judgement or decision, the practical affirmative possibility (i.e. the politics) of post-foundational ethics is limited.

In the first instance, deconstruction is identified as having affirmative or progressive roots, often drawing on the ethical themes outlined above, which nonetheless fail to translate to progressive outcomes. William Connolly, for example, argues that while deconstruction offers important and affirmative resources for demonstrating the unstable nature of foundations, it does not then provide any alternative to that which it puts into question.[32] In order to remain consistent, he argues, the deconstructive project cannot: 'pursue the trail of affirmative possibility very far'.[33] Similarly, Richard Beardsworth claims that that 'the endeavour of deconstruction is to promote alterity and difference',[34] but that this ethical potential cannot translate into real-world political outcomes.[35]

The problem is that deconstruction cannot, on this line of argument, provide better political institutions or affirmative political projects, because of a desire to remain unengaged in the ontological assumptions on which such decisions might be based. Specifically, then, the problem is seen as an inability in deconstruction to provide an account of the decision necessary to legislate for progressive outcomes.[36] Without an ethics which provides either criteria or grounds for judging between competing claims, there are problems in translating that ethics into the practical realm.[37] To overcome the limitation framed in these terms, resources outside of deconstruction or even outside of poststructuralism more broadly are required, in order to cultivate a strategy of 'positive ontopolitical interpretation'.[38]

For those who want to argue that the limitation of the lack of grounds offered by deconstruction can be overcome, the tendency has been to seek better accounts of what might be affirmative or progressive about deconstruction on which to base judgement and decisions.[39] The inquiry then takes the form of determining an 'ethics' of deconstruction of a kind that can inform politics. In this instance, then, the understanding of the affirmative or ethical basis itself is seen as part of the limitation, such that if we want to construct progressive political outcomes, we need to start with a much more systematic and detailed account of the affirmative underpinnings of deconstruction. Once this has been achieved, it is possible to think through how these translate into providing affirmative political resources.

One of the most sustained and influential accounts of the possibilities of making affirmative claims from a poststructuralist position comes from authors engaged in this task of developing accounts of progressive political outcomes, and this project is framed from the beginning in terms of the relationship between ethics and politics. This chapter moves on to consider in more detail two of these accounts, from Simon Critchley and David Campbell.

The Move from Ethics to Politics

Campbell and Critchley offer detailed engagements with the thought of Emmanuel Levinas and Jacques Derrida, whose work is central to a number of the resources identified above. Although much of the work mentioned above takes as its subject 'poststructuralism' in general terms and although in their individual work the authors under consideration draw on a range of thinkers, two elements of similarity are striking. First, when talking in general terms, it is often a deconstructive approach which is argued to be insufficient for ethical and political requirements, as shown in the discussion of the limits of poststructuralist thought. Second, when developing an account of an ethical mode of relation, the work of Emmanuel Levinas emerges as a constant reference point.[40] The authors considered below also provide the most systematic accounts of the dominant way in which Derrida and Levinas have been taken up in poststructuralist approaches.

However, engagement with this work also demonstrates the limitations imposed by framing the investigation in terms of relating ethics to politics. Through contrasting the work of two authors usually understood to put forward opposing arguments about how we might construct a progressive politics in poststructuralism, the discussion will demonstrate how particular dominant features of the debate emerge, which, I suggest, act to limit its scope. Through the reinscription of a particular account of limits and separation, they also – I will go on to argue in later chapters – limit the radical potential of a focus on relationality, which has been previously gestured towards in this chapter.

In framing the analysis in terms of overcoming a limit between ethics and politics, two key features emerge. The first of these is an implicit acceptance of the idea that the theoretical world of ethics and the practical world of politics need to be brought together, the implication being that ethics and politics are separable along the line of theory/practice. The second feature, which follows on from this, is that ethics comes to be treated as both theoretical and foundational. Although this is, in part, a function of the framing of the debate as a response to a perceived limitation in deconstruction (as discussed above), it is also reflective of deeper problematic assumptions that this framing relies upon regarding the nature of concepts, the relation between theory and practice and the way in which these inform particular readings of Levinas and Derrida. The line between ethics and politics functions here to create an ethics that grounds a particular politics; however, later chapters will argue that this line maps on to a series of other distinctions – for example, between singular/plural, face/Third and transcendent/immanent – whose dominant use and understanding needs to be revisited, in order to think through the potential of relationality. It is through engagement with the tensions in the examples below that the book goes on to investigate whether alternative framings are possible.

The politics of alterity

The ethical relation

Campbell starts by defending poststructuralism from the claim that it rejects ethics in its rejection or questioning of universals. He maintains that a poststructuralist position can be ethically relevant and grounded without requiring recourse to the universal, that: 'the demise of the universal does not mean the end of the ethically transcendent'.[41] Further, the demise of the universal, criteria or codes does not, for him, lead to an ethics which is empty of political implication. 'Abandoning principle', he argues: 'does not mean jettisoning ethics ... it is possible to articulate an ethico-political disposition that is both consonant with the complexities of the postmodern world and capable of encouraging us to resist undemocratic practices'.[42] The ethically transcendent on which poststructuralism can draw, argues Campbell, is not a code or law, but our embeddedness in the ethical relation – a 'radically interdependent condition'.[43]

This radical interdependence is, in common with the authors mentioned above, drawn from Campbell's use of Levinas. He thus casts ethics not in terms of 'ethical theory', but 'ethical relation'.[44] Rather than asking how we might engage in ethical politics, for example, he approaches the issue in terms of the way in which we are always already inescapably ethically involved. However, the fact of this ethical relation is insufficient for affirmative ethical practices. Even though we are always engaged, Campbell argues, we need to question whether the nature of particular involvements serves to 'enact or efface the ethical relation we desire'.[45]

On the one hand, then, we are always ethically situated, for Campbell, in a relation of radical interdependence. On the other, this is not sufficient for the practical realm. The ethical relation we desire is not reducible to the fact of inescapable interdependence. There is something more which must be aimed at both in terms of the content of this relationship and its recognition. In the first instance, Campbell argues that the ethical relation that should be aimed at is specifically: 'a responsible non-totalizing relation with the Other'.[46] In the second instance, there is, for Campbell, an ethically transcendent principle in encouraging the recognition of the radical interdependence of being and inescapable responsibility to the Other.[47]

In order to encourage or open the possibility of the ethical relation, we need to acknowledge and recognise our radical interdependence. Campbell argues that it is this recognition which can inform ethical and political judgements, with the criteria being: 'how the interdependencies of our relations with Others are appreciated'.[48] It can, for Campbell, be judged as more ethical to acknowledge our interrelated way of being-in-the-world. In the context of the actions of the United States during the Gulf War, he argues that: 'to be judged as having acted in an ethical way, it would have been more fitting for the United States to acknowledge this heteronomous responsibility than assert its autonomous freedom'.[49] The fact of radical interdependence in itself is not sufficient to ethics, but it points, for Campbell, to the need for a particular disposition, which involves both engagement and recognition:

> While 'radical interdependence' ... is, philosophically speaking, the fundamental situation of a subject's being-in-the-world, the modality associated with that being is something to be politically contested and negotiated. In the place of intervention as that modality, I want to argue that *engagement* with the world is the foundation of an ethical disposition ...[50]

Although Campbell puts forward an account of an ethical disposition with which to guide political judgement, this relationship is not straightforward and does not, Campbell argues, operate on the same terms as the construction of ethical criteria. In fact, Campbell explicitly argues that there is a problem with the tendency 'to believe that the construction of normative frameworks can resolve political questions'.[51] In 'Why Fight', though not drawing on Levinas and Derrida, Campbell's aim is precisely the broader one with which this book is concerned: to resist the 'normative question' of why we should fight, struggle or resist domination.[52] We do not require, he argues, a normative framework in order to formulate a 'progressive' answer to that question.[53] So while Campbell does want to look to ethical commitments to inform politics, he sees this aim as rather different from the construction of normative frameworks to do so. It is this which means that Campbell can also ask, with Michael Dillon, what flows, politically, from his Levinasian 'ethics'; if responsibility to the Other is the ethical starting point, then: 'what articulation and figuration of the political either flows from or is required by this understanding?'[54] The key question, then, is whether this distinction holds, whether Campbell's ethics is sufficiently distinct from a normative framework. As outlined above, however, my contention is that while its relational starting point might achieve this, the fact that the ethics is framed from the beginning in terms of its relation to politics already casts that ethics in rather more traditional terms.

Campbell frames his project as an attempt to fulfil the implications of Levinasian thought for politics, taking the initial account of relationality and responsibility as the starting point.[55] As Campbell recognises, the non-normative ethical demand of responsibility to the Other does not provide political answers in and of itself. The ethical demand of unlimited responsibility to the Other needs, in a political sense, he suggests, to be tempered. The question of how we might do this is, for Campbell and Dillon, part of the question of politics:

> How do we respond to the ethical demand so as to provide an account of discriminating responsibility for our lives that affirms alterity, yet says both 'Yes' and 'No' to the stranger?[56]

It is at this point that Campbell turns to Derrida. The necessity of discrimination between Others, of making judgements and decisions in the light of our situation of responsibility and interdependence is, for Campbell, not theorised sufficiently by Levinas. While, for Campbell, Levinas' work is useful in providing an ethical starting point, there are problems when it comes to the implications of this thought for politics.[57]

Campbell draws on two aspects of Levinas' work to frame the question of the move to politics. For Levinas, the initial relation of subjectivity as responsibility is understood in terms of a 'face-to-face' relation, taken by Campbell to comprise two people, so a relation where choosing between Others is not necessary. We are, in this context, responsible only to the one Other, and it is from this that Campbell derives his ethical commitment to recognising our interdependence with, and responsibility to, this Other.[58]

Campbell then turns to Levinas' concept of the third person, which he understands as an indication that this face-to-face relation is not how things actually are. The third person, Campbell argues, disturbs the responsibility in the face-to-face relation.[59] Their presence introduces an element of choosing and comparing into the relationship. This, for Campbell, is the move to politics. His aim, in terms of politics, then, is to trace how we might expand or apply the notion of responsibility when we move from the one-to-one to the one-and-the-many;[60] where the ethical relation leads once in the realm of practical affirmative possibilities.

For Campbell, Levinas does not provide a convincing account of this movement; he provides an ethics, but no politics.[61] Levinas' refiguring of responsibility: 'does not move us very far towards how, why, and by whom that unavoidable responsibility to the Other should be exercised'; that is, it is not of much use in the practical realm.[62] To answer questions such as these, he argues: 'I think Derrida is better equipped'.[63] In order for a 'progressive' politics to emerge from a poststructuralist position, an account of the decision to 'combat domination' is necessary, and Derrida can provide such an account.[64]

The move from ethics to politics: duty in decision

In order to provide this account of the decision, Campbell turns firstly to Derrida's ethics, since it is this which, for him, underlies the progressive political possibilities drawn from deconstruction. Once we start with a Levinasian understanding of ethics, he argues, deconstruction can be seen as making a series of strong ethical claims.[65] For Campbell, amongst these are Derrida's naming of 'the worst', found in *The Other Heading*, where Derrida refers directly to xenophobia, racism, anti-Semitism and religious or nationalist fanaticism.[66]

If Derrida does subscribe to the (Levinasian) ethical position attributed to him by Campbell, then, Campbell argues, Derrida's account of the decision has a 'duty' within it, which means that deconstruction can provide some guidance as to the content of the decision.[67] Campbell argues that:

Residing within – and not far below the surface – of Derrida's account of the experience of the undecidable as the context for the decision is the duty of deconstructive thought, the responsibility for the other, and the opposition to totalitarianism it entails.[68]

The context of undecidability itself and the demand to decide which is central to this context is, in fact, already a response to this duty: 'The necessity of calculating the incalculable thus responds to a duty, a duty that inhabits the instant of madness and compels the decision to avoid "the bad", the "perverse calculation", even "the worst"'.[69]

The duty Campbell sees, then, is relatively specific: the avoidance of those things named as 'the bad', which, for him, point to totalitarianism. This ethical commitment within deconstruction and the duty within decision to which it gives rise, thus provides a route into particular, practical, political decisions, which are seen as lacking in Levinas' account. The duty, Campbell argues: 'dwells with deconstructive thought and makes it the starting point, the "at least necessary condition", for the organization of resistance to totalitarianism in all its forms'.[70]

The duty within decision is the responsibility to the Other enacted through the opposition to totalitarianism and recognition of interdependence. The specificity of this duty leads to a particular kind of politics. That is, for Campbell, deconstruction, when supplemented with Levinas, addresses the question of politics: 'in an affirmative antitotalitarian manner that gives [deconstruction's] politics a particular quality'.[71] Specifically, this politics foregrounds the relationship with alterity, such that:

> If we seek to encourage recognition of the radical interdependence of being that flows from our responsibility to the other, then we have *a different figuration of politics*, one in which *its purpose is the struggle for – or on behalf of – alterity, and not a struggle to efface, erase, or eradicate alterity.*[72]

The (ethical) duty within the decision, for Campbell, opens up the possibility for a different configuration of politics, which he goes on to describe in more detail as a 'politics of alterity'.

The politics of alterity: democracy

Campbell's 'politics of alterity' is a 'progressive' political commitment. Through this figuration, deconstruction can be read as explicitly providing resources for a progressive politics: 'where progressive politics is understood in terms of a demand to resist domination, exploitation, oppression, and all other conditions that seek to contain or eliminate alterity'.[73] The principle of the struggle for alterity is able to provide this account of progressive politics because of its ethical grounding – 'such a principle . . . is ethically transcendent if not classically universal' – and it is this which leads to its political purchase.[74]

Specifically, the principle of the struggle for alterity leads to a commitment to particularism in opposition to totalitarianism, which points to democracy as the form of progressive politics. The political possibilities of deconstruction, he argues:

> might even be summarized in terms of a general principle for the ethos of democracy, albeit a principle that derives its legitimacy from the transcendentality of particularism. This principle would declare that we should actively nourish and nurture antagonism, conflict, plurality and multiplicity.[75]

In response to the question posed earlier by Campbell and Dillon regarding responding to the ethical demand for a responsibility which affirms alterity and says both 'yes' and 'no' to the stranger, their answer is that in order to enable this response: 'the character of the political must then be democratic'.[76]

However, the democracy that is called for is not any existing democracy or democratic regime, but a: 'new form of democracy'.[77] Campbell is attentive to the risks associated with an ethos of democracy based on Derrida's idea of 'democracy to come'. He accepts that democracy is ultimately 'an empty place' from which progressive political outcomes cannot be guaranteed.[78] His point seems to be that the conditions for the possibility of democracy, although impossible to ever fully realise, should be kept open and that this is the point of any political project associated with deconstruction.

In addition to a commitment to the open form of democracy, Campbell argues that specific political positions can also be derived from the ethics of deconstruction. The cultivation of an ethos of democracy, of the nurturing of antagonism, multiplicity, conflict and plurality are, for him, part of an active affirmation of alterity – one which, he argues:

> *must* involve the desire to actively oppose and resist – perhaps, depending on the circumstances, even violently – those forces that efface, erase or suppress alterity . . . That which in dealing with difference moves from disturbance to oppression, from irritation to repression, and most obviously from contestation to eradication.[79]

For him, then, the politics of deconstruction are certainly not 'bland', but the concern here is that in attempting to provide an account of affirmative politics, Campbell falls into the alternative criticism – of inconsistency – such that the ethical commitment to alterity and particularism reinstates universalist ethical foundations and so closes off thinking in terms of relationality as a route to making affirmative claims without foundations.

If we follow Campbell's line of argument to the more specific practices and commitments which his politics of alterity and ethos of democracy involve, this can be seen more clearly. A commitment to alterity does not entail the welcoming of all opinions; the element of saying 'no' to the stranger is important, and it is here that Campbell provides guidance on the political decision, arguing that:

> these modalities neither sustain a banal celebration of difference nor support a licentious ethic of toleration, for all those dispositions or practices (such as racism or genocide) which discipline the contingent, constitute normality, punish deviance, and deify their own logic are prototypical instances requiring intervention.[80]

Of course, for Campbell, the specific actions flowing from this are not straightforward, precisely because he is aware of the problem of deriving politics from ethics. On the one hand, he wants to give paradigmatic cases of the practices which he would want to resist. We need, he argues, to resist any visions: 'that exclude or suppress the idea of identity as relational, contingent and constructed'.[81] On the other hand, however, he maintains that it is at the point of making this particular decision in specific situations that our decision is no longer secured by anything.[82] It is, he argues, precisely at the point of making decisions about when 'disturbance moves to oppression' or 'contestation to eradication', that we can no longer speak in the abstract.[83] So Campbell retains a commitment to keeping the content of the decision open, but with certain caveats stemming from the duty in decision.

Even this broad claim that the decision needs to keep possibilities open, however, operates on the basis that the Other who practices racism or genocide (for example) is not the Other on behalf of whom we should struggle in our political decisions. Any alterity which itself entails the closing off of possibilities or hostility towards different practices is to be resisted. Racism and genocide are wrong, on this account, once again *because* they violate a prior ethical principle; not because they violate the concept of human rights, but because they: 'discipline the contingent, constitute normality, punish deviance, and deify their own logic'. Relationality, then, despite Campbell's concern in regards to normative frameworks, when attempting to provide an account of politics, becomes just a different ground from which questions can be decided.

The politics of ethical difference

The ethical relation

In *The Ethics of Deconstruction*, Simon Critchley makes a similar argument to Campbell; namely, that deconstruction can be considered ethical if we start from a Levinasian idea of ethics.[84] However, he then argues that Derrida does not provide an adequate account of the movement from ethics to politics (Campbell's duty in decision) and brings in Levinas again as a 'political supplement' to provide an account of the decision necessary to politics.[85] Although Critchley sees the limitations of Levinas and Derrida and the way that they work together in an opposite way to Campbell, certain assumptions are common to them both.

Critchley's argument rests, in the first instance, on a Levinasian conception of ethics, which is similar, but not identical, to Campbell's. There are differences of emphasis; Campbell's concern with alterity is not matched by Critchley, nor does Critchley see the relation between ethics and politics in Levinas in the same way. Although, on the one hand, ethics for Critchley is, in the Levinasian sense, 'simply and entirely' the event of the ethical relation,[86] the immediate context into which that relation is placed is a relationship with politics, such that: 'ethics is ethical for politics'.[87]

Critchley's Levinasian understanding of the ethical relation consists of the questioning of the spontaneity of the self by the presence of the Other.[88] Specifically for Critchley, the ethical relation is one in which, rather than a desire to reduce alterity to sameness, there is instead recognition of this alterity: 'an access to exterior being'.[89] The exterior Other – 'face' in Critchley's reading of Levinas[90] – is the condition of possibility of ethics; it is the relation to the face of the Other which is the ethical relation.[91] However, the ethical relation translates into ethics as such through its political horizon. The exterior alterity disrupts sameness, so ethics, Critchley argues, can be understood as the disturbance or interruption of the political status quo.[92] For Levinas, he claims: 'ethics is the disruption of totalizing politics: anti-Semitism, anti-humanism, National Socialism'.[93] The ethical relation, then, immediately produces interruption as an ethical principle, *because* of its positioning in the political realm.

If we start from this understanding of ethics, Critchley argues that we can then understand deconstruction as both motivated by an initial irreducible responsibility and itself an ethical demand. In the first instance, he argues that the Levinasian rethinking of responsibility provides: 'an unconditional categorical imperative or moment of affirmation . . . the source of the injunction that produces deconstruction and is produced through deconstructive reading'.[94] The originary relation with alterity means that language is always fundamentally addressed to the Other. The structure of this address to the Other underlies the content and meaning of language and destabilises its claims to coherence and mastery, which is what makes language open and deconstructable.[95]

Following on from this, he suggests that once deconstruction is understood as ethically motivated, it can also be seen to produce ethical demands of its own.[96] The ethical purchase of deconstruction, then, does not come entirely from Levinas; for Critchley, like Campbell, there is a 'duty' within deconstruction itself.[97] The pattern of reading produced in the deconstruction of texts, he suggests, has an 'ethical structure'.[98] Insights, interruptions and alterities found through a deconstructive reading of a text are, for Critchley, moments of 'ethical transcendence', in which the ethical emerges from beneath the political (or textual) status quo, such that the alterity of the Other is affirmed.[99] Deconstruction, then, provides a mode of the interruption discussed above and in refusing to cover over the interruption of alterity, it can be understood as ethically affirmative.[100]

The move from ethics to politics: a Levinasian supplement

Although deconstruction on this reading opens up ethical possibilities, this is, Critchley argues, insufficient to politics. Deconstruction provides a means of political critique through demonstrating the unstable foundations on which dominant political regimes rest and so providing tools with which to challenge their legitimacy.[101] However, the limit of deconstruction, Critchley argues, is in the movement from this uncovering of undecidability to an account of the decision which is, he argues: 'essential to the possibility of politics'.[102] How, Critchley asks: 'can one account for the move from undecidability to the political *decision* to combat . . . domination?'[103]

Critchley understands politics in terms of questioning, critique, judgement and decision, the creation of contestation, antagonism and struggle,[104] and Derrida's work, he argues: 'results in a certain *impasse* of the political . . . deconstruction fails to navigate the treacherous passage from ethics to politics . . . from responsibility to questioning'.[105] In response, Critchley proposes supplementing Derrida with Levinas in order to work out a 'politics of ethical difference'.[106] The gap that he identifies can, he argues, be traversed through using Levinas' account of the passage from ethics to politics.[107]

To provide the supplement, Critchley returns to his reading of Levinas' ethics as always already pointing towards politics. This is a complex relationship, in which the ethical and political moments are not chronologically separable, but nonetheless remain distinct in that the ethical is aligned with responsibility to the Other and the political with justice and decision through the figure of the third person. When Levinas talks about ethics, argues Critchley, he is also already talking about politics: 'From the first, my ethical discourse with the Other is troubled and doubled into a political discourse with all the others'.[108] It is the ethical relationship from which the questions and decisions of politics emerge, not as chronologically separate, but as conceptually distinct. Critchley describes this movement from the ethical relationship to politics in Levinas' terms of the transition 'from the proximity of the one-for-the-Other to a relation with all the others whereby I feel myself to be an other like the others and where the question of justice can be raised'.[109]

Levinas' account of ethics, then, for Critchley, already contains within it resources to provide guidance on the content of the political decision. If politics is an extension of the ethical relation, then the Levinasian account of politics is one where its ethical basis is recognised. For Levinas, Critchley argues: 'politics begins as ethics . . . and this leads him to articulate a form of political life that would interrupt all attempts at totalization, totalitarianism, or immanentism'.[110] Recognition of the ethical residue within the political provides a Levinasian politics with a guard against certain political outcomes. Injustice, he argues, 'not to mention racism, nationalism, and imperialism' are the results of a lack of recognition, beginning 'when one loses sight of the transcendence of the Other'.[111] In guiding political decisions towards interrupting totalisation in the name of the ethical basis of that politics, this vision of the political maintains the political community as open and interrupted.[112]

The politics of ethical difference: democracy

The form of politics which allows for this continued recognition of otherness and transcendence is labelled by Critchley a 'politics of ethical difference'.[113] It is played out, once again, in a democratic polity:

> It is only when political space is organized democratically – that is, dis-*organ*-ized as an open, interrupted community – that one can envisage a politics that does not reduce transcendence . . . Democracy is the politics of ethical difference.[114]

Critchley sees democracy as the desirable political organisation, because, in its very structure, it fulfils the requirement that 'the political order is justified only in so far as it is simultaneously capable of being criticised subversively'; that is, the possibility of being interrupted by the ethical.[115] The just polity is, he argues, one that can actively maintain its own interruption as precisely that which sustains it, and democracy is that form which practices the interruption of politics by ethics.[116] Democracy is ethically grounded, then, because it reflects the simultaneity of ethics and politics, the Other and the Third.[117]

Although Critchley is attentive to the way in which ethics and politics are closely related in Levinas, they remain separate realms, such that one can inform the other. This goes some way to explaining the tension between whether ethics and politics are the same gesture (as in Critchley's discussion of ethics itself as interruption) or doubled gestures at the same time (as in the discussion where ethics provides both the momentum and means for interrupting the totalising realm of politics). Critchley most often seems to take the position that they are chronologically simultaneous gestures in different directions, but that the ethical comes first in terms of priority. This separation and ordering is necessary in order for his account of the political decision to be put forward. Although Critchley argues that there is no pure ethical experience and no simple deduction from ethics to politics, he nonetheless maintains that 'we need ethics in order to see what to do in a political situation', and it is his reading of Levinas' account of ethics as the basis for politics which provides this guidance.[118]

If ethics is to tell us what to do in a political situation, to provide resources for informing political decisions, it must be maintained as conceptually distinct from the politics to which it is applied. It must offer, in Critchley's terms, an 'undeconstructable' foundation. The ethical here is the face-to-face relation, plurality and multiplicity, in contrast to (unethical?) totalisation. Politics, the realm of the Third and other Others who demand calculation and totalisation are not ethical and must be constantly corrected by the ethical. By aligning the ethical with the Other and not the third person, we can be assured that totalisation is wrong. This distinction means that ethics can be used to provide an account of reasons, principles or guidelines, as seen in Critchley's argument that anti-Semitism and anti-humanism are wrong and must be resisted, *because* they are instances of totalisation. The potential of ethics as relation is again refigured, such that rather than offering a route to rethinking what ethics might mean in the absence of foundations, it instead provides guidelines or foundations for making affirmative political gestures. The line between ethics and politics functions again to create an ethics that grounds particular politics.

Refiguring the Limit between Ethics and Politics

Refusing ethics

Of course, not all poststructuralist work on ethics and politics engages with the terms of the questions put by the critics in the way that Campbell and Critchley do. The limit encountered in constructing affirmative progressive accounts of politics is not always approached as a limitation to be overcome via a bridge from ethics to politics. As I have suggested, it is this starting point and the context in which it situates a discussion of ethics and politics which leads to the limiting of accounts of post-foundational ethics. Poststructuralist authors who call on alternative contexts thus offer a range of questions with which to interrogate the key moves that are made in the dominant accounts of poststructuralist ethics and politics. These alternatives point towards lines of enquiry that the book pursues in later chapters.

The first important move opened up for analysis is the way in which Critchley and Campbell's accounts of progressive politics proceed by identifying an ethical basis from which to derive guidelines for a better politics. A 'politics of alterity', 'politics of ethical difference' or commitment to democracy, although seeking to avoid the closures and abstraction of totalisation and universalisation, can only guarantee this ethical openness if based initially on a closure. In attempting to bring ethical concerns about difference, alterity and response to the Other to inform political organisation, there is also the risk, as Jenny Edkins points out, of a return to abstraction and generalisation.[119] Thus, Campbell's insistence on the importance of retaining political decisioning in specific cases comes after he has argued that this decisioning must have within it a duty to protect alterity. Deconstruction, Campbell argues, leads to a political ethos of democracy, which gives rise to general principles.[120] So the decision will always already have been made, at least in part. In providing foundations with which to resist programming and prediction as a strategy for keeping the possibility of decision open, the decision to resist programming is already made.[121]

On one reading, these problems of a return to abstraction and generalisation are problems which necessarily accompany any engagement with ethics. Rather than searching for an affirmative ethics on which to build an affirmative politics, the argument here is that, in fact, ethics closes down the possibility of politics. The 'limit' of deconstruction outlined above, in terms of providing alternative theories and progressive outcomes, is approached here as an opening, rather than a limitation.[122] It is this limit which might allow for politics, as distinct from the application of principles and programmes, in the first place. The attempt to overcome this limit is, then, an ill-advised move, which threatens the very possibility of politics.

In particular, on this reading, the introduction of ethics as a means to bridge the limit is a threat to politics. Alex Thomson argues, for example, that only the move away from the ultimate goal of an ethical starting point allows for a move towards 'politicisation'.[123] For Thomson, the political aspect of deconstruction is occluded by this reliance on ethics. In order for deconstruction to be thought of as a political practice, it requires 'a suspicion of ethics'.[124] On this argument, politics is expressly not about providing an account of the decision, but happens in the absence of a secure account of the decision. The broader question pertaining to ensuring affirmative or progressive politics is then refused: the task of deconstruction is not to legislate for the better political outcome, but is 'a challenge to ensure that there might be decisions at all'; it is a politics of: 'resisting the programming and prediction which threaten to end politics itself'.[125]

Of course, this critique is aimed at a 'traditional' account of ethics. As Mark Franke puts it, ethics, here, is a question of 'what should be done', which is a question that must be posed as answerable.[126] The critique also relies on the separation of ethics and politics in precisely the same way as Campbell and Critchley, such that ethics is aligned with the provision of grounds for decision.[127] On this argument, it is only when justifications – the business of ethics – fail that politics begins.[128] If Campbell and Critchley end up with a position which closes down the possibility of decision and politics, this is because they engage with ethics; even a poststructuralist account of ethics is too closely tied to grounds and foundations to be exempt from the criticism.

The reconfigured understanding of politics as not requiring an account of the decision leads to a rejection of ethics as the realm from which this account might otherwise be drawn. In one sense, this alternative approach to politics does offer some potential to disrupt the dominant context in which ethics is engaged. If Campbell and Critchley are marshalled towards a foundational account of ethics because of the function they need it to fulfil with regard to politics – specifically, informing an account of the decision necessary for progressive politics – then it would seem that an alternative account of politics might enable a different engagement with ethics. But, in fact, the alternative approach to politics is most often employed alongside a wholesale rejection of ethics.

So while sympathetic to this refiguring of politics, it strikes me that the accompanying rejection of ethics in fact means that the analysis is reliant on the same underlying assumption as that which it critiques. Ethics and politics remain separate in this approach, and ethics remains understood in terms of grounds and foundations. Its wholesale rejection does not really help us to think about what the context of its relation with politics does (because, in both cases, the relationship with politics is the same) or what a relational account of ethics or politics might look like once this context is put into question. In short, while Campbell and Critchley can be read as figuring attempts to overcome the limit separating ethics and politics, the authors rejecting ethics are very mindful of keeping the limit in place. As such, both approaches (re)produce the separation of ethics and politics as the context for their analysis.

The separation of ethics and politics

To return to Edkins' critique of the risks of abstraction and generalisation, the second way of approaching this problem might be to suggest that, rather than a product of attempts to link ethics and politics such that politics can be derived from ethics, the important move is, in fact, the separation of ethics and politics in the first place. As R. B. J. Walker has argued, it is this separation of ethics and politics which leads to thinking of politics in terms of application or extension.[129] The second important move for analysis in the approaches I have explored is the way in which ethics and politics are rendered separable by these authors. This is, I suggest, at least in part a function of particular readings of Levinas and Derrida and the way in which they are seen to be related.

Both Campbell and Critchley's arguments ultimately rely on the assumption that the realms of ethics and politics are separate, such that one can and, indeed, should inform the other. In order for ethics and politics to fulfil the roles assigned to them under this assumption, ethics needs to be understood as a relatively unproblematic realm; difficulties and negotiation enter the picture only with its extension to politics. For both authors, this is a position drawn from their readings of Levinas, who is employed to offer an original ethics.

The concept of the ethical in Critchley is used to derive the politics of ethical difference and, hence, democracy. His use of Levinas is intended to bridge a gap in deconstruction between ethics and politics.[130] This use of Levinas to offer a passage from ethics to politics only works if it is accepted that ethics comes first for Levinas and politics or questioning is separate from this. Similarly, in Campbell's reading, Levinas provides an original and relatively straightforward ethics of: 'a responsible non-totalizing relation with the Other'.[131] Indeed, it is precisely because this relationship leaves no room for negotiation, questioning and politics that Campbell feels the need to bring Derrida in to theorise the move to politics. For both authors, Levinas' separation of ethics and politics is the basis on which he provides a useful supplement to fill a perceived gap in deconstructive thought, which is itself problematised as such precisely by this same distinction between ethics and politics through which it is read.

One approach to escaping the context of the separation between ethics and politics is offered by a return to Thomson's argument. The problem in work such as Campbell's, he argues, starts with the use of Levinas to supplement Derrida. On Thomson's reading, Levinas and Derrida do not dovetail quite as neatly as Campbell and Critchley suggest, because Derrida's work is a critique of precisely the oppositional philosophy which allows for the separation of ethics and politics in Levinas.[132] For Derrida, Thomson argues, the opposition between ethics and politics cannot be sustained, so the prioritising of one over the other or deducing of one from the other cannot be either:[133]

> By refusing to deduce politics (totality, violence) on the basis of ethics (the relation to the other, transcendence) but by showing both gestures to be possibilities inscribed within the (non-finite) totality, Derrida insists instead on the irreducibility of violence.[134]

Despite Derrida's problematisation of the separation of ethics and politics, however, ultimately, for Thomson, Derrida remains a thinker of politics and Levinas a thinker of ethics.[135] For Thomson, Derrida's work calls for a focus, albeit strategic, on politics and a 'suspicion' of ethics.[136] Thomson then comes down ultimately on the side of the authors above, who move away from ethics in order to retain politics, but his analysis opens up the question of the use and relation of Levinas and Derrida as a central site for rethinking the relationship between ethics and politics, which I take up in later chapters.

Working at the limits of theories

How, then, might it be possible to think through ethics and politics without reproducing the oppositional separation by favouring one side over the other? Some indications are provided by work which refuses the terms of the question posed by the critics; work which is not engaged in the first place in an attempt to set out in a systematic fashion a response to the claim that poststructuralism leads nowhere or to demonstrate its progressive political potential.[137] Edkins' critique of Campbell's 'politics of alterity' is part of a broader claim that the responsibility of the intellectual is to refuse to give an abstract or generalising answer to the ethico-political question.[138] The issue at stake, then, may not be that poststructuralist approaches do not go far enough, do not have enough content and are not affirmative enough, but that there may be, in some work, a tendency to go too far, to try to appease those asking for affirmative and positive accounts of ethics and politics and to provide it in the terms imposed by the questioners.

If the primary task is not figured in terms of demonstrating that deconstruction leads somewhere in a progressive manner, then the limit between ethics and politics takes on a different character. Rather than starting with ethics to ground politics or refusing ethics to start with an ungrounded politics, the possibility emerges of disrupting the dichotomy itself, hence Edkins' use of the 'ethico-political'. Starting and remaining engaged with precisely the limit of ethics and politics and the modalities of its disruption has given rise to specific, limited and empirically based engagements. Rather than asking in general terms how we might institute a politics which allows for interruption and multiplicity, for example, Maja Zehfuss demonstrates – in the context of the Iraq War – the way in which a post-foundational ethics as an approach does not ground politics, but rather illuminates the already interrupted nature of ethical and political claims.[139] Elizabeth Dauphinee, rather than providing an account of a politics of multiplicity and pluralisation based on the claims of alterity, shows how these categorisations, as well as universalising or totalising accounts of obligation, responsibility and politics, are in fact problematised in the face of alterity.[140]

It is this 'ethico-political' insight, developed largely in specific empirical contexts, which my analysis seeks to build on by taking a step back and exploring the conceptual underpinnings that might enable an alternative to the dichotomous framing of ethics and politics. What conceptual work is needed to move from a framework which reproduces a foundational account of ethics to one which sustains the initial relational insights offered by post-foundational approaches? How might we think through the conceptual possibility of refusing a general answer to questions of ethics and politics, of remaining at, and reconfiguring, the limit?

Chapter 2
Emmanuel Levinas: Ethics as Relation

Introduction: Ethics, Politics and the Third Person

Levinas is, in many ways, an obvious starting point for an investigation of non-theoretical and post-foundational ethical approaches.
His work is central to the configuration of ethics as relationality,
which was introduced in Chapter 1. He is explicitly concerned with
offering an alternative to universalisation and totalisation, which he
does through reconfiguring the idea of relation with a focus on the
Other. This leads to two key interrelated insights, which shape the
rethinking of ethics in terms of relationality: first, the presentation
of subjectivity as relational and responsible; second, the immediate,
pre-conscious and thus non-theoretical nature of responsibility.

Levinas is perhaps a less obvious resource for questions of politics.
Certainly, for the authors considered in the previous chapter, he
is the thinker of ethics, rather than politics. For them, limitations
emerge in his thought when it comes to relating ethics to politics. The
approaches outlined in Chapter 1 share a reading of Levinas in which
ethics is seen as separable from politics and prior to it.[1] Levinas is
understood to provide a relatively unproblematic ethical starting
point,[2] and whether the subsequent move from ethics to politics is
seen to be a strength or weakness in his work presupposes that such
a move is necessary, due to the initial separation of the two realms.

If, as I have suggested, this foundational reading emerges in the
context of a relationship between ethics and politics understood in
such a way that there is a perceived requirement to provide an account
of ethics which is 'politically useful', then a suspicion towards this
starting point opens up the possibility of alternative readings. The
alternative that I argue for in this chapter is a reading of Levinas in

which the implications of relationality are not constrained by the questions imposed by a prior distinction between ethics and politics. The depth, extent and complexity of Levinas' approach to relationality are lost, I suggest, if he is approached as a thinker of a 'simple' ethical obligation to the Other. His approach to thinking ethics without theory or foundations is, on this reading, not one which can then be used to ground politics, but rather one in which the political is always already implicated.

In order to develop this reading, the chapter emphasises the role of the 'third person' as the figure which complicates the separation of ethics and politics in Levinas' work. Existing approaches sideline this essential theme or give it merely secondary status to a pure ethical relation with the Other. The separation of ethics and politics and the corresponding suggestion that there is a pure ethical realm in Levinas' work is made possible precisely by this reading. Even in work which attempts to foreground the role of the Third, an essential separation between ethics and politics remains, with their interrelation described in terms of 'contamination' and 'haunting'.[3] However, it is the suggestion that the Third plays a potentially more complex role which I draw on as a starting point in an attempt to move beyond the current consensus. This idea can be seen, for example, in Diane Perpich's argument that the Third implicates ethics and politics 'prior to every origin';[4] in Bob Plant's suggestion that the Third is Levinas' figure for the 'mutual contamination' of the ethical and political realms;[5] and even in Simon Critchley's assertion that: 'ethics . . . entails and has to entail, a relation to politics conceived as . . . the third party'.[6]

From this starting point, the chapter presents a reading of Levinas in which the Third and the Other are equally important and assesses the implications for thinking the relation between politics and ethics that this approach entails. If the implications of the Third are fully appreciated, then the unproblematic and uncontested responsibility found in the relation to the one Other that is often drawn from Levinas' work is neither something that is possible, nor something on which a politics can be built. Instead, the Third points to the idea of relationality understood in terms of plurality. An examination of the concept of the face and the face-to-face relationship from which responsibility emerges demonstrates that the Third is present in that face-to-face relationship from the very beginning; in fact, it is an integral part of the face itself. As such, the ethical relation often relied upon is always already also political within itself. Ultimately, ethics and politics are not separable realms for which an account of relationship has to be found, but are necessarily inseparable and contained within one another.

Chapter 1 pointed to the importance of engaging with the limit between ethics and politics in order to sustain the initial relational insights offered by post-foundational approaches. This chapter explores the resources to be found in the work of Emmanuel Levinas for such an engagement. The chapter employs Levinas' work to think through the conceptual possibility of refusing a general or foundational answer to questions of ethics and politics in light of the pre-originary relational reformulation of ethics that he offers.

The first section begins by introducing Levinas' work on the Other, alterity and subjectivity as central to his approach to relationality. It then traces the implications of this relationality for thinking about ethics through a consideration of the concept of the face and the non-theoretical, immediate and asymmetrical responsibility that it enjoins.

The second section of the chapter elaborates on the concept of the face and the face-to-face relation through a reading which highlights the immediate presence of the third person. The implications of this reading are then traced through a discussion of its impact on Levinas' conceptualisation, first, of responsibility and, second, of justice, charity and the state as instructive for the way in which he conceives of the interrelation of ethics and politics. This section suggests that the concept of the ethico-political, in contrast to the notion of a pure ethical starting point, offers the possibility for deeper engagement with the consequences of Levinas' radical approach to relationality, which disrupts any ordering around the concepts of ethics and politics through its exposure of the aporetic plurality at the heart of responsibility.

The Other

Ontology, knowledge and totalisation

Levinas' concern throughout his work is to identify and attempt to move outside what he sees as a tendency towards totalisation in Western philosophy. The problem with this tendency, and the possibility of an alternative to it, is demonstrated, for Levinas, by the identification of a contradiction within the political structures of the West. On the one hand, the idea of European peace, he argues, has been based on ideas of the diverse uniting and the stranger being assimilated on the basis of universal knowledge and truth.[7] This is the model that has been used to try to perfect the political structures of the West in terms of reducing violence through, for example, human rights legislation, genocide conventions and immigration policies. On the other hand, however, this political tradition is also what has provided the conditions of possibility for the violences of genocide, imperialism and colonialism.[8] The tradition fails to recognise within itself this integral element, approaching cruelties and oppressions as aberrations or deviations from the progressive universalising ideals which found its political structures. For Levinas, these problems are not aberrations, but rather are symptomatic of the very priority given to unity, rationality, truth and knowledge, which determine a particular way of approaching or thinking the Other: 'it is in the knowledge of the Other as a simple individual – individual of a genus, a class or a race – that peace with the Other turns into hatred; it is the approach to the Other as "such and such a type"'.[9]

This violent disjuncture at the level of political structures is identified by Levinas as indicative of a much broader problem with the way in which Western philosophy is based in ontology, understood in terms of a tendency towards panoramic overviews and thematisation. The thematic exposition of being through knowledge is central to Western philosophical tradition, and it is this totalising trend which, he argues, has allowed the worst violences to occur.[10] The ontological tradition of which Levinas is critical includes all approaches which think in terms of comprehending otherness, of being able to have knowledge and understanding of it or of being able to grasp it and place it into a frame of understanding in which the same and the Other could be approached as terms in a relationship or as examples within a common genus. He is, for example, critical of the idea of human rights in this context, as he sees it as predicated on a view of individuals subsumed under the category of human through ideas of recognition, sameness, understanding and equality. This dominant ontological approach is insufficient to understanding our relations with Others, both in that it has violent consequences and it obscures the elements of the relationship which are not subsumed under understanding or comprehension. These are the elements to which Levinas turns his focus as a route to thinking about ethics outside of this totalising framework.

Levinas attempts to articulate the way in which we find ourselves to be responsible and responsive to the Other, suggesting that the idea of an originary state of conflict which is then regulated by ethical rules (as suggested by the universal commands of human rights, for example) does not do this effectively. He asks: 'Does the social, with its institutions, universal forms and laws, result from limiting the consequences of the war between men, or from limiting the infinity which opens in the ethical relationship of man to man?'[11] He suggests instead that we should think in terms of starting with a non-totalising 'ethical' relationship to the Other (which is simultaneously corrupted, as will be discussed below). For example, the question 'why does the Other concern me?' only has meaning, Levinas argues, if it is first assumed that the ego is concerned only with itself.[12] In this situation, it would indeed be incomprehensible that the Other concerns me, but Levinas' argument is that the Other does concern me in various ways and thus that the basis of enquiry should acknowledge that an originary war of all against all may not be the most appropriate way of understanding human relations.

Thus, Levinas proposes an alternative, whereby rather than thinking about the ethical as a controlling or limiting factor acting on subjects, ethics is approached instead as a structure on which both subjectivity itself and all our intersubjective relationships rest. Levinas, then, does not provide a theory of ethics in which knowledge would enable the construction of ethical principles, but rather approaches ethics as the name for the relation to the Other. He argues that, in a pre-originary way, we begin in a peaceful relation with the Other, rather than in conflict with them. Responsibility, for him, is the form that this relationship takes.

Alterity and relational subjectivity

Levinas' approach to the Other, then, is as absolutely other, outside of the realms of knowledge and understanding where they might be considered knowable, recognisable or like us. Approaching the Other in terms of knowledge, understanding or recognition, Levinas argues, is violent towards them: 'Thematization and conceptualization ... are not peace with the Other but suppression or possession of the Other'.[13] This is because, for Levinas, knowledge would subsume the Other within the self and bring it into the realm of the self. Knowledge confers a degree of ownership, as the thing known is brought within the self's comprehension; it becomes possessed or possessable.[14] However, the Other, he argues, is more than an object which can be placed in one of my categories and, as such, be allowed a place in my world.[15]

The Other, Levinas argues, resists these attempts at categorisation, because they are completely other. They are not just different in their characteristics, a different person, but still a person *like me*, under a genus, categorisable, an example of a type, not 'another self with different properties and accidents but in all essential respects like me'.[16] Levinas refuses this idea of difference which places the self and Other in common and instead adopts a more radical view, arguing that 'the alterity of the Other does not depend on any quality that would distinguish him from me, for a distinction of this nature would precisely imply between us that community of genus which already nullifies alterity'.[17] The Other is completely other for Levinas – an absolute alterity, outside the realms of knowledge to which we may try to reduce them. They are absolved from 'all essence, all genus and all resemblance'.[18]

This alterity, then, is not dependent on characteristics of the Other, rather, Levinas suggests, it is otherness itself which is the content of the Other. It is not that differences (of characteristics, of identity) constitute this absolute alterity, but that alterity is what allows for differences in the first place: 'It is not difference that makes alterity; alterity makes difference'.[19] It is not that we know the Other as such and such a type or as an example of a category which is differentiated by particular aspects or characteristics, but that this initial 'such and such a type' or 'example of a category' is removed, that the difference is not in the attributes, the content or the identity of the Other that differentiates, but rather that 'its formal characteristic, to be other, makes up its content'.[20] The alterity of the Other, then, for Levinas: 'does not result from its identity, but constitutes it'.[21]

Thinking of the Other as absolute alterity in Levinas has implications for the way in which he conceives of interpersonal relationships and sociality. Rather than concern for the Other arising from commonality between us, Levinas sees it as arising precisely out of the lack of commonality. It is not that community is the basis for concern, but that community is the result of the concern which arises from the fact of absolute alterity, claiming that: 'it is not because the neighbour would be recognised as belonging to the same genus as me that he concerns me. He is precisely *other*. The community with him begins in my obligation to him'.[22] Levinas thus reformulates the interpersonal relationship as a relationship with something completely outside the self and the self's powers to bring it into its grid of understanding and possession. If Others are rendered, through knowledge, a part of the self, it becomes impossible to enter into a social relation with them. The knowledge-based relationship is, for Levinas:

> . . . a relation with what one equals and includes, with that whose alterity one suspends, with what becomes immanent, because it is to my measure and my scale . . . there is in knowledge, in the final account, an impossibility of escaping the self; hence sociality cannot have the same structure as knowledge.[23]

For Levinas, the relation with something completely other and impervious to my powers of comprehension and control is about complete separateness. True togetherness is about separation, rather than about any degree of synthesis.[24] We are not together, for Levinas, in the commonality of being individuals within a genus, an analysis where the fact of the elements of sameness amongst us would come first: 'that sphere of the common which every synthesis presupposes is absent between men'.[25] The way in which we are together is rather, he argues, through first being completely different and strange to one another. Community and togetherness only then emerge through the obligation that this alterity enjoins. Community does not found obligation, rather obligation founds community. Togetherness is not found through being in common, but only through being utterly uncommon.

Once Levinas takes as a starting point the non-totalising relationship with alterity, an alternative conceptualisation of subjectivity also emerges. The self as separate, for Levinas, is not a quality of the self alone, but the result of the self's encounter with the Other. Importantly, this encounter is not posited in terms of there being an already existing self who is then confronted with a particular Other, thus leading to a modified subjectivity. He argues that we do not *establish* a relationship with the Other, but that we begin in relation with them; there is not, he argues, 'a period of pure interiority'. Indeed, we do not begin 'in solitude';[26] rather, the event of subjectivity is always already structured by the possibility of there being otherness, things which are outside of the self and its understanding and control. There is not first the subject and then disturbance, rather subjectivity itself is already disturbance, structured as 'the other in the same'.[27]

Importantly, this disturbance and putting into question of the idea of the self by the Other is not a special case of self-knowledge; it is not a matter of being conscious of being put into question, but rather of putting consciousness itself in question.[28] Subjectivity is 'irreducible to consciousness and thematization' and decoupled from the concept of autonomy.[29] Levinas instead posits the subject as held together by the accusative voice from elsewhere and so as necessarily relational.

In particular, this relationality takes the form of responsibility, which, for Levinas, is: 'the essential, primary and fundamental structure of subjectivity'.[30] Subjectivity, then, is understood in terms of the Other. Rather than the addition of responsibility to an already existing self, Levinas places the relation with the Other as prior to, and constitutive of, the self or ego. The self is created as a summons from the Other to respond. It is not that the I is conscious of the need to respond to the Other, as if it were something about which it could make a decision, but rather, for Levinas, the very position of the I *is* responsibility.[31]

It is through responsibility that, for Levinas, the subject can be understood as unique, singular and irreplaceable. The demand placed on the self by the Other renders the subject unique, rather than any attributes of the self; uniqueness is understood in terms of chosenness.[32] What renders the I unique is this relation of responsibility, where no-one can be responsible in my place and where the call of the Other is something to which only I can respond.[33] It is only in responsibility for the Other that the self can be considered both singular and irreplaceable:

> . . . in the relationship in which the other is a neighbour, and in which before being an individuation of the genus *man*, a *rational animal*, a *free will*, or any essence whatever, he is the persecuted one for whom I am responsible to the point of being a hostage for him, and in which my responsibility, instead of disclosing me in my 'essence' as a transcendental ego, divests me without stop of all that can be common to me and another man, who would thus be capable of replacing me.[34]

Uniqueness lies in the fact that I, and only I, am called and commanded by the Other to respond: 'At the moment when I am responsible for the Other I am unique. I am unique inasmuch as I am irreplaceable, inasmuch as I am chosen to answer him'.[35]

The face

Levinas describes the relation with the Other, with something completely other and impervious to the self's powers of comprehension and control, in terms of the concept of the face and the face-to-face relation of complete separateness. The face, for Levinas, is fundamentally the point at which we are exposed to the otherness of the Other and, as such, is what determines my relation with the Other. However, the face is also what points towards (or, as I will argue, *is*) the Third – the other Other or third party. The following section is an attempt to present a rereading of the concept of the face, not as an encounter with a unitary self-identical or autonomous Other, but rather as pointing towards fragmented and interrupted subjectivity, towards an Other other to itself, another within the Other. This is the starting point of my argument that, for Levinas, politics and the multiple always inhabit ethics and the singular.

Importantly, although the term 'face' immediately suggests a human face in terms of features – a nose, eyes and a mouth – as an image or as something recognisable, Levinas' use of this term is somewhat different. Levinas refuses the idea of the face as an image or object of perception. He suggests that to encounter the 'face', one cannot look at a human face in the usual way. To look, he argues, involves knowledge and perception and so negates the possibility of entering into a non-totalising relation with the Other, because it brings the Other into our own sphere of ownership. It would thus be tantamount to entering into a relation with oneself.[36] It is the idea of the face in terms of recognisable features which, in fact, creates the Other as an object. For Levinas:

> You turn yourself toward the Other as toward an object when you see a nose, eyes, a forehead, a chin, and you can describe them. The best way of encountering the Other is not even to notice the colour of his eyes.[37]

While it is possible to be in a social relationship where elements of perception exist, this is not the case, Levinas argues, if these are the full content of the relationship. Although the relationship with the face can be dominated by perception, he points out that what is specifically the otherness of the face – what allows for sociality or relation – is precisely what cannot be reduced to perception[38] or what overflows perception.[39] The reason that understanding the face in terms of images is problematic for Levinas is that he sees images as being immanent to one's own thought: 'as though they came from me'.[40] To appear to me, the Other would have to, in some way, make themselves intelligible to me, to signal to me in such a way that I could understand and thus make my own. Thus, for Levinas, the neighbour as Other does not appear.[41] The face does not represent or signal the Other which we might think of as lying behind it, the Other (as in Derrida's reading of Levinas) 'is not signalled by this face, he is this face'.[42] What sort of signalling, Levinas asks, 'could he send before me which would not strip him of his exclusive alterity?'[43]

It is in this sense that the face is something which contacts me outside of the world of my understanding, knowledge, comprehension or ownership, outside of the power and mastery of my self, my ego and my identity. My relation to the Other is not something that can be subsumed within consciousness or reduced to a theme. It is the nature of this relationship as other than consciousness that gives it its disquieting impact; it is foreign, causing 'disequilibrium . . . delirium, undoing thematisation, eluding principle, origin and will'.[44] The Other as face contacts and affects me otherwise, outside of my consciousness, power, knowledge and control. It is in this sense that the face places the ideas of my autonomy and identity in question.

Rather than perception, Levinas understands the face in terms of exposure, in which the Other is both destitute and commanding – in fact, commanding because destitute. Encountering the face entails an awareness or realisation of the mortality, material misery, defencelessness and vulnerability of the Other: 'the face . . . is like a being's exposure unto death; the without defence, the nudity and the misery of the Other'.[45] The discovery of the Other as defenceless and before death is, for Levinas, intimately interwoven with the Other's call to me and demands on me, and it is this combination of exposure and command which, for Levinas, is the face: 'this discovery of his death, this hearing of his call'.[46] Through exposure to the defencelessness of the Other in the face, the self is called to responsibility for, and subjection to, that Other.[47] Specifically, the face is, for Levinas, the commandment not to kill: 'The face is what one cannot kill, or at least it is that whose *meaning* consists in saying "thou shalt not kill"'.[48]

Responsibility

The responsibility instituted by the face's commandment not to kill is unlimited at the cost, ultimately, of the complete abnegation of the self. Through the commandment 'Thou shalt not kill', the right of the self even to be is put into question by Levinas' argument that 'in society such as it functions one cannot live without killing, or at least without taking the preliminary steps for the death of someone'.[49] It is this threat that the self inextricably poses to the Other that leads, for Levinas, to the question of whether I have the right to be:[50] 'Is being in the world', Levinas asks, 'not taking the place of someone?'[51] The commandment 'Thou shalt not kill', for Levinas, means much more than a command to not kill directly. Rather, it renders us responsible for *everything* that we do not do for the Other – taking their place, putting concern for the self first, even persisting in being of the self – for the reason that, ultimately, this might lead to the death of the Other. [52] Levinas' responsibility here, then, refers to harm in a very real sense, in terms of a concern with the Other's material misery: 'it is a matter, eventually, of nourishing him, of clothing him'.[53]

The relationship with the Other is, for Levinas, one of unlimited responsibility, regardless of whether we act on or assume this responsibility. He argues that: 'The tie with the Other is knotted only as responsibility, this moreover, whether accepted or refused, whether knowing or not knowing how to assume it, whether able or unable to do something concrete for the Other'.[54] It is because of this idea that we are always already placed in a situation of responsibility; that responsibility, for Levinas 'cannot begin in my decision'.[55] Any responsibility which began in me, in the sameness of the self, could not be a response to the Other, because the Other makes demands in a realm other than this consciousness. Indeed, for Levinas, it is the Other who, in their call, institutes consciousness. Levinas describes responsibility in terms of a paradox in consciousness: 'that I am obliged without this obligation having begun in me, as though an order slipped into my consciousness like a thief'.[56] This is, he continues 'impossible in consciousness', thus: 'we are no longer in the element of consciousness'.[57]

Responsibility, then, comes before any decision, because it comes before consciousness. This explains Levinas' argument that 'no-one is good voluntarily', not because being good or responsible goes against will or instinct on the part of the ego, but because responsibility comes before the concepts of will, decision, freedom or the possibility of doing something voluntarily.[58] Levinas' concept of responsibility for others 'could never mean altruistic will, instinct of "natural benevolence" or love' nor social rules or norms or the duty that one has because of certain relationships or which is brought on by choice, action or inaction of the self.[59] Responsibility is unchosen and so passive: 'a passivity that is more passive than the passivity that is opposed to action'.[60] It is in this sense that, for Levinas, as Jill Robbins argues, responsibility is immediate; I am obligated straight away without recourse to, or by way of, the theoretical.[61]

Responsibility, then, for Levinas, does not begin with my actions, decisions or consciousness. This leads to what Levinas considered one of the most important themes in his work, that: 'what is important is the notion of responsibility preceding a notion of a guilty initiative'.[62] That is, the idea that my being responsible for the Other is not something in which my actions have any import. I am responsible regardless of whether the destitution of the Other could be considered any fault of my own. I am not responsible because of, or for, my action or inaction, but immediately for the Other and, by extension, for their action and inaction. Responsibility is 'responsibility for what is not my deed, or for what does not even matter to me; or which precisely does concern me, is met by me as face'.[63]

The responsibility that I have for the Other is always greater than any they may have for me, because the unlimited nature of my responsibility means that I am responsible for the Other's responsibility.[64] The call of the Other for me to respond to them – their command not to kill – is a call to do everything for them, to take on responsibility for them with no limitations, to substitute myself for them to the point of complete self-sacrifice. Levinas thus argues that 'in this responsibility which we have for one another, I have always one response more to give, I have to answer for his very responsibility'.[65]

In line with Levinas' disjoining of responsibility from a guilty initiative, it is also divorced from any consideration of the self. For Levinas, responsibility is not reciprocal, nor is the consideration of my duties and obligations to the Other extendable to the Other's duties or obligations. Although this question of extending duties to

Others is not clear-cut in Levinas because of the Third, as will be discussed below, he provides no direct resources for prescribing the obligations of the Other or extending the unlimited duties by which I am bound to the Other. Only I, for Levinas, am subject to the Other. This is not an ethics which could be used to formulate or prescribe general rules for how I, Others or people 'in general' should behave. Instead, it is radically asymmetrical, unlimited, immediate and outside of choice, decision and consciousness.

An approach to ethics understood in terms of responsibility to the face of the Other is, then, from the beginning, not universal or universalisable and does not offer any general principles, because it is outside of the realm of principle. It offers, rather, a relational starting point, from which attempts to put 'ethics' to use, extend it, apply it, develop it or use it as a foundation cannot proceed. Once ethics is understood in terms of the Other, it is decoupled from theory and so from the theoretical avenues along which such accounts might be developed. The immediate unlimited responsibility to the Other in the face-to-face relation which is often put forward as the Levinasian ethical starting point with which to construct an ethical politics, on this reading, resists such an appropriation. However, in addition to the limit encountered when attempting to 'progress' from this starting point, the very idea of unlimited immediate responsibility to the Other can also be seen to be put into question when we consider the role of the third person in Levinas' thought.

The Third Person

The immediacy of the Third

The face-to-face relationship is problematised for Levinas upon the introduction of the third person. The figure of the Third introduces the elements of justice, comparison, universality and politics, which in some readings are approached as secondary to Levinas' discussion of charity, singularity, alterity and ethics[66] or which Levinas is seen as requiring supplementation (with Derrida in this case) in order to adequately address.[67] Rather than the Third as a secondary element coming after the face-to-face or as less important than it, I instead want to suggest that the ethical, the face-to-face and the infinite responsibility it demands is inextricably entwined with the ideas of the Third, justice and politics in Levinas' work.

Levinas is clear about the position of the Third, stating that: 'The Others concern me from the first'.[68] There is not first the Other and then the Third, but rather the Other and the face-to-face relationship with them always includes the Third. It is not that there is another person necessarily in the relationship (although in practice there always is – we do not live as part of an isolated pair), but that:

> The third party looks at me in the eyes of the Other [. . .] It is not that there first would be the face, and then the being it manifests or expresses would concern itself with justice; the epiphany of the face qua face opens humanity.[69]

That is, that the concerns of humanity as a whole, which are the concerns of justice (as will be discussed below), are themselves part of the relationship with the Other.

The use of Levinas discussed in Chapter 1, in which the face-to-face is taken as the interruption of totalisation – the pure ethical moment which we must seek to instantiate or protect – relies on rendering the Third secondary. For example, Martin Hagglund argues that the Third acts to corrupt an existing relation of perfect responsibility, that there is first sincerity and hospitality and then these values are compromised:

> Levinas's thinking describes a metaphysical opposition between a positive principle [sincerity, hospitality, ethics] – which ought to reign supreme – and a negative principle [the corruption of sincerity etc.] that unfortunately has taken hold of our existence.[70]

However, Levinas is clear that the Third does not enter or interrupt a prior relationship of perfect responsibility in the sense of the 'real world' getting in the way of responsibility:

> It is not that the entry of a Third party would be an empirical fact, and that my responsibility to the Other finds itself constrained to a calculus by the 'force of things'. In the proximity of the Other, all the others than the Other obsess me.[71]

Diane Perpich also offers a useful way of thinking about the immediacy of the Third and the way that it is already present in the face-to-face, arguing that:

[I]t would be a mistake to understand the difficulty described here only as that of an ego who is suddenly overburdened with extra responsibilities or who experiences a kind of divided loyalty; after all, the ego's responsibility to and for the Other was already *infinite* . . . responsible for the Other's responsibility, thus already responsible to and for the other of the Other.[72]

The face-to-face relation itself is about both complete responsibility to the Other *and* the demands of deciding between Others; for Levinas: 'Everything that takes place here "between us" concerns everyone'.[73] He goes even further in places, suggesting that the face itself is already the third person: 'The presence of the face, the infinity of the Other, is a destituteness, a presence of the third party (that is, of the whole of humanity which looks at us) . . .'[74]

The Third then alters the way in which we can think about or respond to our infinite responsibility to the Other, and it does this from the very beginning. The relationship with the third party, Levinas argues 'is an incessant correction of the asymmetry of proximity . . . and thus a decree in which my anarchic relationship with illeity is betrayed'.[75] However, the Third does not limit the degree of responsibility. We are, for Levinas, in a relation of infinite responsibility to both the Other and the Third. The Third places yet more demands on us and does not in any way let us out of our duties to the Other: 'I never deal with only one person; I am always dealing with a multitude of persons . . . That is what limits, not my responsibility, but my action'.[76] The general context of infinite and impossible responsibility, which is further extended by the Third, informs Levinas' approach to the necessary negotiation between the Other and the Third and underlies his position on the relations between ethics and politics, charity and justice, infinity and totality.

The Third ushers in a requirement for weighing up, calculating and choosing between Others – what Levinas calls justice.[77] It requires what Levinas terms 'morality': an institutionalisation of ethical guidelines and a series of rules regulating social behaviour.[78] It also institutes the realm of politics, institutions and processes by which the competing claims of the Other and the Third are mediated, negotiated, limited and organised, and this set of practices is required by justice. Justice is a realm of abstraction, generality and calculation, precisely the sphere of totality which Levinas initially seems so wary of: 'As soon as there are three, the ethical relationship with the Other becomes political and enters into the totalising discourse of ontology'.[79] The fact of the other Others and my responsibility to them leads to (and, for Levinas, requires) an institutionalisation and universalisation of responsibility as a way of choosing between or weighing up my responsibilities. The Third demands justice, and, for Levinas, politics is the way in which we try to respond to this demand.

If the Third is taken seriously in Levinas' work then, there is an insistence that ethics cannot be separated from politics and responsibility cannot be separated from irresponsibility. The implications of this foregrounding of the Third in Levinas impact on how we might go about thinking about the possibilities of deducing an ethics or politics from his work or using it as a grounding for a deconstructive approach. The Third entangles totality and infinity in such a way that we can no longer use Levinas' work to provide an uncorrupted ground. The following sections will explore the manifestations of this relationship in Levinas' treatment, first, of responsibility and irresponsibility and, second, of ethics, charity, politics and justice.

The impossibility of responsibility

While for Levinas we may always be responsible in the sense of being obligated infinitely to the Other and the other Others, there is a second element to the idea of responsibility touched upon above in the discussion of responding to the call of the face or the obligation under which it places us. Levinas is clear that the obligation placed on us by the Other, of our responsibility for them, does not entail the taking up of this responsibility. It does not entail a responsible response, whereby we fulfil our obligations to the Other(s). Responsibility, then, has two interlinked strands: as accusatory – having a responsibility – and as a reference to the response to this obligation in terms of behaving responsibly, taking the responsible course of action and so on.

This second aspect of responsibility in Levinas is more concerned with the particular way in which we respond, an encounter with the Other in which we approach them as face – what Levinas calls a social relationship – as opposed to a relationship of totality.[80] It is in this context that Levinas seems to make initial pronouncements on what a 'good' relation to the Other would look like; initial because this is always already complicated by the Third. Levinas argues that responding to the face as face, rather than proceeding from universality, is 'good' – that is, the idea of responsibility in this sense is one situated in the realm of choice or decision, where proceeding from universality is a possibility. There is virtue, it seems, in a type of response to the face that is not 'proceeding from universality' – that is, not turning away from the face.[81] Levinas states that: 'It [goodness] consists in going where no clarifying – that is, panoramic – thought precedes, in going without knowing where'.[82] The good, ethical and responsible thing to do is to respond to the call of the Other: 'responsibility is . . . to respond to the Other, to approach the Other as unique, isolated from all multiplicity and outside collective necessities'.[83]

Levinas is concerned – in a similar way to his concern with the Other's 'material misery' – with a concrete approach to the Other of 'affective warmth, feeling, and goodness', arguing that this constitutes 'the proper mode of this approach to the unique'.[84] There is 'holiness or the ethical in relation to oneself in a comportment which encounters the face as face'.[85] Responding to the face as face is 'good' for Levinas, because it is what the Other asks of us – that is, there is goodness in being attentive to the call of the Other, rather than necessarily in the content of that call.

However, we can never live up to what the Other demands of us. We can never fulfil our responsibilities, never be assured that we have taken the responsible course of action or 'done the right thing'. The demands of the Other upon us are already infinite, because we are charged even with their responsibilities to Others, and we are always also confronted with our infinite responsibilities to the Third. If the face-to-face – my complete responsibility to the Other – is necessarily a one-on-one situation, the presence of a Third immediately moves relations into a different realm, for in attempting to fulfil my absolute responsibility to the first person, I betray my duty to the second and so on: 'responsibility for the Other . . . is troubled and becomes a problem when a third party enters'.[86]

If the Third is immediate, this problematisation of responsibility is immediate. We are always simultaneously obligated to one Other *and* to all the other Others, as well as to the generality, rules, institutions and norms which adjudicate between these responsibilities. These demands are necessarily incompatible, because responding to the face via duty, rules or law is immediately to do violence to its alterity by approaching it as an instance of a type. This is, emphatically, not to say that the general, universal, rules, norms, law and so on have no place in Levinas' thought, nor are they in any way secondary. What is key about Levinas' approach is the interpenetration of the general and the particular; he is concerned with 'Totality *and* Infinity' (emphasis added), rather than a hierarchy or choice between the two terms.

The Third means that our obligations are not clear and that we can never fulfil them, because the infinite nature of the responsibilities that we have to the Other and the Third makes them necessarily incompatible. We are, then, always irresponsible in any attempt to be responsible. We are, in this sense, always turning away from the face of the Other, sacrificing them and reneging on our responsibility to them. This is in part because what is demanded of us is infinite and excessive, but it is also because the demand itself and the structure of the way that it is relayed to us calls for both responsibility and irresponsibility. The Third is always already there in the demand, in the face of the Other. Importantly, this impossibility is not a limit, weakness or oversight in Levinas' work. It is the very fact that the call of the Other does not determine a particular response and that it is always in competition with the incompatible calls of other Others and provides no way of adjudicating between these demands that means that the possibility of responsibility, rather than the violence of an obsession with the one Other or a clear knowledge of what we should do is maintained.

Levinas' approach of aligning responsibility with the *choice* to respond to the Other as face rather than in a totalising way means that even in a hypothetical face-to-face relationship without the Third, there would be no possibility of decision and, as such, no possibility of responsibility. It is the possibility of the approach of proceeding from universality and entering into a totalising relation with the Other that conditions the possibility of the response not being predetermined; we can approach the face as face or we can approach it in a totalising way. The possibility of there being a decision only occurs when the Third enters (otherwise we would be completely commanded and our response would be determined by the face of the one Other), so the element of choice that Levinas seems to see as necessary for responsibility or goodness is only possible with the Third; it would not be possible to be responsible in this way in the face-to-face.

Responsibility, in terms of a responsible response rather than in terms of obligation, only makes sense with an appreciation of the

Third in Levinas' work. It is the Third which opens up the possibility of responding in an unpredetermined way, but the Third simultaneously renders this responsibility impossible, since there is no response which could meet my responsibilities to both the Other and the Third. Levinas then might be read as articulating an aporia of responsibility from which he does not offer a way forward, not because of a failure of his theorising at this point, but because of an acknowledgement that it is the aporia itself which conditions the very possibility of responsibility. As such, the idea of Levinas' face-to-face relation as providing the horizon or grounding for thinking about responsibility and politics becomes problematic.

Problematising ethics and politics: justice, charity and the state

This interpenetration of the responsible and the irresponsible in the figure of the Third is extended to Levinas' discussion of ethics and politics. Levinas is sometimes read as calling for a critique or disruption of the political in the name of the ethical, as discussed in Chapter 1.[87] Similarly, the idea of a passage or movement from ethics to knowledge, the Other to the Third and so on characterises much of the debate regarding Levinas' political utility.[88] However, this approach relies on a categorical and temporal distinction between these realms, which, I suggest, is not to be found in much of Levinas' work. His understanding of ethics and politics is, I argue, more complex than this separation suggests and can be more usefully characterised by the idea of the ethico-political.

Levinas' approach to politics concerns the need to create institutions, rules, universalisable and generalisable structures as required by the Third. It also encompasses a more traditional, concrete understanding of politics, addressing issues such as the state and democracy, although these issues arise out of the same concerns. It is ultimately justice which requires institutionalisation and politics: 'Justice is necessary, that is, comparison, coexistence, contemporaneousness, assembling, order, thematisation, the visibility of faces'.[89] Justice is the mechanism by which the claims of Others are compared and judged. Justice as calculation and legislation, although aligned with the realm of the general, abstract and universal, plays an important 'ethical' role: 'against the persecution which targets Others and especially those close by, one has to have recourse to justice'.[90]

Justice is necessary because of the Third, who is immediately present in the face of the Other. In approaching the Other, Levinas argues: 'A third party is also approached; and the relationship between the neighbour and the third party cannot be indifferent to me when I approach. There must be a justice among noncomparable ones'.[91] The demand for responsibility to the Third and, in this, to a multiplicity of Others requires that what may initially seem to be a commitment to infinite responsibility to one Other also entails that there must be comparison and calculation. It is this that makes charity or responsibility possible among many Others: 'justice and the just state constitute the forum enabling the existence of charity within the human multiplicity'.[92] However, calculation and comparison also threaten this possibility, if separated out from a continued concern with the infinite responsibility of the face-to-face (as discussed below).

Levinas' introduction of the Third requires a consideration of justice and comparison, and it is the state which institutionalises this necessity: 'This multiplicity of human beings must be organised, calculated. I can cede my responsibility within a society organised in a State, in justice'.[93] The state is not put forward as purely positive or negative, as ethical or unethical (although these categories are themselves problematic in this context). The Third both extends and limits our responsibility, and this difficulty is reflected in the state and institutions. It is for Levinas 'necessary in order to make comparisons, judge, have institutions and juridical procedures, which are necessary'.[94] However, as well as being necessary, the state is unavoidably violent, as all limits to infinite responsibility to one singular Other are violent: 'You find . . . the necessity of the state. Violence, of course, in relation to the charity rendered necessary precisely by the charity inspired by the face of the neighbour'.[95] The state both supplements and denies the 'work of interpersonal responsibility'.[96] As such, the state and institutionalisation are not necessarily a corruption of an ethical relationship; in the light of the Third, the relationship between ethics, charity and politics or justice becomes more complex.

Levinas does, however, raise concerns about an approach which separates politics and justice from concerns of charity. Although charity, for Levinas, is impossible without justice and the state, justice is 'warped' without charity.[97] It is from this starting point that Levinas criticises the state and justice as problematic when approached as sufficient in, or legitimised by, themselves. Again, this is a reflection of the aporia of the ethico-political relation – the insufficiency of either the face-to-face or the relation to the Third to the demands of responsibility. Justice, taken by itself, inseparable from formalised and sedimented institutions: 'risks causing us to misrecognise the face of the other man'.[98] The judgement required by justice is, for Levinas, violent, in that it transforms faces into:

> [O]bjective and plastic forms, into figures which are visible but defaced, the appearing of men, of individuals, who are unique but restituted to their genera. With intentions to scrutinise and acts to remember.[99]

It is in response to this (unavoidable) violence that Levinas argues that 'love must always watch over justice', in order to provide a foil to its totalising tendencies, to negotiate the violence done in its name (although in the name of another violence aimed at the Third).[100] Justice is, for Levinas, an impossible concept, precisely because of its position with regards to the competing demands of the Other and the Third. Justice, Levinas argues: 'remains justice only in a society where there is no distinction between those close and those far off, but in which there remains the impossibility of passing by the closest'.[101] Justice, then, might be understood as the very impossibility at the heart of the ethico-political relation, whereby we are under obligation both to the immediate absolute demand of the Other and the realm of generality, rules and norms which adjudicate between Others.

The complexity of the relationship between justice and charity is what complicates Levinas' approach to politics and the state. Levinas does not see all politics as totalising or inimical to a concern with the ethical. Rather, he is concerned with emphasising the danger in an idea of pure politics, of generalisation, universalisation and a concern only with the Third in an abstract sense: 'Politics left to itself bears a tyranny within itself; it deforms the I and the Other *who have given rise to it*, for it judges them according to universal rules, and thus as in absentia'.[102] It is this approach which would deny the roots of politics in the negotiation of unlimited responsibilities demanded by the face. Politics is always already about a negotiation between the Other and the Third, always already the ethico-political.

Levinas contrasts the liberal state with a totalising state, arguing that one leaves space for charity and the interpersonal, while the other attempts to bring everything within 'pure' politics or institutionalisation. Levinas' work on the liberal state is relevant because of the way that it highlights the importance of charity within justice in contrast to the totalitarian state, which he sees as an attempt at closing down this dimension of charity and the interpersonal, but which, importantly, always fails in this task. His discussion of the totalising state also illustrates his concern with the fragility of charity in the face of totalising justice and politics.

Levinas suggests that the liberal state recognises, at least to an extent, the impossibility of the concept of 'pure' politics. Because the state is an institutionalisation of the aporetic ethico-political interpersonal relationship, it contains within itself contradictory elements and so potentially openness: space for the personal and institutional and an acknowledgement of the singular and particular as that which demands the universal and general. The liberal state allows for this openness. For Levinas, there is 'an appeal to mercy behind justice' in the liberal state – an acknowledgement of the duty we have to the Other at the same time as our duties to the Third and the generality, that is, to justice.[103] A state which recognises this has the possibility, for Levinas, of not excluding charity and retaining an acknowledgement of 'the presence of the singular in the universal'.[104]

It is, however, only in the liberal state, for Levinas, that the violence to the singular and unique, of which he is wary, can be checked. This is because of an element of openness that he sees in the liberal state, a structurally guaranteed possibility for change, contestation and, most importantly, a space or the possibility of space outside of the direct control of totalising, universalising institutions, policies or control in which the interpersonal relation can exist unmediated by totalising and violent (though, for him, necessary) institutions: 'A state in which the interpersonal relation is impossible, in which it is directed in advance by the determinism proper to the state, is a totalitarian state'.[105] In contrast, there is at least the possibility for both the universal and particular to coexist in the liberal state through contestation, negotiation and interruption. The notion of perfectibility that he sees at the heart of the liberal state is essential to his position:

> the universality of the law in the state – all this violence done to the particular – it is not licence pure and simple, because as long as the state remains liberal its law is not yet completed and can always be more just

than its actual justice. Hence a consciousness . . . that the justice on which the state is founded is, at this moment, still an imperfect justice.[106]

Levinas makes these arguments on the basis of the position that the state is itself an institutionalisation of (or in the case of non-liberal states, an attempt at resolution of) the aporia between the demands of the Other and the Third found in the ethico-political relation. For Levinas 'the political, the state and institutions presuppose the starting point of the one-for-the-other of responsibility';[107] that is, for Levinas, the state emerges not as a result of a 'war of all against all', a tool for limiting violence, but rather as a tool to control and limit our excessive responsibilities.[108] The commitment to the relation to the Other and, with the entry of the Third, to justice is, for Levinas, reflected in the order of the state. It is the Third who calls for the state in causing 'the relation with the I to become with a we and thus to aspire to a state, laws, institutions and universality'.[109]

For Levinas, charity and justice cannot be separated. However, his emphasis on the liberal state points to his concern that some (for him, non-liberal) structures might threaten the claims of charity. This can be read as a prioritising of charity over justice or as an argument that justice must be kept 'in check' by charity, but in the same way as with ethics and politics, I suggest that this is not the overall tone of Levinas' argument. He is rather, I suggest, concerned with the fragility of charity, responsibility and the interpersonal in the face of the necessarily totalising tendencies of justice and the state. His concern is that the interpersonal aspect of the ethico-political relation may disappear 'in the justice that it requires and in the politics that justice requires'.[110] The possibility of responsibility itself being extinguished through being fully subsumed under a totalising and universalising system – indeed, being extinguished by that which is both a necessary part of it and demanded by it – is not a rejection of these totalising and universalising moves. Universalisation, justice and calculation, a response to the demands of the Third *in the face of the Other*, both condition the possibility of responsibility (because for responsibility to be responsible, it must be a response to both the infinite responsibility demanded by the Other *and* to the generality demanded by the Third) and pose great risk to it. In the face of this risk, Levinas is concerned with ensuring the continued possibility of, and space for, interpersonal relationships to coexist with the totalising tendencies of justice, such that, he argues: 'to soften this justice, to listen to this personal appeal, is each person's role'.[111]

To put this theme into context, Levinas' work in this area draws heavily on Vasily Grossman's *Life and Fate* ([1980] 2006), in which the focus is the totalising reach of the Soviet state and its attempts and ultimate failure to regulate and control the interpersonal. Levinas draws on Grossman's idea that the 'little goodness' from one person to his neighbour risks being lost and deformed: 'as soon as it seeks organization and universality and system, as soon as it opts for doctrine, a treatise of politics and theology, a party, a state and even a church'.[112] As such, Levinas is concerned with the moment that the 'senseless incidental goodness in the human, the compassion proceeding from one private man to another' becomes 'preaching, ideological beginning', because it is at this point that it risks betraying itself.[113]

Charity may be fragile, but the politics from which it is under threat is a politics institutionalised in the name of charity. Politics itself, then, is not pitted against responsibility, but is an attempt at responding to the incompatible demands which emerge at the very starting point of the encounter with the face. It is part of, and not in opposition to, what might usually be understood as the ethical in Levinas' work.

With this in mind, Levinas' pronouncements on the necessity of critiquing the political with the ethical take on a rather different tone. The problem, when recast in this way, is with the idea of 'pure' politics and, I would argue, the corresponding idea of 'pure' ethics or responsibility. Levinas' argument that 'politics must be able in fact always to be checked and criticised starting from the ethical'[114] and that 'politics must be held in check by ethics'[115] can be seen as linked to his desire to limit any move to totalisation by politics or the state. These moves are precisely those of attempting to foreground the inseparability of the two concepts, rejecting any tendency towards instituting or attempting to institute a realm of politics divorced from ethics in this case. Rather than being seen as an assertion of the primacy of a realm of pure ethics, when put within the broader context outlined here, these statements can be seen as corresponding with Levinas' argument that the Third and politics always inhabits ethics or responsibility.

By arguing that ethics, charity or the interpersonal can or should interrupt politics, the suggestion is that politics is a separate realm, which could pre-exist the ethical or be founded without reference to it. However, Levinas' approach is one where the political is, even in its most traditional definition, an institutionalisation of the impossibilities already within the ethical, an institutionalisation necessary in the name of (and yet always insufficient to) justice. The ideas of responsibility and the difficulties within them are, for Levinas, what necessitates this formal politics, but this movement is not a chronological progression.

This interrelation suggests that Levinas' work requires thinking in terms of the ethico-political. It is not only that the ethical always permeates the political, an insight that is quite widely accepted and acted upon in existing poststructuralist literature, for example, by problematising the notion of political decisions as ethically neutral.[116] The political is also always within the idea of the ethical or responsible. If the ethical or responsible is approached as always entwined with the political, then it becomes impossible for, first, one to be derived from the other and, second, for ethics to be considered as a ground. Ethics and responsibility, if the Third is taken seriously, need instead to be conceptualised as already containing within themselves the notions of multiplicity, negotiation, categorisation and aporia. The ethico-political is always undoing any notion of the ethical from within, for Levinas, through the Third – a figure of the aporia at the heart of any conception of ethics, responsibility or charity.

Relationality as Plurality

Levinas' approach to politics is frequently regarded as a weakness or 'Achilles heel' in his work.[117] While he is often used to provide relatively clear-cut resources in terms of an ethical starting point, his treatment of the relation between ethics and politics and the position of the Third in his work has been the subject of rather more controversy. However, throughout this debate, there is an assumption that ethics and politics are, for Levinas, separate realms to varying degrees, that ethics can and should interrupt politics and that Levinas' work can provide a foundation from which to deduce a politics through his discussion of the relationship between the Other and the Third.

While Simon Critchley has argued that Levinas' 'deduction' between ethics and politics should be replaced with a 'hiatus' drawn from Derrida,[118] this chapter has put forward a reading of Levinas in which hiatus and aporia already characterise this relationship. I have argued that, for Levinas, the ethical and political are immediately interconnected through the figure of the Third. It is possible through this to read Levinas as foregrounding the difficulty in responsibility and politics – that there is no pure responsibility without the element of violence and negotiation that the Third brings. The interconnectedness of the Other and the Third, the particular and the universal, charity and justice, ethics and politics is reflected throughout his work. There is no pure ethical relation to which we might try to return: the ethical is always already political, and it is this which may allow for the possibility of responsibility. It is for this reason that the Levinasian approach to responsibility is not one which can uphold a political project.

Levinas offers resources for thinking outside foundational and theoretical accounts of ethics by recasting questions of ethics in terms of relation. Often this is taken to mean that there is a pure ethical relation in the face-to-face, but this is in part because Levinas' thought is being used to try to provide a non-foundational foundation from which to develop a politics. If we suspend this initial separation of ethics and politics, a different reading emerges in which the relationality that Levinas explores is a relation with plurality: with the Other and with all the other Others who are immediately present, with the contradictory demand to approach as face and as an instance of a type. The separate realms of ethics and politics and the distinction between the one-to-one relation and the one-to-many relation on which these are founded no longer hold. Relationality understood as plurality cannot provide general or theoretical answers. Nothing can be built on or deduced from it.

This plurality, the aporia within the concept of the ethico-political, is not something which is a failing or limitation. While it does have consequences for the extension and application of Levinas' thought to questions about how we might construct an ethical politics, it simultaneously suggests a rethinking of the way in which we ask questions of ethics and politics. The consequences of a reading of Levinas' thought which does not provide a pure vision of ethics or responsibility, of foregrounding his argument that the Third is present even in the face of the Other, means that Levinas cannot be used to provide an ethical ground, returning us once again to the risk and uncertainty which may allow for responsibility and politics.

Chapter 3
Jacques Derrida: The Im-possibility of Responsibility

Introduction: Theory, Im-possibility, Limits

There are two key themes offered by the work of Jacques Derrida which offer resources for thinking how we might avoid reproducing a mode of analysis in which the potential of post-foundational approaches to ethics are limited by its positioning as a ground for politics: first, an explicit focus on the limits of, and in, theory; second, the development of the concepts of the im-possible, aporia and hiatus. These are the starting points for the analysis offered in this chapter.

In the first instance, Derrida's engagement with the limitations of theory and theorising offers a way to move outside of the question concerning what ethics can do for politics, for thinking about ethics as non-theoretical and non-foundational and for exploring the implications of this reorientation for politics and the political. Deconstruction explicitly 'resists theory',[1] offers a focus on 'what threatens, exceeds, or destabilizes the *stanza* of a coherent theory'[2] and seeks to 'exceed the theoretical'.[3] That is, rather than rejecting theory, deconstruction offers a way of engaging with its limits.[4]

The second theme is a more specific articulation and development of this question of limits. One of the ways in which the limits of theory are traced in Derrida's work is through the concept of the im-possible: 'the edge that forms the union and the separation of the possible and the impossible, the dash between them – the im-possible as possible or the possible as im-possible'.[5] This provides a route by which the discursive positioning of ethics as grounding or foundational by the authors identified in Chapter 1 might be disrupted. The im-possible offers a way of conceptualising ethics that engages with the difficulties internal to the concept as its very condition of possibility; that the condition of possibility of any ethics or responsibility is that it is without stable foundations.

The chapter proceeds by developing the implications of these broad themes for approaching ethics and politics in the absence of secure foundations. There are three elements in the reading of Derrida presented here which are central to my argument. The first element is the contention that if the Other as outside, transcendent or face no longer marks a simple (if excessive) ethical demand, then a reading of Derrida's work emerges in which the im-possibility of ethics, responsibility or justice cannot be resolved. The concepts most often associated with the 'ethics' of deconstruction – for example, the unconditional, which provides David Campbell's 'duty in decision', or the moments of interruption, to which Simon Critchley assigns an ethical status – rely on a resistance to totalisation as an ethical demand drawn from this outside. However, I will argue that the idea of the im-possible illuminates the necessary and immediate contamination of the outside or undeconstructable, which both implicates and locates the ethical from the very beginning also in the realm of totalisation.

Following on from this, the second element to my argument is that this contamination signals the interpenetration of ethics and politics. If deconstruction does not provide an account of an undeconstructable outside in which to locate ethics, then it cannot provide the corresponding account of a realm of totalisation in which we might locate politics. It is, in fact, the interpenetration of these realms which renders ethics and responsibility im-possible. This offers the potential to shift the context in which we might think about ethics away from the dominant question of its 'relationship' with politics, as outlined in Chapter 1, by positing the interpenetration of the two concepts such that to then theorise the relationship between them as if they were initially separate no longer makes sense. As I have suggested, it is in part the assumed separation of ethics and politics which leads to the continued reliance on foundational accounts of ethics. I suggest a rereading in which ethics cannot be positioned as a ground for politics, because the condition of possibility for any ethics or politics is precisely the way in which they are rendered im-possible by the interpenetration of the two realms.

Third, and informing these readings, the chapter engages with the implications of Derrida's argument that: 'Deconstruction . . . is what happens. Deconstruction is the case'.[6] This means, I will argue, that the type of resources offered by deconstruction are not ones which might allow us to formulate or derive principles, rules or guidelines. Rather, Derrida offers an exploration of the way that texts, discourses and concepts, including those of ethics and politics, are unfinished, insecure and aporetic.[7] A deconstructive approach cannot determine in advance the meaning of 'ethics' or 'politics' and so cannot provide an account, theory or guideline for the political or ethical decision, but rather shows how the grounds on which any such guideline might rest are deconstructed. The chapter then draws from Derrida a rethinking of the ethical and political, rather than an ethics or a politics as such. The implications of this undermine any attempt to derive affirmative ethical or political gestures from a deconstructive position. As Derrida states, a deconstructive approach to 'the concepts . . . of responsibility, decision, justice . . . are anything but reassuring to those who wish to reassure themselves in ethics and politics'. [8]

The chapter has three parts. First, it offers an overview of the idea of the responsible decision as one of the key ways in which Derrida engages the themes of responsibility and ethics and which he employs to demonstrate the ways that responsibility is both aligned with, and exceeds, the realms of thought, consciousness and reason through the figure of the Other. The aporia at the heart of decision illuminates the limits of knowledge and subjectivity as possible starting points for thinking about ethics. The second part of the chapter moves on to consider the implications of this reading for constructing an ethics of deconstruction. It argues that the concepts of the unconditional and absolute duty on which an ethics of the Other might be built are always necessarily destabilised by risk, undecidability and im-possibility; it is only through the Other that decision might be responsible, but the Other renders responsibility impossible. The third section analyses the implications of this reading of ethics for the possibility of a 'politics of deconstruction'.

The Responsible Decision

The limits of knowledge

The most sustained engagement with the concept of responsibility in Derrida's work can be found in his interrogation of the responsible decision, as well as his decentring of the concept of decision, which is discussed below. Only a decision, he argues, can be responsible; without decision, there is no possibility of responsibility or ethics.[9] We can only be responsible for a decision – that is, we can only call responsibility ours or take responsibility for a decision. Without a decision, we are simply in the realm of the technical application of knowledge. Following rules or being guided by knowledge is not something for which we can take responsibility. If we only look elsewhere for guidance or rules, then responsibility is taken out of our hands. As Thomas Keenan argues, it is only when 'there are no alibis, no elsewhere to turn in the instant of decision' that the decision can be called 'ours'.[10]

The first 'elsewhere' to which we might turn is the ground of knowledge, theory or rules. Derrida is concerned to show that rather than responsibility residing solely in reason, sense or consciousness, it is also aligned with the suspension of these faculties.[11] All 'decisions' which are reached through calculation or in accordance with a programme are, Derrida argues, effectively pre-coded. The responsible decision cannot consist simply of carrying out or applying a rule or norm:

> Wherever I have at my disposal a determinable rule, I know what must be done, and as soon as such knowledge dictates the law, action follows knowledge as a calculable consequence: one *knows* what path to take, one no longer hesitates. The decision then no longer decides anything but is made in advance and is thus in advance annulled. It is simply deployed, without delay, presently, with the automatism attributed to machines. There is no longer any place for justice or responsibility.[12]

Derrida's approach is not an attempt to abandon knowledge or underplay its importance, but rather is an insistence that decision itself is heterogeneous to knowledge. There is, in decision, an element of urgency; the moment of the decision is always now, it cannot be indefinitely postponed while all possible knowledge is gathered:[13]

> [A]s if absolute urgency were not the law of decision, the event and responsibility, their structural law, which is inscribed a priori in the concept. Centuries of preparatory reflection and theoretical deliberation – the very infinity of a knowledge – would change nothing in this urgency. It is absolutely cutting, conclusive, decisive, heartrending; it must interrupt the time of science and conscience, to which the instant of decision will always remain heterogeneous.[14]

The urgency of decision means that knowledge will never be sufficient, but there is also a broader structural difficulty in the passage from knowledge to decision. Even if complete knowledge could secure the decision, thus insuring the outcome, it would no longer be a decision, but rather the application, consequence or effect of this knowledge.[15] The urgency of decision, its break with knowledge, is not an unfortunate 'fact of life' which undermines attempts at decision, but rather is a structural feature of decision itself – an im-possibility, a fault line or limit inscribed within the very concept. That is, decision *demands* both knowledge and non-knowledge. As Derrida explains:

> [W]e need to have knowledge, the best and most comprehensive available, in order to make a decision or take responsibility. But the moment and structure . . . of the responsible decision, are and must remain heterogeneous to knowledge. An absolute interruption must separate them, one that can always be judged 'mad', for otherwise the engagement of a responsibility would be reducible to the application and deployment of a program.[16]

Derrida's problematisation of the notion of decision and its link to responsibility places this responsibility at least partially in the experience of the unknown. This translates to a tension in the very way that we might approach an attempt at understanding or theorising responsibility. On the one hand, for responsibility to be understood or thematised, it must be treated as if it were a matter of knowledge or technical application, which would negate the possibility of responsible decision.[17] On the other hand, there is a necessity for a thematisation or understanding of what responsibility might be, in order for decisions to be responsible. To make a decision outside of knowledge, to be unaware or unconscious of what one is doing, would also negate the possibility of responsibility.

So while this account might initially seem to point to decision, for it to be worthy of the name, as entirely outside of rules, norms and knowledge, for Derrida, it also requires a regard for rules and knowledge. It is the limits of knowledge, theory and rules with which he is concerned, rather than a rejection of them. While responsibility is not served if a decision follows programmes or formulae, it is also not possible if rules and law are suspended entirely or if in the confusion of non-knowledge, the decision itself is suspended, if in making a decision:

[H]e doesn't refer to any law, to any rule or if, because he doesn't take any rule for granted beyond his own interpretation, he suspends his decision, stops short before the undecidable or if he improvises and leaves aside all rules, all principles.[18]

The role of knowledge is not secondary in thinking about responsibility and decision for Derrida. A decision made without regard to knowledge would not be responsible. There can be no responsibility if we ignore rules and stop trying to make new, better and more nuanced knowledge and laws. And yet there can be no responsibility if this is *all* we do or if this determines events such that nothing can happen:

> [T]o be responsible in ethics and politics implies that we try to programme, to anticipate, to define laws and rules ... the challenge is to do our best to predict, to prepare, to programme, to organise ethics and politics ... master the surprise, without, if possible, erasing the heterogeneity, the alterity of what is coming, and that is the political and the ethical challenge.[19]

The necessity of decision thus leaves us with a double imperative, which we cannot escape; to suspend calculation and rules, but simultaneously to be mindful of these realms, to push them to their limits and beyond. The passage from knowledge and rule to invention and decision, then, is ultimately unsecured – a passage through non-knowledge and non-rule.[20] As Thomas Keenan argues:

> One can, and must, oppose as militantly as possible all the new obscurantisms, fight for the extension and radicalisation of all enlightenments ... and still insist: no matter how bright the light, the crossing occurs at night.[21]

This double gesture requires that the law or rule both be followed and suspended. Responsibility is not about an absence of rules and knowledge, but: 'a reinstitution of rules which by definition is not preceded by any knowledge or by any guarantee as such'.[22] Derrida links decision and responsibility with invention or reinvention, arguing that whichever rule, norm or knowledge would govern a decision needs to be both confirmed, in terms of interpreting it, and invented each time anew, as if no rule or programme existed:

[T]o be just, the decision of a judge, for example, must not only follow a rule of law but must also assume it, approve it, confirm its value by a reinstituting act of interpretation, as if ultimately nothing previously existed of the law, as if the judge himself invented the law in every case. No exercise of justice as law can be just unless there is a 'fresh judgement' ... This 'fresh judgement' can very well – *must* very well – conform to a preexisting law, but the reinstituting, reinventive and freely decisive interpretation, the responsible interpretation of the judge requires that his 'justice' not just consist in conformity, in the conservative and reproductive activity of judgement. In short, for a decision to be just and responsible, it must, in its proper moment if there is one, be both regulated and without regulation: it must conserve the law and also destroy it or suspend it enough to have to reinvent it enough in each case.[23]

The limits of the subject

The requirement that a decision be singular, as if invented each time anew cannot be simply resolved for Derrida with a turn to the subject as the origin of the decision, by an approach whereby decision is understood as 'active, free, conscious and wilful, sovereign'.[24] The subject cannot be the starting point for decision, since it is the decision which invents the subject each time: 'if there is a decision it presupposes that the subject of the decision does not yet exist and neither does the object'.[25] Subject and object would render the decision predetermined. A reliance on the subject, agency or identity as grounds for action would be, in Keenan's terms, just another 'alibi' or 'elsewhere' to which we might turn.

Derrida suggests that a 'purely autonomous movement' would not be a decision, because it would 'simply deploy the possibilities of a subjectivity that is mine'.[26] A decision, Derrida argues, cannot be a product of identity or subjectivity in any straightforward way:

If you describe an individual as a set of possibilities, a set of capacities, a set of predicates – I am this or that . . . If the decision is simply the consequence or what follows from this set of possibilities, then it's not a decision.[27]

An approach to the subject where it is autonomous, sovereign and fully in command and in control of itself would mean that anything which originated in it would be already determined by the pre-given characteristics, identity and consciousness of the subject. This type of subject could not engage in decisions, because it would be merely acting out what it already was or what was already within it. As Derrida argues: 'If a decision is simply an expression of myself, my identity or nature, if it just follows from what I am, it is not a decision';[28] and elsewhere: '[I]f what I'm doing and deciding is simply what I can decide or what belongs to my possibility, if this is in me, then this is not a decision'.[29] The 'being mine' of a decision acts both to make a responsible decision possible and threaten its possibility.[30]

A decision, then, would not be something which the subject could take in any unproblematic way. The decision must come from outside the capabilities of the self-identical subject; it is something, for Derrida, which must come from the Other – that which exceeds existing structures of meaning, whether in the other person or not:

> If I make a decision which I can take, that is something which I'm able to do, something which I'm strong enough or have the capacity or the ability to do, so that the decision then follows my potentiality, my ability, my possibility – then there is no decision. For a decision to be a decision, it has to be, to look impossible for me, as if it were coming from the Other.[31]

The decision, although in some ways remaining mine, at least in terms of responsibility for it, must, to be a decision, also be taken 'in the name of the Other',[32] prompted by the Other's demands on me, a response to the Other's call to me. Yet to be a decision, and one that is impossible for me to take: 'it is . . . necessary for me to receive from the other, in a kind of passivity without parallel, the very decision whose responsibility I assume'.[33] There must be something passive in a decision, something which remains outside of my mastery:

> If a decision is wholly under my control, if it is predicated of a subjectivity, if I am the one who decides for the decision, and it is totally active in that sense, then what follows as an effect of the decision is programmed. However paradoxical it may sound I must be affected by my own decision.[34]

The role of the Other in decision, then, does not in any way let me 'off the hook', as it were. For a decision to be responsible, it must still be something for which I remain responsible, a decision which is not mine, but which is made through me, something beyond my capabilities, impossible for me and yet still my decision. Derrida argues that:

> In order to be a decision ... My decision should not be mine, it should be, as impossible, the decision of the Other, my decision should be the Other's decision in me, or through me, and I have to take responsibility for the decision which is not mine.[35]

The idea of the Other's decision in me, such that the responsibility is mine for something which I do not control, seems less paradoxical when we consider Derrida's approach to subjectivity. By starting with the Other (in a similar way to Levinas), the link between subjectivity, autonomy, sovereignty and self-identity is put into question. The subject, for Derrida, is not complete and whole in itself; it is different from itself, there is a gap in identity.[36] This gap within identity is, he argues, mirrored in an untraversable gap between oneself and the other person. There is something other within myself and something other within the Other: 'I cannot appropriate the alterity of the Other, whether in the other person or in myself. In myself there is something irreducible to identity, to the ego, which is infinitely resistant to appropriation'.[37] The subject rethought in this way is inseparable from the Other; it is, in fact, the product of an 'underivable interpellation from the Other'.[38] The Other comes first, as for Levinas; it calls the subject into subjectivity, thus making the structure of subjectivity once again one of responding to the call of the Other:

> It is a singularity that dislocates or divides itself in gathering itself together to answer to the Other, whose call somehow precedes its own identification with itself, for to this call I can *only* answer, have already answered, even if I think I am answering 'no'.[39]

This incompleteness of the subject is key to Derrida's approach, because it is what allows for relation, decision, responsibility and, ultimately, I will argue, for politics. For Derrida, alterity is, in a similar way as it is for Levinas, the very condition for the relation to the Other:

> [It] is a duty, an ethical and political duty, to take into account this impossibility of being one with oneself. It is because I am not one with

myself that I can speak to the other and address the Other. That is not a way of avoiding responsibility. On the contrary, it is the only way for me to take responsibility and to make decisions.[40]

In order for there to be relation, society, community, love, friendship or even war, there must remain, for Derrida, separation from the Other.[41] This is a relation with the Other where they remain absolutely 'transcendent'; they cannot be reached and cannot be known from the inside.[42] This complete separation is not an obstacle, as might be imagined, but rather the very condition of relation.[43] The Other can be addressed only 'to the extent that there is separation, so that I cannot replace the Other'.[44] In places, Derrida uses the ideas of an 'ethical' relation to the Other and a 'just' relation to the Other interchangeably,[45] arguing that justice *is* this particular relation with the Other; it is: 'the experience of the Other as other, the fact that I let the Other be other'.[46]

The subject, then, is not an originary source. It is, as Howells argues, an 'effect of difference', an element in a relationship.[47] The subject is incomplete, other to itself, in relation and yet it is also singular, and this singularity is the condition for the relation in which it finds itself. Subjectivity, for Derrida, is an effect of structure, rather than an origin in itself. However, Derrida's argument is that this structure of language and social being has a lack, in that, as Caroline Williams puts it, there is 'no centre or origin to the system within which we are determined'.[48] If, for Levinas, the subject is a response to the call of the Other – understood most often as the other person – such that responsibility is always for the Other, for Derrida, we might think of the subject as a response to 'otherness' more generally; as an effect of a structure which is always undone by alterity. Decision and responsibility, for Derrida, are also always of the Other: 'even if it's the Other in me'.[49] This lack at the centre of subjectivity permeates all of the following discussion of ethics, politics and responsibility in Derrida's work. It is, as Howells argues, an understanding of the subject as not identical to itself which lies at the root of Derrida's approach to ethics as aporetic.[50] For Derrida, the responsible decision must be made by, and with reference to, the Other, not only in terms of the other person, but also in terms of an other knowledge, an-other set of rules or way of thinking.

Thus, Derrida argues that the responsible decision would be an experience that we are unable to experience – a non-road of aporia, non-traversable and which does not allow passage; an experience of the Other.[51] This experience of aporia is an experience of the moment when the decision is 'not insured by a rule', a subject or any knowledge.[52] Without this im-possible experience of aporia, there can be no responsibility:

> ethics, politics, and responsibility *if there are any*, will only ever have begun with the experience and experiment of the aporia. When the path is clear and given, when a certain knowledge opens the way in advance, the decision is already made, it might as well be said that there is none to make: irresponsibly, and in good conscience, one simply applies or implements a program. Perhaps, and this would be the objection, one never escapes the program. In that case, one must acknowledge this and stop talking with authority about moral or philosophical responsibility.[53]

The Ethics of Deconstruction?

Response, the Other and absolute duty

The aporia in the responsible decision means that any attempt at identifying a duty which might provide guidance in making responsible decisions necessarily encounters a limit. As discussed in Chapter 1, one central framing of the debate on the ethics of deconstruction revolves around the question of whether we can draw from it any principle which might enable the making of better decisions; if there is something that we can identify as more responsible. Themes in Derrida's work, such as a commitment to alterity, the unconditional or undeconstructable, are often called upon to provide this principle. However, these do not, I will argue, in any way temper, domesticate or offer a way out of the aporia of decision. Moreover, were they to do so, the very possibility of responsibility would be lost. In short, it is only to the extent that the formulation of an ethics of deconstruction is rendered impossible that a deconstructive approach might remain ethically engaged.

The tension between the realms of rule and non-rule in Derrida's discussion of the responsible decision is, I suggest, a reflection, in part, of our situation with many Others. Derrida draws on Levinas' concept of the Other and the Third here, and there are clear parallels between the two authors, in that it is the tension between the Other and the Third which both opens the possibility of responsibility and ethics and which also makes them impossible. This im-possibility can be traced through a consideration of the three modalities within 'our culture and our concept' of responsibility as identified by Derrida:[54]

> One says 'to answer for', 'to respond to', 'to answer before'. These three modalities are not juxtaposable; they are enveloped and implied in one another. One *answers for*, for self or for something (for someone, for an action, a thought, a discourse), before – before an other, a community of others, an institution, a court, a law. And always one *answers for* (for self or for its intention, its action or discourse), *before*, by first responding *to*: this last modality thus appearing more originary, more fundamental and hence unconditional.[55]

Within responsibility, there is both a reference to the Other as singularity and to the generality of other Others. There is both a demand to answer *before* as making intelligible, explaining oneself, entering into the ethical generality and responding to the absolute and singular demand of the Other. It is this which renders responsibility im-possible.

Derrida draws out these im-possibilities very clearly in his discussion of Abraham in *The Gift of Death*. In this example, Abraham's ethical duty is a responsibility to his family, the wider community and ethical rules and norms, which he must neglect in order to undertake absolute duty, as demanded by God as the Other. Absolute duty demands that he must, in the moment of the sacrifice of Isaac, hate that which these ethical codes bind him to. However, he must simultaneously love it – that is, he must love his son – as to sacrifice something that one hates is no longer a sacrifice, and Abraham would therefore no longer be acting in the name of the absolute duty required of him.[56] Duty and responsibility, thus construed, binds one to the Other as a completely inaccessible absolute singularity demanding a response outside the ethical generality. But in an echo of Levinas' approach, this relationship to the absolutely Other is not quite as simple as it might initially seem. There is never only the one Other to whom we must respond; there are always other Others and the demands that they place us under are incompatible: 'you cannot be just for everyone and for every single one'.[57]

Acting in accordance with absolute duty and in infinite responsibility for the one Other necessarily leaves open the fate of all the other Others. The realms of rules, the ethical generality, calculation and so on act to protect the other Others; they are instituted in the name of the incalculable responsibility that we have to the Other in the same way that, for Levinas, morality and justice are required by ethics and charity. To extend this principle, the ethical, generalisable duty, the realm of knowledge and theorisation must be acknowledged, respected, regarded and perpetuated in the same moment that it is betrayed: 'in a word, ethics must be sacrificed in the name of duty'.[58] It is for this reason that Abraham cannot speak of what he has to do and that he must not speak. To explain his actions would entangle him in the justifications of the ethical generality, but, in any case, he would be unintelligible unless he had already acted with reference to theorisable rules which would allow him to give reasons and justifications.[59]

Thus, the sacrifice of the realm of generality is, for Derrida, a sacrifice of the other Others, who are protected by the generality that has been sacrificed.[60] To respond to the Other, to be responsible, *requires* the sacrifice of the other Others and the ethical generality:

> [A]s soon as I enter into a relation with the Other ... I know that I can respond only by sacrificing ethics, that is, by sacrificing whatever obliges me also to respond, in the same way, in the same instant, to all the Others.[61]

This sacrifice and betrayal cannot be resolved or justified, it must remain painful, secret and, by remaining so, by making these unjustifiable decisions binding us to one singularity over the generality of singularities, absolute duty might be done.[62]

However, this one singularity – the absolute Other (God in the example of Abraham) – is also every Other, since all Others are completely other, inaccessible and absolute singularities to whom we are infinitely responsible at every moment.[63] For Derrida: 'every Other (one) is every (bit) Other';[64] every Other is completely other, absolutely other, but there is also, as Thomson argues, an 'unstable equivalence between the absolute alterity of each Other and the being alike in being other of every Other'.[65] If we think in terms of the Other as the other person, then the complete otherness of every Other means that the generality of ethical norms which protects the other Others cannot be disregarded in the name of absolute duty. In the name of these other Others, we must pay heed to rules, knowledge and calculation, while acknowledging that these are inescapably violent to an understanding of every Other as every bit other; they focus on the being alike in being Other at the expense of their each being every bit Other.

Further, for Derrida, in the same way as for Levinas, the Other is already also the Third; the other Others do not come along later and corrupt a relationship of absolute unproblematic responsibility, rather 'the relation to the singularity of the Other also passes through the universality of law'.[66] Not only is the tension between the Other and the Third the condition of there being any responsibility or justice (as will be discussed below), but the Third is not a secondary element which could otherwise be put aside. The Other is the Third, so even in my responsibility to the Other, I always already also have an incommensurable responsibility to the Third: 'I have a relation to the Other in his/her singularity or uniqueness, and at the same time the third one is already in place. The second one is a third one'.[67]

As concepts, responsibility and ethics contain within themselves contradictory imperatives, a duty to singularity entailing silence and secrecy and to the generality which calls for justification, explanation and a regard for norms and rules. The responsible is thus always also irresponsible. For Derrida, responsibility, in general, is incompatible with absolute responsibility.[68] This 'absolute responsibility' must necessarily remain outside of thematisations and conceptualisations of responsibility. Indeed, it needs to be 'exceptional or extraordinary' and so must remain unthinkable and thus irresponsible.[69] There are, then, two contradictory demands with which we are faced, rendering responsibility impossible. Yet this impossibility is precisely the condition for responsibility:

> It is even impossible to conceive of a responsibility that consists in being responsible for two laws, or that consists in responding to two contradictory injunctions ... But there is no responsibility that is not the experience and experiment of the impossible.[70]

Ethics and responsibility are ultimately, Derrida argues, on the side of both the incalculable and absolute, and on the side of rules and processes.[71] They are not, as suggested by a reading which might look to incalculability as the better way forward, only on one side of this divide. Rather, their ethical or responsible nature is dependent on this position at the limit, separating and connecting the two realms, and this means that there is no notion of pure responsibility by which to measure the more or less responsible. It is not only that we are always acting irresponsibly in any attempt to be responsible, but more broadly that we cannot even mitigate such irresponsibility; there is no 'more responsible' towards which we might strive.

The unconditional

If responsibility is a necessarily aporetic concept, might we look to Derrida's notion of the unconditional or undeconstructable to offer resources for developing an affirmative account of deconstructive ethics? As discussed in Chapter 1, if a duty in decision to resist totalisation can be identified, this is usually done via an appeal to the unconditional, a development of Derrida's 'unconditional injunction' at the heart of deconstruction, that: 'I have to welcome the other . . . unconditionally . . . I have to keep it open or try to keep it open unconditionally'.[72] In order to argue that what initially seems to be a simple and straightforward ethical injunction is, in fact, a double imperative, complicated and rendered im-possible by precisely the same movement at work in the concept of responsibility, in this section I trace its development in Derrida's work through the specific contexts of hospitality and justice.

Hospitality, for Derrida, is, at its most basic: 'a very general name for all our relations to the Other'.[73] Derrida draws on Levinas to articulate a 'radical' conception of hospitality in contrast to the traditional cosmopolitical right to universal hospitality, which is 'only political, always determined by citizenship'.[74] In this formulation, pure hospitality would be hospitality to an Other 'neither expected nor invited' and not within our control.[75] This is, necessarily, risky. We do not know what or who we might be welcoming, yet without this element of risk, Derrida asks, would it be true hospitality?[76] Offering hospitality to what I know, control, predict, can limit or decide on would, he argues, betray the unconditional within hospitality. It would not be an open welcome to the Other, but a limited and regulated welcome designed to protect myself and what is mine and welcome the Other only to the extent that these things are not threatened. Justice might similarly be approached in terms of this relationship with the Other, such as when Derrida argues that:

> What I would call justice has always to do with the absolute singularity of the Other – the Other not considered as a person or as an ego – absolute

singularity exceeds the order of the subject, the calculable unit of the subject as voter or citizen.[77]

Justice, however, also points to a relation with otherness in terms of an-other future, it is 'inextricably bound with the unanticipatability of the future'.[78]

Unconditional hospitality and justice, then, offer one necessary horizon of the ethical.[79] Without the concept of the unconditional, there would be no duties to the Other and the Third to negotiate between, there would not be anything outside of law and regulation to inform our relations with the Other, and there would be no thought of approaching the Other as Other. What, Derrida asks, 'would an ethics be without hospitality?'[80] Without the thought of unconditional hospitality 'we would have no concept of hospitality in general and would not even be able to determine any rules for conditional hospitality'.[81]

It is in this vein that Derrida contrasts hospitality with tolerance. Tolerance is, he argues: 'conditional, circumspect, careful hospitality'; it is: 'the opposite of hospitality'.[82] Tolerance may suggest the trappings of hospitality, but it is carefully limited; it does not welcome the Other unconditionally, laying the self open to whatever the Other may bring. Instead, it keeps the self in a position of superiority and control. Tolerance, Derrida argues, is:

[A] kind of condescending concession always on the side of the reason of the strongest, it says to the Other from its elevated position 'I am letting you be . . . I am leaving you a place in my home, but do not forget that this is my home'.[83]

However, although critical of tolerance, Derrida insists that, ultimately, unconditional hospitality is not something that is possible or, more importantly, desirable. First, unconditional hospitality would not, practically, be possible. It is not something which could be legislated for or organised. If it were to be organised, it would lose its unconditionality, its orientation fully towards the Other, and it would also lose the element of unpredictability, becoming arranged and predetermined. For Derrida, one cannot, by definition, organise the concept of unconditional hospitality, it 'can have no legal or political status. No state can write it into its laws'; it is thus impossible in a practical sense.[84]

Second, unconditional hospitality is not the figure of an ideal state towards which we should aim. Unconditional hospitality, Derrida argues, *must* be conditioned and tempered with laws, rights, borders and so on.[85] Pure hospitality is neither possible nor desirable: 'I am not even sure whether it [pure hospitality] is ethical, insofar as it does not even depend on a decision'.[86] We cannot offer unconditional hospitality to everyone, and it is partly in responding to 'everyone' that decision and responsibility become possible. If 'ethics is hospitality', it is in the sense of the necessary negotiation between the conditional and unconditional.[87]

Similarly, Derrida makes it clear that his conception of justice is 'paradoxical' and 'impossible'. For this reason, it does not conform to the usual ideas of morality, ethics or concrete concerns, such as minimising cruelty.[88] The unanticipatability of the future is of key importance here. The future may not be what we want and it may not be 'good'; indeed, the 'to come' might be the worst. Derrida's idea of justice has no guarantees in terms of being aligned with the good:

> I am not happy with people saying that in fact deconstruction is very ethical, with a high sense of responsibility etc. No; when I say justice . . . I distinguish it from love, and even morals and the usual sense of ethics.[89]

The unconditional, then, is a risky openness; it does not provide incontestable ethical precepts. Furthermore, it is an openness which is already embedded within all conditional concepts. Concepts such as unconditional justice are themselves already entangled with the conditional, both in practice and as part of their structure:

> I would not simply oppose, on the one side, the field of politics, ethics and rhetoric, and, on the other side, justice. We have to pay attention to their heterogeneity, I would insist on that, and because of this one calls for the other: they are indissociable. Decision, an ethical or a political responsibility, is absolutely heterogeneous to knowledge. Nevertheless, we have to know as much as possible in order to ground our decision. But even if it is grounded in knowledge, the moment I take a decision it is a leap, I enter a heterogeneous space and that is the condition for responsibility.[90]

Without the unconditional, discourses of hospitality, justice or forgiveness: 'would not have meaning'.[91] It inspires, motivates and gives meaning to notions of responsibility and 'inflects' politics, change and the law.[92] As Caputo argues, justice is not a thing, not present or future-present, not existing, not real and not an ideal:[93] 'justice is the absolutely unforeseeable prospect (a paralyzing paradox) in virtue in which the things that get deconstructed are deconstructed'.[94] The unconditional is the horizon of possibility contained within the conditional, with the two poles separate, but indissociable and in constant tension.

The double bind of the conditional and unconditional is necessary.[95] It is what allows for the very possibility of responsibility. A commitment to unconditional justice or hospitality, the absolute Other or alterity would spell the end of ethics and responsibility, rather than their ideal manifestation. In the example of pure, unconditional forgiveness, Derrida argues that:

> If one wants, and it is necessary, forgiveness to become effective, concrete, historic; if one wants it to *arrive*, to happen by changing things, it is necessary that this purity engage itself in a series of conditions of all kinds . . . It is between these two poles, irreconcilable but indissociable, that decisions and responsibilities are to be taken.[96]

The idea of a 'just' or ethical relation with the Other is always already complicated. The conditional and the double bind it engenders protects against what Derrida calls the 'violence' of the unconditional in the same way that the Third in Levinasian terms protects against the violence of the pure face-to-face.[97]

Undecidability

The inseparability of the three modalities of responsibility means that the concept of responsibility is placed in the realm of what Derrida calls the 'undecidable'. As discussed above, for there to be a decision, the path must not be clear. There can only be a decision when it would be impossible to know what to do, when one is in the midst of the undecidable. Undecidability is not the opposite of decision, not a failure to decide, nor is it indeterminacy, rather it is 'the competition between two determined possibilities or options, two determined duties'.[98] Undecidability is always a 'determinate oscillation' between possibilities of meaning, but also of acts.[99] The possibilities themselves are strictly defined in any given situation.[100]

It is for this reason that deconstruction does not lead to indeter-minism.[101] As in Keenan's reading of Derrida, undecidability is not uncertainty:

> It is not a matter of knowing or not knowing where to draw the line cor-rectly, nor of some ultimate disappearance or erasure of the border in a fog of confusion. There is aporia only because there are frontiers, because we must pass from one side to another, to the other. And there would be no passage, in any rigorous sense of the word, without the experience of the impasse, without the darkness of a certain undecidability.[102]

Responsibility itself is, I would argue, ultimately undecidable. For Derrida, one must take account of undecidability to be able to act, assume responsibility, decide, indeed: 'to even be able to think the concepts of decision and responsibility'.[103] Rather than making decision and responsibility impossible, it is the condition of their possibility:

> A decision can only come into being in a space that exceeds the calculable program that would destroy all responsibility by transforming it into a programmable effect of determinate causes. There can be no moral or political responsibility without this trial and this passage by way of the undecidable. Even if a decision seems to take only a second and not to be preceded by any deliberation, it is structured by this *experience and experiment of the undecidable*.[104]

It is not that the tension in responsibility creates only difficulties or that the incommensurability of the Other and the Third corrupts a responsible relation, but that this tension is the condition of possibil-ity of there being responsibility or justice: 'This terrible situation of two and three . . . is not simply a trap, it is a condition of justice. If there is a justice it has to go through this terrible situation where there are two and three'.[105]

This undecidability leaves us in a precarious position. In short, we do not know what to do, we have no guarantees and whatever we might do will be necessarily insufficient. But this does not leave us free of the demand to be responsible. The demand with which we are faced, on this reading, is not from the absolute Other, unconditional justice or hospitality, but the demand of the undecidable. Unde-cidability calls for decision.[106] It refers not only to the oscillation between competing imperatives, but the experience of the demand to make a decision and of its incalculability. The undecidable is the demand to give itself up to the impossible decision.[107] The aporia of undecidability, the double bind of responsibility to every Other, is precisely that which demands and makes necessary decision:

> Although *aporia, double bind*, and *autoimmune process* are not exactly synonyms, what they have in common, what they are all, precisely, charged with, is, more than an internal contradiction, an indecidability, that is, an internal-external, nondialectizable antimony that risks paralysing and thus calls for the event of the interruptive decision.[108]

There is an element of urgency and immediacy to the decision, which means that a Derridean approach does not entail an intellectualising of ethics or responsibility. Not knowing does not absolve us of our obligations, but instead makes them more far-reaching:

> [W]e have no criterion to decide whether a decision is good or bad, it may always be a bad decision . . . One's ethical duty would be to nevertheless try and make good decisions without given or safe norms.[109]

The lack of guarantee means that there is no way of securing against the worst, of identifying and guarding against evil, whatever that might be. Knowledge should not and cannot guide us in terms of determining good and bad if we want to preserve the possibility of responsibility. At each moment, we must make a decision, and each decision is a risk: '[W]e should not know, in terms of knowledge, what is the distinction between good and evil'.[110]

There is then, in responsibility, both chance and threat, with chance dependent on there being threat. Without the possibility of evil, of the worst, there would be no decision, because the way forward would already be determined by knowledge: 'Without the possibility of radical evil, of perjury, and of absolute crime, there is no responsibility, no freedom, no decision'.[111] The possibility of responsibility must always entail running a risk; it must always go through the aporia or double bind, and this contains both 'threat and chance, not alternatively or by turns promise and/or threat but threat *in* the promise itself'.[112]

The undecidability through which decision must pass, which conditions the possibility of decision and responsibility: 'is not a moment to be traversed or overcome'.[113] Derrida's work does not call for more or better knowledge in order to be able to move outside of the undecidable. It is not something to be resolved: 'The crucial experience of the *perhaps* imposed by the undecidable – that is to say, the condition of decision – is not a moment to be exceeded, forgotten or suppressed'.[114] Undecidability is how things are. There is no full stop, no point at which things become clear, and this is the case in terms of meaning, decisions and possibilities. That is, we cannot ever saturate a situation with knowledge, programme or create rules and norms which are sufficient to the Other that demands them, or secure a decision that we may have to make. Undecidability also persists after the decision, always unravelling it from within such that we can never know if a decision has taken place. The inescapability of undecidability has the effect of rendering 'all totalization, fulfilment and plenitude impossible'.[115]

The Politics of Deconstruction?

Deducing politics from ethics

If undecidability undoes the concepts of ethics and responsibility from within, then we are left with an unstable ground from which to determine a better politics. The undecidability of ethics and responsibility means that there is no non-violent starting point. Violence is not only introduced with the entrance of the Third, universality, conditionality and generality. As Thomson argues, for Derrida, there is no 'first term' from which another could be derived; there are 'no first places, only second places'.[116] Furthermore, undecidability means that the very concept of politics loses its status as an autonomous realm: how can we rethink the politics of deconstruction when it is already indissociable from the im-possibility of ethics and responsibility?

In the same way that ethics refers not only to the realm of the unconditional or incalculable, politics does not refer only to the realm of the calculable. It certainly has elements of calculation and knowledge, which, as Derrida argues, might seem to distinguish it from ethics or responsibility:

> Some might then be tempted to say ... that this is actually the border between pure ethics and the political, a political that would begin by choosing and preferring the like, knowledge, cognition and recognition, technique and calculating law, all of which require knowing and recognizing the like and the same as units of measure.[117]

However, politics does not mark only the pole of institutions, calculation and universalisation. Similarly, ethics does not mark only the pole of singularity and incalculability. Ethics and politics are both located in the difficult terrain between the conditional and the unconditional. Both concepts are on the side of the right and law and on the side of justice, split across the two:

> I try to make a sharp distinction between 'justice' and 'right'; that is, I try to make a sharp distinction between 'justice' and 'the law' or 'the right'. On the side of the right you would put what you called, a little hastily, politics, ethics, rhetoric *(ethics and politics for me are also on the other side)*.[118]

The distinction between ethics and politics in deconstruction then becomes complicated: 'The border between the ethical and the political here loses for good the indivisible simplicity of a limit'.[119] There is not politics as the conditional and ethics as the unconditional in Derrida's work, but rather, I suggest, ethics, politics and responsibility are names for the limits and openings which occur on the line where the conditional and unconditional meet.

This complication of the relationship between ethics and politics in turn complicates the idea of deducing a politics from an ethics in Derrida's work. On the one hand, Derrida seems to want a hyperbolic vision of justice or ethics to inform politics, but, on the other hand, the necessarily always already political nature of the just or ethical renders this deduction unsatisfactory.

Deriving a politics from ethics is necessary, argues Derrida, because particular political interventions must be made, and they must be made in an attempt to make the 'right' decision. As discussed above, this attempt at making a 'good' decision must be furnished with as much knowledge as possible. It is necessary, argues Derrida, 'to deduce a politics and a law from ethics. This deduction is necessary in order to determine the "better" or the "less bad"'.[120] To find the 'better' or the 'less bad' requires 'a negotiation between the non-negotiable'.[121] There remains, in Derrida's work, a demand to determine the better course of action.

However, this deduction is impossible, Derrida argues; there is: 'a silence between ethics and politics, ethics and law'.[122] From Levinas' ethics as hospitality, which Derrida draws on in positing an ethical or just relation, Derrida argues that a law or politics of hospitality cannot be deduced; 'one cannot *deduce* from Levinas's ethical discourse on hospitality a law and a politics, some particular law or politics in some determined situation today'.[123] There is a demand, but the political content which is assigned to it remains undetermined. Indeed, it is:

> Still to be determined beyond knowledge, beyond all presentation, all concepts, all possible intuition, in a singular way, in the speech and the responsibility *taken* by each person, in each situation, and on the basis of an analysis that is each time unique.[124]

The content of any politics is left open. There is a silence between ethics and politics; a silence 'concerning the rules or schemas', which might enable us to formulate a politics in the name of this ethics.[125]

This silence, which elsewhere Derrida calls a 'hiatus', while denying the utility of a deconstructive approach for developing a set of general political tenets, is also what enables it to remain ethically and politically engaged and retain the possibility of ethics, politics and responsibility:

> Without silence, without the hiatus which is not the absence of rules but the necessity of a leap at the moment of ethical, political, or individual decision, we could simply unfold knowledge into a program or course of action. Nothing could make us more irresponsible; nothing could be more totalitarian.[126]

Rather, it is the interconnectedness of, and simultaneous silence between, ethics and politics which keeps open the possibility of the Other, of decision, of anything happening and of deconstruction's orientation to the future. The lack of guidelines from an ethical starting point means that there is still the possibility of decision and responsibility:

> Would it [the hiatus between ethics and politics] in fact open – like a hiatus – both the mouth and the possibility of another speech, of a decision and a responsibility (juridical and political if you will), where decisions must be made and responsibility, as we say *taken*, without the assurance of an ontological foundation?[127]

The deductive move from ethics to politics fails then on two counts. First, the ethical is always already undecidable and contains within it the concerns of calculation and conditionality with which we might first associate politics. It is not separate from these things and so is not, ultimately, something pure from which a politics could be deduced. There is a silence within ethics. Second, ethics and politics (understood in terms of any particular intervention, guideline or political position) are separated by a silence. There is a hiatus across which a demand is made for decision and political interventions, but also across which the content of these interventions does not travel.

Political in(ter)ventions

For some authors, the lack of an ethics from which to deduce politics ultimately leaves deconstruction politically unengaged.[128] Derrida has been accused of eschewing politics or political engagement and failing to encompass normative or ethical concerns in his insistence on undecidability and the non-closure of context. On this reading, there is a failure of politics in deconstruction, because it does not offer any guidance to the content of the decision or how it should be made. Political or ethical intervention and engagement are argued to be problematic in the absence of explicit formulations of political or ethical positions, and it is for this reason that Critchley argues that Derrida requires supplementing with a Levinasian normative foundation.[129] The possibilities of political or ethical engagement are viewed here as dependent on a 'positive grounding' for decision.[130]

   This assumption neglects somewhat the way in which Derrida attempts to rethink the concept of the political itself and in particular the separation between political engagement and theorising regarding it. Deconstruction cannot provide a theory of politics, precisely because it operates at the limits of theoretical questions; deconstruction, for Derrida 'defies all questions in the form of "what is" and of "what does it mean?"'.[131] It does not offer an answer to what politics *is* and, as Thomson argues, this is what enables it to be politically engaged. We can only recognise the 'excessive and disconcerting' political implications of deconstruction if we do not determine in advance what politics is.[132] Derrida himself is clear on this issue, arguing that his project is not to propose 'a new political content within the old framework but to redefine or think differently what is involved in the political'.[133] Similarly, in defending deconstruction against the claim that it is politically neutral or even politically suspect, Derrida argues that: 'everyone can use this motif [deconstruction] as they please to serve quite different political perspectives, which would seem to mean that deconstruction is politically neutral', but that ultimately it is this which allows for 'reflection on the nature of the political and a hyper-politicisation'.[134]

If there is no ethical principle which might offer guidance on how to make decisions in the undecidable, then one refiguring of the politics of deconstruction would be the suggestion that the undecidable itself must be protected or promoted in order to ensure the possibility of decision and responsibility. This move is made by, for example, Alex Thomson, who argues that a politics informed by deconstruction would entail making space for decision, ensuring that there can be decisions at all by resisting programming and prediction. Similarly, David Campbell argues that the principle drawn from deconstruction is that we need to find ways of keeping the undecidable open; it in this context that he argues for democracy as the politics which might best do this.[135]

However, the reading of decision and the undecidable presented above suggests that, for Derrida, the context of undecidability is inescapable. As such, all decisions, if there are any, are placed within it. If undecidability *is*, nothing is secured, however hard we may try to ensure that it is. Deconstruction, Derrida argues 'is what happens. Deconstruction is the case';[136] similarly 'Deconstruction, if there be such a thing, happens; it is what happens'.[137] It is not just that undecidability is not something towards which we should work, but that the fact of undecidability, that deconstruction is the case, already undoes the terms of an approach whereby we might determine theoretically, generally or in principle that any way forward is better, including that which seeks to institute or recognise undecidability.

For Derrida, deconstruction is how things are; it is descriptive, a matter 'of saying that this is the way it is'.[138] Deconstruction is not something invented or introduced by Derrida, but is at work constantly, regardless of whether anyone claims to be 'deconstructing' anything: 'Deconstruction is not a philosophy or a method, it is not a phase, a period or a moment. It is something which is constantly at work and was at work before what we call "deconstruction" started'.[139] Ultimately, we are enmeshed in a world in which things are not clear-cut, where they are outside of our control, difficult, fragmented, unable to be tamed by knowledge, unpredictable and in which the decisions we might try to make are always in the context of this undecidability.

This does not necessarily entail the celebration of this undecidability. Rather, Derrida suggests that we should and, indeed, do attempt to control and extend knowledge:

> We should question again and again, deconstruct and endlessly accumulate knowledge, memory, awareness, in order to control the uncontrollable. Thus we have to circumscribe or surround a decision with the maximum of guarantees, knowledge, precautions, and so on, *even if* we know that a decision belongs to an order which is heterogeneous to knowledge.[140]

The emphasis on that which is heterogeneous to knowledge in deconstruction does not translate into a rejection of knowledge, programming and prediction. Derrida insists that deconstruction does not lead to a deliberate policy of suspending decision, relinquishing attempts at control and mutely waiting for the Other, the maybe or the future. If anything, it suggests that we question and try to saturate a context with knowledge and that these are not necessarily negative things, but that they will always, to some degree, fail:

> What I describe here as the modality of the maybe does not imply that we should teach ourselves or deliberately choose the maybe, it is not a matter of choice. We try all the time to resist the perhaps, to protect ourselves against the absolutely unpredictable coming. But, even if we succeed in anticipating or predicting everything, what happens is surprising.[141]

We are not tasked with creating the openness with which deconstruction is concerned, rather deconstruction shows us how things are always already open. We will always be surprised, regardless of whatever we might do in order to try to make this otherwise: 'we are exposed to the perhaps. And we have to take into account the fact that, however prepared, protected, resisting we may be, we remain exposed to what is coming'.[142] Deconstruction shows how we are always already vulnerable and exposed to, and in relation with, the Other. For Derrida: 'I don't have to open it [my space, my home, myself] because it is open, it is open before I make a decision about it'.[143]

If deconstruction is taken seriously as what happens, the implications pose challenges for any project which seeks to use the approach in order to better understand or intervene in a particular way in concrete political and ethical problems, particularly for one which might seek to establish guidelines for doing this. If deconstruction is how things are, then we are always confronting the aporia at the limits of knowledge, regardless of whether we take a self-consciously deconstructive approach:

> [I]nvention (we could translate invention by 'decision' as it were) doesn't owe anything intrinsically to theoretical or historical knowledge, it is heterogeneous to a knowledge. Then anyone, without having deconstructed anything or without having interrogated the tradition, could and should invent new ethical and political decisions, could be able and ready to make such decisions . . . One does not therefore need the activity of questioning in order to be responsible, to have authentic relation . . . to the Other, at every moment.[144]

We are left not with an ethics or a politics, which would determine in advance the meaning of ethics and politics, but with the very lack of determined meaning which means that we are always engaged in ethics and politics. All political or ethical interventions are already political and ethical interventions, and deconstruction allows them to be interrogated as such.

Im-possibility and the trace

Perhaps instead of 'deduction', Derrida's call for ethics to 'enjoin' a politics offers scope for conceptualising the limits of ethics and politics.[145] The unconditional or undecidable contains within itself a call for conditions and decision. Those terms that we might associate initially with the ethical infuse this call with the requirement to find the less bad, but do not provide guidance on how this might be done or even what 'less bad' might mean. What remains is, in Derrida's terms, a trace; the ethical does not and cannot inform politics, but the idea of a pure ethical or unconditionally just or hospitable relation to the Other, however enmeshed this may already be with politics and conditionality, nonetheless marks thinking about politics:

> No politics, no ethics, and no law can be, as it were, *deduced* from this thought. To be sure, nothing can be *done* with it. And so one would have nothing to do with it. But should one then conclude that this thought leaves no trace on what is to be done – for example in the politics, the

ethics, or the law to come? . . . On it, perhaps . . . a call might thus be taken up and take hold: the call for a thinking of the event *to come*, of the democracy *to come*, of the reason *to come*.[146]

But this is only ever a trace, only ever a second place. There are no originary terms here from which to start the analysis; we always start in the middle, on the limit which both separates and conjoins the conditional and unconditional, the possible and impossible. The potentials, possibilities and limitations of ethics and politics are to be found precisely at this limit. The trace renders the concepts of ethics and politics im-possible by leaving within them a mark of openness to the Other. This openness is the condition of possibility for any politics or ethics, for everything not already having been decided. But it is not an openness to the Other as pure ethical experience. The trace of alterity left is the im-possible demand to respond to every Other (one) as every (bit) Other.

In Derrida's rethinking of ethics and politics then, we find ourselves at the limit of theory. The unconditional operates at the limits of theory and knowledge and yet calls for it, which leaves a trace of this limit within all attempts at theory and knowledge. The trace left is not an ethical demand for unconditionality, because, as I have argued, the unconditional is not a first place. It is not outside theory, but operates at its limits, always indissociable from the conditional for its very condition of possibility. The concepts are never closed or finished. It is this trace which implicates the conditional and unconditional in one another from the beginning. That is, within the demand for unconditional justice, absolute duty and so on, there is always already, immediately, the necessity and demand to submit to the demands of generalisation, calculation and conditionality. It is this double imperative, from the limits of theory, which undoes the certainty of all of theoretical claims.

The resistance within and limits of theory are of central importance, because it is this which means that deconstruction's demonstration of the aporetic relationality within and between concepts cannot be co-opted into a project to determine an ethics or a politics. Deconstruction resists all attempts at doing this. There is 'no possible limit to the gesture of deconstruction'.[147] The 'clause of non-closure' through which the outside penetrates the inside also applies to any attempt to close the realm of theory and knowledge.[148] We cannot demarcate a stable inside nor, by extension, a stable outside. Rather, we operate only on a mobile and shifting limit, which renders the two indissociable. Working at this limit, rather than seeking to overcome it, is one way to displace the positioning of ethics as a ground for politics and, more broadly, to move away from a framing which starts from an attempt to theorise the relationship between them.

Chapter 4
Jean-Luc Nancy: The Transimmanence of Ethics

Introduction: Starting at the Limit

The preceding chapters offered readings of Emmanuel Levinas and Jacques Derrida, respectively, which drew out the importance of limits in post-foundational approaches to ethics. In the absence of ethical grounds or foundations, the task at hand is to begin thinking from these limits. This chapter turns to the work of Jean-Luc Nancy to develop the implications of such a starting point for conceptualising ethics and politics.

Nancy's work is apposite to this task because it offers an explicit focus on the limit. It is precisely the tension between the Other and the Third, conditional and unconditional, absolute and relative around which the discussion of ethics and politics has so far centred that Nancy takes as a starting point. There is, in his work, a focus on how we might think about these relationships of separation, interpenetration and indissociability, without resorting to polarities, purity or originary terms. Nancy offers instead an ontology of the singular-plural of being, in which the limit operates as the central term, such that we start only with second places. There are two specific elements of this ontology on which the argument in this chapter draws to develop an account of ethics and politics that remains at, and is mindful of, this limit as the very condition for their emergence.

First, for Nancy, the starting point of the limit is understood as relationality. In the absence of first places or initial separation, Nancy offers a conceptualisation of singularity not as *in* relation, but *as* relation. The potential of relationality as an approach to post-foundational ethics becomes limited in accounts which entail a focus on the nature of the parties to the relationship, but Nancy's work allows for a loosening of such constraints. As such, the categories of same and Other are displaced; rather than starting with the primacy of the Other, we start with the primacy of relationality. Nancy offers a way of keeping the focus on relationality by giving it first place, but a first place that is a non-place, without content.

Second, underlying this shift in focus to relationality is a broader move away from a reliance on transcendent alterity as the only means by which we might think through the possibility of resistance to totalisation. That is, Nancy offers resources by which we might conceptualise resistance to totalisation that take into account the destabilisation of the realms of a pure outside, ethical starting point, or originary grounding, as demonstrated in the previous chapters. Nancy introduces the concept of transimmanence as a way to conceptualise existence itself structured as a beyond, such that there is no opposition between immanence and transcendence. We do not need to look to an outside as pure exteriority in order to disrupt totalisation, because the singular-plural of being itself is structured as resistance.

The implications of these insights for reframing the question of post-foundational ethics are developed in three key ways in the argument that follows. First, once we can move outside the oppositional framing of immanence and transcendence, we can also rethink the relationship of singular/plural, absolute/relative, Other/Third, conditional/unconditional and so ethics/politics. If the indissociability of these concepts is taken as the starting point, then responsibility cannot rest with one side or the other, nor can it be approached as a negotiation between the two poles; it emerges only on the line which both separates and connects. Ethics and the political here are both refigured as the resistance of the singular-plural transimmanence of being, such that neither is the starting point or first place.

Second, Nancy offers a way to think about making ethical claims without, or at the limits of, theory by recasting the relationship between ethics and ontology. His work allows for a way of thinking ontology as the transcendence of being, whereby the starting point of relation and transimmanence means that ethics can be recast *as* ontology, rather than in opposition to it. The transimmanent or relation as origin opens up the possibility of thinking not in terms of an originary ethics, but of ethics as origin. This is an ontology in which singularity is only ever produced as on the limit of conflicting demands – that is, demands which are not informed by, on the one hand, a duty to the same and, on the other hand, a duty to absolute alterity, but by a duty to the singular-plural, such that they cannot initially be separated, ordered or put in a hierarchy. The question of how to respond to these demands is necessarily left open.

Third, Nancy offers an alternative way into thinking about ethics without grounds or foundations. The singular-plural does not offer a foundation for ethics, rather it *is* ethics; ethics itself is originary. The starting point of the singular-plural of being is always open or transimmanent, a relation without content. As such, this originary ethics has no content, but is rather aligned with what Nancy calls 'ethos' or conduct. We cannot derive from this any ethical or political guidelines, but we can refocus the way in which we approach ethics as at the limits of theory – the point where theory no longer insures conduct.

The chapter is arranged into three sections. It begins by offering a reading of Nancy's ontology of the singular-plural of being, in which the central importance of relation and the hyphen, line or limit is drawn out. The development of this ontology in the context of politics and the political is then addressed, in order to show the ways in which the political is refigured when we are left with a starting point without content. Once the political is recast in this way, different possibilities open up for thinking about ethics, to which the final section turns its focus, in order to argue for the potential in conceptualising ethics in terms of conduct.

The Singular-Plural of Being

The 'with' and the hyphen

Nancy offers a conceptualisation of existence as coexistence or being as 'being-with-others' or 'being-in-common'. We begin, according to Nancy, together. Existence is always coexistence or being-with-others, but in a very specific way, in which neither the idea of being, nor that of togetherness or the common is primary.[1] This leaves the 'with' as the central term, and it is the theorisation of this 'with' that animates much of Nancy's work.

The 'with', for Nancy, is not in addition to a prior being; rather, it is at the heart of being.[2] That is, we do not start with being as a whole or with beings that are then added together. The 'with', relation or bond does not presuppose the pre-existence of the term upon which it relies.[3] This pre-existence would suggest that there could be such a thing as being that was not 'with' – a being alone. However, the very idea of being alone already rests, Nancy argues, on a prior notion of being-with, because aloneness is reliant already on the absence of an other. Aloneness does not make sense without an idea of being-with; the 'with' haunts the concept, even in its negation. So in being-in-common, 'being' does not come first; the 'with' is not a reference to pre-existing individuals coming together. 'Together' is not something applied to pre-existing entities, it is not 'The "together" of juxtaposition *partes extra partes,* isolated and unrelated parts'.[4]

However, if there is nothing pre-existing the together or the in-common – no pre-existing terms which are then joined together – neither, for Nancy, does the 'common' come first. While we do not start off as beings alone, nor do we start off as common in the sense of all being examples of a type or parts of a whole or unity. Nancy is concerned with distinguishing his approach from one that might be thought of as 'beings together'; 'Being is together, and it is not a togetherness'.[5] The situation is not one of a pre-existing group or unity which determines or shapes someone, 'someone with others is not someone in others', not someone 'dissolved in some prior unity' and not 'someone by others' – a product of conditions.[6] The 'with' problematises any concept of an organic whole of society or community and of the individual as constituted by their involvement in society; indeed, the 'with' 'does not indicate the sharing of a common situation'.[7] Rather, the 'with' displaces the notions of *either* pre-existing individuals or of types or essences: 'From the very beginning then, "we" are with one another, not as points gathered together, or as a togetherness that is divided up, but as a being-with-one-another'.[8]

Nancy develops this idea through the elucidation of an ontology of the 'singular-plural of being'.[9] In this, the terms singular and plural are at the same time different from one another and indistinct. Neither term comes first, relies on or presupposes the other and nor are the two terms clearly separable.[10] For Nancy, being is always being-singular-plural, such that none of the terms precedes or grounds the others, but rather where 'each designates the coessence of the others'.[11] The hyphenation is what is of importance here, playing a role like the 'with' in that it both links and separates, leaving neither term primary or uncontaminated by the other:

> This coessence puts essence in the hyphenation – 'being-singular-plural' – which is a mark of union and also a mark of division, a mark of sharing that effaces itself, leaving each term to its isolation *and* its being-with-the-others.[12]

For Nancy, the very idea of the singular already entails that it is both separated from, *and* inescapably connected to and with, other singularities. It is not that a singularity is amongst other singularities, because this would take us back to the starting point of individuals which are then brought together. Someone does not, Nancy argues, enter into a relationship with other someones, rather: 'the relation is contemporaneous with the singularities'.[13] That is, for Nancy, we cannot conceive of singularities in relationship, rather singularity *is* relationship; it is plural in its very concept.

The singular implies in itself, Nancy argues, its singularisation, 'and therefore its distinction from other singularities'.[14] It belongs to the register of 'one-by-one' and suggests a counting in this manner, rather than, for example, being an instance of a type or a part of a whole or pre-existing togetherness. This would be, perhaps, a 'one of many' or one among many. The singular, Nancy argues, is not about being one within a group, it is 'different from any concept of the particular, since this assumes the togetherness of which the particular is a part, so that such a particular can only present its difference from other particulars as numerical difference'.[15] The singular is not one particular instance of a type, one particular human being among a pre-existing community of human beings, a particular which is subsumed under a prior togetherness.

On the other hand, the singular is not a self-contained and autonomous sovereign, which would return us to the starting point of the lone individual. The singular, for Nancy 'is primarily *each* one and, therefore, also *with* and *among* all the others'.[16] Not one, alone first and then added to others, nor many ones starting off alone, but from the beginning one-by-one, one-with-others. The singular is always plural.[17]

One way to approach Nancy's treatment of the relation between the singular and the plural that does not reduce one to the other or combine the two in a whole is through his discussion of lines and surfaces. From one singularity to another, he argues, 'there is contiguity but not continuity'[18] – that is, there is togetherness which is without a prior separation, but which is not togetherness as one. The lines of touching and separation on which singularities are produced rely on both separation and contact, with their separation as a condition for their contact: 'All of being is in touch with all of being, but the law of touching is separation; moreover, it is the heterogeneity of surfaces that touch each other'.[19] Singularity entails both separation and touching; it is necessarily 'at once detached, distinguished, and communitarian'.[20]

This is not to suggest that the singular itself is a bordered entity. It might rather be thought of as the border itself or the line on which the inside is exposed to the outside. The singular is not a pure inside which may then become exposed – 'cut open, lacerated, and so exposed' – but an inside which is always in its very being also entirely exposed to the 'outside'.[21] This exposure on the limit is, for Nancy, the primordial structure of singularity.

It is in this sense that Nancy argues that the logic of the 'with' – of what is between two or several – is the logic of inside-outside; it is what belongs neither to pure inside nor pure outside, but 'belongs to all and to none and not to itself either'.[22] The 'with', hyphen or singularity is neither inside nor outside, but on the line which might distinguish them. Not a line which is essence for itself, but rather a line made up only of the exposure of inside and outside, of which it is neither. Hence Nancy's argument that the common, which might be thought of as the essence of the line, is in no way more originary than the 'being' in being-in-common. This is 'the logic of the singular in general';[23] neither pure inside nor pure outside, neither self-contained individuals nor a pre-existing group. Rather, singularity is exposure itself; it is that 'which, each time, forms a point of exposure, traces an intersection of limits on which there is exposure'.[24]

Being-together, Nancy argues, describes being at the same time in the same place[25] or the sharing of a 'simultaneous space-time'.[26] Thus, it is always specific; there is no general or stable mode of being-together. 'We', for Nancy, is always an expression of our specific entanglement and division, not a unique subject or a 'diffuse generality'.[27] The singular-plural is not a generalisable or abstract relation: '"one" is not "with" in some general sort of way, but each time according to determined modes that are themselves multiple and simultaneous (people, culture, language, lineage, network, group, couple, band and so on)'.[28] That is, singularity itself takes specific and multiple modes. People, culture, language, network and so on as specific modes of being-together are in themselves singularities, rather than a way in which singularities find themselves in relation.

Importantly, the line on which exposure takes place is not static, because the suspension between inside and outside is always being decided 'at each instant'.[29] The singular, then, is not something which can be simply identified or pinned down. The lines on which it emerges are not static or simple ones, rather they are: 'trembling, mobile, and fleeting'.[30] So we cannot know where, precisely, what Nancy calls the 'sharing' of a person or a stone may begin or end; we cannot know what or who may be an 'existing singular':[31]

> The delineation is always wider and at the same time more narrow than one believes when one grasps it . . . Each existent belongs to more groups, masses, networks or complexes than first one recognises, and each also detaches from them and from itself, infinitely.[32]

It should be becoming clear that, for Nancy, singularity is not the same as individuality in either structure or nature.[33] Thinking in terms of the individual would return us to assuming the primacy of the first term in 'being-with-others'. This would be the logic of 'me' and 'you', but the singular is never these things.[34] Rather, it is 'what is distinguished in the distinction'[35] or, as Jenny Edkins suggests, what lies on the line of touching and separation, between the inside and outside.[36] However, it is not that the individual is not a singularity, but rather that singularity exceeds the scope of thinking in terms only of individuals: 'I say "singularities" because these are not only individuals . . . Entire collectives, groups, powers and discourses are exposed here, "within" each individual as well as among them'.[37]

Sharing, exposure and the in-common

It is being which we share or have in common, and being is not a thing we could possess in common like a common property.[38] Being is, Nancy argues 'only when shared *in common* or rather whose quality of being, whose nature and structure are shared (or exposed)'.[39] Further, what is in common here is not a quality, but is a lack, so it is not in-common in the usual sense of the word. We do not and cannot share any quality or attribute, since 'we' are not prior to the in-common. This means that no foundation can be built on the in-common; there is, in a sense, nothing there. The human condition is, argues Nancy, 'that there is no first or last condition, no unconditioned that can be the principle or origin'.[40]

What is shared, then, or what we have in common 'is sharing itself'.[41] We have in common that which differentiates us – not the content of the difference, but the differentiation itself. For example, Nancy argues that 'what I have in common with another Frenchman is the fact of *not* being the same Frenchman as him, and the fact that our "Frenchness" is never, nowhere, in no essence, in no figure, brought to completion'.[42] It is everyone's non-identity, both to themselves and others, which is shared.[43] For Nancy, the Other and the same are alike, not through their identification or identical-ness, but in that identity itself is always shared, always non-identity.[44] We are alike, for Nancy, not in terms of similarities or even differences (in the Levinasian sense of difference of characteristics or identity). 'Alike' suggests one resembling another, but Nancy removes this hierarchical structure or concept of an origin or original identity; 'a like being', he argues, '"resembles" me in that I myself "resemble" him, we "resemble" together . . .'[45] A like-being, he continues, does not resemble me as a portrait resembles an individual, one does not come first, one is not more originary or authentic than the other.[46] It is not, then, that the Other would be like me in such a way that it would be subsumed into the same, because the same is already opened up in its resemblance with the Other; the central categories of same and Other are undone here.

This sharing and exposure which are central for Nancy are precisely what constitute being-in-common. Sharing and exposure are, for him, understood in terms of communication. Communication *is* being, or being is communication: language is not an instrument of communication, and communication is not an instrument of being.[47] Rather, in communication, what takes place is our exposition, it is finite existence exposed to finite existence, exposure of our common limits, co-appearing.[48] The 'dislocation and interpellation' that is communication in fact constitutes being-in-common. Singularity exists only by, and through, exposure to an outside and, as discussed above, the outside is not a general structure, but the exposition of another singularity.[49] This exposure or sharing, Nancy argues, is what gives rise to the mutual interpellation of singularities, prior to any address in language.[50] It is the condition of possibility of language.[51]

As such, Nancy is opposed to what he calls the 'intersubjective myth of dialogue' and proposes the interruption of this 'myth':

> the dialogue is no longer to be heard except as the communication of the incommunicable singularity/community. I no longer (no longer essentially) hear in it what the other *wants to say* (to me), but I hear in it that the other, or some other speaks and that there is an essential archi-articulation of the voice and of voices, which constitutes the being *in* common itself: *the* voice *is* always in itself articulated (different from itself, differing itself), and this is why there is not a voice but the plural voices of singular beings.[52]

What is exposed in communication or being-together is at the heart of Nancy's approach. It is not the exposure of individuals which could, in theory, be contained and unexposed, not the showing of some pure 'inside' which is corrupted or penetrated. Exposure, for Nancy, happens; it is the cornerstone of the way we are in the world, the way in which we appear *with* or compear, and what is exposed is this key fact: 'What is exposed in compearance is the following, and we must learn to read it in all its possible combinations: "you (are/ and/is) (entirely other than) I". Or again, more simply "*you shares me*"'.[53]

Nancy uses the figure of touch to think about relation in the context of the singular-plural. Touch neither separates completely, nor subsumes one into the other. It is, as Watkin argues, not a communion, but 'an indication of both proximity and distance, contact and impenetrability'.[54] Exposure and community are, for Nancy, structured as touch, as each up against one another. Importantly, exposure relies on the idea of the limit – a relation of those who have nothing in common, not a relation where one is subsumed into the other.[55]

It is touch, Nancy argues, that differentiates the identification photograph from the portrait, with an identification photo being a 'descriptive record', as opposed to an image.[56] The image touches, for Nancy, in that 'it pulls and *draws* . . . in that it *extracts* something, an intimacy, a force'. In this sense, all images are portraits.[57] It is not the representation which is important here, but this touching, pulling and intimacy, and so Nancy argues that the image, in this sense, is not only visual, but rather that the visual plays the role of a model: 'it is also musical, poetic, even tactile, olfactory or gustatory, kinesthetic and so on'.[58]

Image relies on relation and, in particular, on the relation of touch – that of being-together. Image as exposure 'does not belong to the domain of objects, their perception and their use, but to that of forces, their affections and transmissions'.[59] The image is not something to be assessed or understood from a safe distance, but is instead affecting and involving: 'There is no image without my too being in its image, but also without passing into it, as long as I look at it, that is, as long as I show it *consideration*, maintain my regard for it'.[60] There is, then, in the idea of touch and exposure, something of Levinas' concept of the face. There is more than the descriptive or identificatory aspects which might confront us. It is what Levinas might call the expressive, but which, for Nancy, is more obviously relational – an involvement in the image.

Politics without Essence

Totalisation and the resistance of community

To conceptualise the in-common in a way that does not rely on unity, completeness or essence either as properties of the individual or the group, Nancy turns to the concept of community. If being-with is how things are, then community *is* always already, rather than something to be created or formed. This insight entails a different understanding of community, its potential and limitations, and the refiguring of community is a key element in Nancy's ontology. Martin Coward highlights two etymologies of community which are useful in orienting Nancy's thinking here: first, as a fusion of *com* and *unus* – that is, together as one; second, as *com* and *munis* – that is, obligated together.[61] These two conceptions broadly link, Coward argues, to a socialist and nationalist approach in the first instance and a social contractarian approach in the second.[62] However, both positions rest on logic of identity and closure, either of self-identical individuals coming together or of a unified and stable community, and it is this shared logic to which Nancy offers an alternative.

In contrast to these approaches, Nancy argues that community is neither a coming together of individuals, nor a pre-existing nature to be fulfilled – that is, neither fusion nor production.[63] Instead, he offers an account of an 'inoperative' community, which can also be translated from the French as an 'unworkable' community. The notion of 'work' here refers to producing or production, and it is this which Nancy sees as the danger in, for example, nationalist and socialist approaches to community, but also in advanced liberal societies.[64] In these instances, he suggests, a common substance or defining principle for community is produced – for example, capital – which places the identity and generality of production and products above community.[65]

The inoperative community takes communal identity as itself a singularity (a singular-plural, a being-with), rather than a sum of singularities.[66] That is, communal identity – in fact, all identity – is an unstable intersection of limits and relationality. Community is not an essence or shared identity, an organic 'togetherness', but nor is it a pre-existing totality into, or through which, subjects emerge. Community is a manifestation of 'being-with', in which it is not just that togetherness does not in some way 'come first', but that singularities, selves or subjects do not 'come first' either. For Nancy, we have neither one common being, nor beings that are utterly distinct.[67]

This conception of community does not have a fixed structure or mode. By virtue of the specific and protean relationality of which it consists, community itself 'is' only in each specific articulation: 'this communitary "ground" or condition of existence is an unsublatable differential relation that "is" only in and by its multiple singular articulations (though it is always irreducible to these) and thus differs constantly from itself'.[68] The inoperative community offers a way of thinking about the multiple which maintains or allows for the instability of the singular-plural.

What needs to be emphasised is that, for Nancy, community – albeit a specific and novel understanding of community – is how things are. It would be impossible to 'lose' it, since 'community is given to us with being and as being, well in advance of all our projects, desires, and undertakings';[69] there is being only in, and as, community.[70] Whatever attempts are made to co-opt, put to work or disavow community, it never ceases to resist; it is, Nancy argues, 'resistance itself'.[71] Community or being-with underlies all attempts at closing off this or that particular community, at putting forward an essence, project, stable identity or foundational 'myth'. What resists is the in-common; not anything we *have* in common, rather that we *are* in common.

Nancy's rethinking of being-with and community is directed towards questions of political organisation, although in addressing them, it also challenges the way in which they are formulated.

Nancy's question, in one particular articulation, is that if we no longer think in terms of either singularity or plurality:

> how can this community without essence (the community that is neither 'people' nor 'nation', neither 'destiny' nor 'generic humanity' etc.) be presented as such? That is, what might a politics be that does not stem from the will to realise an essence?[72]

This is, for Nancy, a question of the politics of the political, and the separation of these two terms is a key factor in his approach here.

Politics, for Nancy, refers to the everyday empirical practice of politics, of order and administration or, more specifically, to 'the play of forces and interests engaged in a conflict over the representation and governance of social existence'.[73] The political, on the other hand, is the site of contestation over meaning, where 'what it means to *be* in common is open to definition'.[74] The political is not the organisation of society, but the openness and sharing at the heart of community, the 'disposition of community as such'.[75] The political informs and orients politics and is – as is the community of which it is an experience – irreducibly open. Politics, then, can be thought of as the system of particular guarantees or assumptions of an order – for example, commitments to God, the market, communism and so on – and related questions of the meaning of community and subjectivity and the administration of that order under or within this guarantee. The political, on the other hand, refers to the realm of the guarantees and assumptions, their negotiation, questioning and ultimate groundlessness; in other words, the realm of community without communion. It is in this context that, if 'everything is political', as Nancy argues, it is in the sense that '"everything", the "whole" should in no way be total or totalised'.[76]

In the light of this, Nancy is concerned with what he sees as the totalisation of politics, through the idea that everything is, or should be, political.[77] If everything is political, he argues, there is a concern that nothing is anymore, because the term loses all its specificity.[78] In encompassing all spheres, the political excludes every other area of reference and so becomes totalitarian.[79] Everything becomes subsumed within this completion: 'What "completes" itself ... is the great "enlightened" progressivist discourse of secular or profane eschatology ... the discourse of the re-appropriation of man in his humanity, the discourse of the actualisation of the genre of the human'.[80] That is, the conditions of existence and meaning of society or humanity are already answered through the answer to the political.[81] Everything falls under the umbrella of 'enlightened progressivist' discourse, so that specifically political questions are assumed to be already answered. In place of these questions, Nancy argues, we are then left only with management or organisation.[82]

Political questions (or the political as a question) cannot emerge in this totalising environment, because there is no space for them. The political as grounding and foundation is assumed, taken to be 'well known' or 'obvious'.[83] Nancy is concerned that the political as a question has been closed down, that 'the thinking of community as essence – is in effect the closure of the political'.[84] For Nancy, this, when the political is assumed or made self-evident, is the route to totalisation and totalitarianism. Totalitarianism, then, might be understood as encompassing any political or social organisation which answers the very questions which need to remain posed as questions. It is an attempt to bring into understanding and knowledge that which ultimately resists these – that is, the in-common. The route taken to this by the current incarnation of totalitarianism, argues Nancy, has been through the 'dissolution of transcendence', which renders all spheres of life devoid of alterity.[85]

In response to this totalitarianism, Nancy and Lacoue-Labarthe call for a retreat or retreating of the political. This has two related meanings: first, referring to the neglect, assumed lack of importance or taken-for-granted-ness of the political – a retreat of transcendence or alterity.[86] In the second meaning, the retreat refers to the need for the political to be re-treated, rethought and opened up again for debate. Retreating is, in this sense, 're-tracing'; raising the question in a new way as 'the question of essence',[87] which is precisely the question of relation, being-with and community.[88]

The re-treating of the political must be mindful then of the openness of community, as it is here that it is exposed and presented. Politics must henceforth be understood, Nancy argues, 'as the specific place of the articulation of a non-unity' – that is, as a place of detotalisation.[89] It should be noted that, while Nancy diagnoses totalitarianism as proceeding from the retreat of transcendence, he does not argue that a retreating of the political should be a repeat of an appeal to transcendence.[90] Although the specific 'form of life' which Nancy identifies as having grown old is autonomy, this does not imply that the way out should be sought in heteronomy.[91] The retreating of the political is informed by the need to think in terms of neither autonomy nor heteronomy, neither the law of the same nor the other, but rather in terms of exonomy, as a potential move outside this binary, unappropriable by the same or Other.[92]

Similarly, the retreat of transcendence or alterity (the two are linked for Nancy) does not call for a renewed appeal to it. Any appeal to transcendence – god, man, history and perhaps even the Other – installs totalitarianism and the immanence of life in common by providing an originary grounding.[93] So the question of relation, of the essence of the political or being-in-common needs, for Nancy, to be addressed in the light of his rethinking of being-singular-plural. That is, starting not from the same or Other, but from what is between in the singular-plural.

Nancy then is suspicious of appeals to both transcendence and immanence. On the one hand, community itself, for him, is a 'resistance to immanence' and so is itself transcendence.[94] However, this is transcendence without any 'sacred' meaning: 'signifying precisely a resistance to immanence (resistance to the communion of everyone or to the exclusive passion of one or several)'.[95] It is in this sense that the dissolution of transcendence has rendered all spheres of life devoid of alterity. In order to pursue an approach to the question of the political which relies on neither transcendence nor immanence, Nancy introduces the idea of transimmanence.

Transimmanence is, in part, a rethinking of transcendence which attempts to free it from the idea of purity or what is completely beyond. As such, it also entails a rethinking of immanence. Transcendence has to be understood, Nancy argues: 'not as that which might transcend existence towards a pure "beyond" . . . but as that which structures existence itself into a "beyond" . . .'[96] This existence structured as 'beyond' is transimmanence – an open immanence which is not in opposition to transcendence, but rather where something in immanence itself transcends immanence or where immanence itself is transcendent, opened up within the world.[97] The transimmanent is neither immanent nor transcendent, but is 'what exceeds the phenomenon in the phenomenon itself'.[98]

Community, then, is a resistance not only to immanence, but also to transcendence. The community is, in this new terminology, transimmanent, since transimmanence points to the impossibility of closure. It is neither relation nor non-relation which resists knowledge

or immanence for Nancy, not the singular or the plural, but relation/
non-relation, the law of touching as separation, the singular-plural.
It is precisely this transimmanence which underlies the structure of
singular plurality.

The politics of transimmanence

The implications of starting with transimmanence are disconcerting
for attempts to account for politics and the political decision. Transimmanence does not offer the kind of starting point that an appeal
to the Other as transcendent might – that is, it explicitly decouples
politics from any possible ground. Rather, it offers one possible
mapping out of thinking through politics without an appeal to foundational or transcendent ethics and offers a focus on relationality,
which does not return to, or rely on, a theorisable or foundational
ethical ground.

In terms of providing guidance for 'practical' politics, Nancy
leaves us in a similar position to Derrida and Levinas, with only
minimal interventions, none of which are of a systematic or
programmable nature.[99] This has led some authors to suggest that
there is a failing or limitation in his work when faced with political
questions. Andrew Norris, for example, criticises Nancy for failing
to provide guidance for political judgement. Nancy, he argues is:
'too content to rest with deconstructive aporias, and not sufficiently
attentive to the inevitability, the necessity, and the dignity of
political judgement'.[100] That is, Nancy gives us insufficient advice
on how to make a decision, and he 'does not indicate on what
grounds such a choice might be made'.[101] Ian James argues that if
community *is*: 'it can only be affirmed or denied, cannot be lost or
gained, regretted in past or projected in a program for the future'.
The decision becomes only whether shared finitude is recognised
and affirmed or negated, and this, for James, is of little use for 'real
politics'.[102]

However, this critique arises because Nancy offers a different
starting point for considering politics and the political decision,
such that political engagement is radically reconceptualised; the
question of shared finitude is at the heart of politics. If the question
of the essence of the political is the question of relation, then any
guidelines would be both inadequate and irresponsible. Being-with
is never in a determined mode, but is inherently in flux. How we

are together is not something that can be pinned down, but is rather (re)created at every instant and site of intersection of singularities. As such, it is always a question, and it is this question which Nancy refers to when describing community as resistance. His concern is precisely that the political be re-opened as a question, something which can only be done if the thinking of community is refigured; otherwise, the answers are already presented. As such, his work does not provide new, or at least not final or complete, answers. Any guideline would act as an attempt to answer the question, an attempt to fix and essentialise community and so would ultimately be a totalising move. Nancy's rethinking of community, then, provides no grounds on which guidelines might be based. In fact, he is concerned precisely with thinking about community without ground or foundation.

For Nancy, the lack of ground does not lead to nihilism or relativism. This would be only the substitution of another ground or, in Nancy's terms, moving myth into the place of figure. It is not, then, that there can be no decisions or political interventions, but rather that these can never be fully resolved or totalising. In fact, he argues that using philosophy to inform politics in any straightforward way has dangerous implications. As James explains, Nancy sees the expectation of such a movement as 'deeply implicated' in the recent history of European totalitarianism.[103] That is, a simple derivation of politics from a philosophical position immediately renders mute any specifically political questions by providing a new ground or 'quasi-transcendental fictional myth'.[104]

However, as will be elaborated on below, this lack itself acts in some way as a ground, and it is from here that Nancy's minimal guidance on 'practical' politics emerges. This is often in terms of negative guidance, since questions of the political open only at the limits of knowledge. Nancy suggests that these limits – the 'there isn't' – can and should be recognised. While this means that we cannot know, predict or command our world, for Nancy, it also means that we need to try to create political configurations which acknowledge this impossibility. We can, he argues: 'act in such a way that this world is a world able to open itself up to its own uncertainty as such'.[105]

The political question, then, is how to 'induce the group to configure itself as a space of sense (as in being-toward) as opposed to truth'[106] – that is, as a space of uncertainty, which recognises the irreducible openness of the question of relation. Being-toward, then, would be without saying toward-what or toward-whom. Elsewhere, Nancy describes this in terms of 'making a world' in which everything is not already done or decided,[107] in which no answers are taken as givens and in which the 'obviousness' of the political is challenged. This keeping open of the question is, in Nancy's work, what offers up the potential to resist totalisation.

Nancy is not suggesting a complete openness to whatever may come in terms of a suspension of, or retreat from, the realm of politics. Being-with cannot lead to particular political prescriptions, and it disrupts the grounds on which much of our political thinking is based. However, as well as resisting a world in which everything is already played out, Nancy sees the need to 'make a world for which all is not . . . still entirely to do (in the future for always future tomorrows)'.[108] We are left, for Nancy, before a double imperative, where:

> It is necessary to measure up to what nothing in the world can measure, no established law, no inevitable process, no prediction, no calculable horizon – absolute justice, limitless quality, perfect dignity – and it is necessary to invent and create the world itself immediately, here and now, at every moment, without reference to yesterday or tomorrow.[109]

At one and the same time, we need to affirm and denounce the world as it is – that is, not at one moment to affirm and one to denounce, nor to think in terms of working as best we can towards some ideal within the constraints of the 'real world', but to create a world where these contradictions are opened up:

> not to weigh out as best one can equal amounts of submission and revolt . . . but to *make* the world into the place, never still, always perpetually reopened, of its own contradiction, which is what prevents us from ever knowing in advance *what* is to be done.[110]

In doing this, we become unable to give simple answers. There is no system of organisation which can be built upon 'being-with', because 'being-with' destabilises such systems. Nancy cannot provide alternative forms of organisation, but rather opens up already existing formations and already existing gaps and limitations. These must, he argues, be paid heed to, but not in the interests of building a new improved project around them.

Ethics without Transcendence

The ethical and the ontological

Nancy's politics emerges out of an absence of foundational or transcendent ethics. Ethics is here liberated from its positioning as a ground for politics, such that they are both refigured through the singular-plural. While it may initially seem that Nancy devotes less time to questions of ethics and responsibility than politics, this indicates the problematic nature of these categories in the terms of his work. Ethics and politics cannot be easily separated here. In the same way that politics cannot be derived from a prior philosophical starting point, but is instead part of this starting point, ethics cannot be derived either.[111]

The singular-plural disrupts the very notion of first places, absolutes or origins, so all of Nancy's work is, in a sense, an attempt to think outside of the ethics/politics, absolute/relative and Other/Third framings. There is not the singular on the one hand and the plural on the other, with ethics and politics emerging somewhere between the two or shuttling first to one and then to the other. The idea of purity is displaced by that of the border, line or limit. Following on from this, for Nancy, we might think in terms not of a line between ethics and politics, but of ethics and politics as the line.

In the absence of first places, Nancy also moves away from an appeal to the (pre)originary transcendent alterity of the Other as prompting the ethical relation. Being-in-common does not take a determined mode, so relationality, for Nancy, is a relationship without content. To be on the limit of inside/outside, as discussed above, is 'not yet even to be face-to-face', because this exposure on the limit occurs before identification: 'before entrapment by the stare that takes hostage'.[112] In one sense, the relation in which we find ourselves would not be always already 'ethical' as it is for Levinas, for this would be to confer meaning and content on the relationship.

A number of critics argue that Nancy's approach to ethics is problematic in that this lack of content leads to neglecting alterity or demonstrates a return to an ontology that reduces everything to the same. More specifically, Critchley accuses Nancy of leaving us standing 'shoulder-to-shoulder', rather than face-to-face, and argues that this creates problems for thinking about ethics, because it risks turning into a relation of reciprocity.[113] In Nancy, the relation of height we find in Levinas is flattened, Critchley argues, and asymmetry is lost; 'The other becomes my colleague, my comrade', rather than the widow, orphan or stranger.[114] Nancy, Critchley argues, leads us back to an ontological tradition that 'is incapable of acknowledging that which resists knowledge' as the source of ethical experience.[115]

Certainly, there are suggestions of this focus on how we are alike for Nancy, but, importantly, the like is not the same. We are in-common in terms of having our exposure in common, rather than in-common in terms of characteristics or membership of a group. The in-common is being-in-common, not beings that are then in common, nor the common dissipated through beings, as an idea of the in-common as characteristics or group membership would necessitate. The collegiality of the shoulder-to-shoulder is at odds with Nancy's focus on separation and the beyond knowledge. We are alike precisely in that which resists knowledge. Being-with is not positioned in opposition to separation and alterity, but rather the two are mutually reliant on one another. Separation is what allows for exposure, sharing and touching. This touching is not a subsuming into the same, but an experience of the simultaneous distance and proximity in which we are together. There remains a place for alterity in Nancy's work, but without its positioning as originary or transcendental.

Critchley's argument aims, in part, at a difficulty that he sees with Nancy's commitment to ontology. As discussed in Chapter 2, for Levinas, an ontological relation subsumes the other into the same and so makes ethics impossible. For Levinas, we need to look outside being – 'otherwise than being' – to encounter alterity. For Nancy though, Critchley argues, 'the particular being is always already understood within the pre-comprehension of being'; both singularity and plurality are understood from within being, not as otherwise than it, not as transcendent.[116] Ontology and ethics are thus set up as in opposition.

The broader question at stake here, then, is the nature of the relationship between ethics and ontology for Nancy. The singular-plural of being as an ontology without first places entails that rather than seeking to disrupt totalisation by an appeal to ethics as the pre- or extra-ontological which we might read Levinas as doing, Nancy's concept of the singular-plural of being locates ethics already in an ontology refigured as open and exposed – as transimmanent. This is an ontology which does not reduce the Other to knowledge or the same, because there is no same to start from; we are always already placed in question in the 'disturbance of violent relatedness'.[117] While in Critchley's formulation there is being within which singularity and plurality might then be understood; for Nancy, being *is* being-together, the singular-plural, which is a very different ontology to the one critiqued by Levinas.

Ethics and ontology, then, are not in opposition, because, for Nancy, ontology itself is structured as ethics. Coexistence or being-with is not an 'idea, notion, or concept', but is already 'a *praxis* and an *ethos*'.[118] As Critchley puts it, for Nancy: '*fundamental ontology is ethics and ethics is fundamentally ontological*'.[119] Being-singular-plural has the same structure as responsibility in that both point to an originary structure of im-possible being-together. Thus, Nancy argues that: 'Not only is there an ethics but ethics becomes the ontology of ontology itself'.[120] Ethics here does not describe the content of the relationship, but the very fact of relationality itself. Ethics, then, is not a matter of choice; we are, in being-together, always already in an ethical relation in which, as Coward argues, 'we cannot but respond'.[121] This does not return us to an originary ethics, ethos, code of conduct or mode of relation. Rather, the origin *is* ethos: 'Thinking the origin as *ethos* or conduct isn't the same as representing an originary *ethos*'.[122] The origin as ethos or ethics is a function of the transimmanence which structures existence itself as beyond. On this basis, Nancy argues, the transcendence of being (transimmanence) 'can and must be expressed as originary ethics'.[123]

Nancy does not follow the path of beginning from the Other, because thinking in terms of either the one or the Other denies being-with.[124] We are *with* the Other. As such, the Other as metric of complete otherness risks a covering over of the *with*, while at the same time being its condition of possibility; we cannot be *with* the same. There can be being-with only with alterity. Thinking in terms of the Other, Nancy argues: 'both represents the incommensurability of Being as being-with-one-another *and* runs the risk of covering over or deferring this Being's realm . . . insofar as it is the measure of this incommensurability'.[125] So, on this reading, we are left with a Nancy who admits a central place for alterity in his thought, which nonetheless does not occupy the first place. In being-singular-plural, there are no first places, only the hyphen; a first place without content, a non-place. That is, relation, but relation without content, is primary. More accurately perhaps, it is not that we are *in* relation, a state which already suggests separation, but that we *are* relation. We *are* only on the border which both separates and joins.

Nancy's starting point of the one-by-one in which we are both separated and together places emphasis on the hyphen, not singular and plural, but singular-plural. Rather than a project of disrupting ontology (or showing how this ontology disrupts itself), Nancy offers an ontology from which we can start thinking – a starting point of responsibility, community and being-together that makes none originary or derivable, so necessarily leaves the question of ethics, the political and community always open.

The invention of justice

The demand made by thinking being as singular-plural might also be thought of as an ethical demand to the extent that the singular-plural is originary ethics. What is demanded here is the im-possible task of thinking justice to the singular and plural as inseparable, without hierarchy or origin. This is more far-reaching than it might seem. Individualism, human rights, utilitarianism, humanism, communism and natural law all depend on the privileging of one term over the other, as does an approach in which openness to absolute alterity is prioritised. We find it difficult to think, it seems, in the singular-plural.

The inseparability of singular and plural is not the same as their identity, and the negotiation of this inseparability without identity is, for Nancy, the work of justice; justice is to be done to the singular-plural. This does not entail 'a unique justice interpreted according to perspectives or subjectivities' – an interpretation which would prioritise the singular and might stray close to relativism.[126] It points rather to the same justice equal for all, but, crucially, in a way that does not prioritise the plural; a justice without common measure, which is 'irreducible and insubstitutable from one to the other'.[127] Because we do not know where each singular existent begins and ends, as discussed above, we cannot know 'what must be rendered to each singular existent'.[128] The singular and the plural are not clear or stable in their demarcation, and justice to a singular existent does not make sense in being-with – it ignores the hyphen – so, for Nancy:

> What is appropriate is thus defined by the measure proper to each exist-
> ent *and* to the infinite, indefinitely open, circulating and transforming

community (or communication, contagion, contact) of all existences between them.[129]

As suggested above, this double imperative does not have a hierarchical structure. Furthermore, the imperative is not 'twofold', but is 'the same'.[130] We are not called by two competing imperatives – this would retain the assumption of the singular and plural as separable and in conflict. The imperative is, then, 'the same', not the same in terms of the community and the existent being identical, but in terms, once again, of the hyphen or the line as the central object of analysis. Justice is to be rendered to this line, which both separates and makes contact:

> Justice is thus the return to each existent its due according to its unique creation, singular in its coexistence with all other creations. The two measures are not separate: the singular property exists according to the singular line that joins it to the other properties. What distinguishes is also what connects 'with' and 'together'.[131]

This justice to the line is, Nancy argues, 'visible nowhere',[132] and its task is one of creation and invention, to 'create a world tirelessly' – that is, to create a space of 'unappeasable and unsettled' sovereignty of meaning.[133]

The demand for justice, then, cannot be used to develop any generalised principles: 'It defines neither *a* politics, nor *a* writing, for it refers . . . to that which resists any definition or program'.[134] As with the previous authors that have been discussed, for Nancy, this is explicitly not a limitation or failing:

> What I have said . . . sets out no values onto which one can hold, or to which one could respond. But is it precisely this which is important . . . we must have in sight that which escapes any sign. Of necessity we have to invent the direction to take, and to invent it knowing that this invention can never claim to 'know' for everybody . . .[135]

This is a necessity imposed by the very structure of our being-together. There is an obligation which is imposed by this being-with-others, because, for Nancy, each singularity is an origin of the world, which is inaccessible to other singularities:

> One cannot know what being or existence is for each person, every time. One has to invent it. One must consequently act according to this

obligation to invent, to allow to be invented, each person's meaning of being.[136]

This is a commitment to (re)invention or being-toward without knowing toward-what. It is only through the 'eruption of the new' – an orientation that allows for such eruption – that totalitarianism, in terms of a world where everything has already been decided or answered, can be resisted.[137]

So the ethical demand in Nancy is as difficult as those discussed in previous chapters; invention and an understanding or acknowledgement of the difficulties that this lack of guidance leads to. Nancy is more explicit than either Levinas or Derrida about the need to 'bring into view' or try to acknowledge our being-with-others – that is, to bring into view that which resists knowledge or understanding. This is, in fact, an 'ethical demand' for him:

> To bring into view that which we cannot 'see' – that which conceals itself as the origin of the other, in the other – and to bring 'into view' that fact that we cannot 'see' it: that is what today makes an ethical demand.[138]

It is the lack of ground which, for Nancy, needs to be recognised or taken into account. The ethical demand, however, is not a general one; rather, it refers to Nancy's diagnosis of the contemporary operation of particular modes of totalisation associated with the retreat of the political. Nancy's prescriptions, if they can be termed such, would be the suggestion that the whole should not be totalised, that the space of the question, the space of the political should be kept open as a question. This is precisely the recognition of the 'there isn't' which prevents Nancy's own interventions from taking on the mantle of an answer to the question of ethics and politics. It is because of this lack of guidance that, for Nancy, we have to invent and that there is an obligation or ethical demand to do this.

Ontology, ethos, limits

For Nancy, the 'with' and coexistence are at the heart of being. Nancy's work takes as a starting point that we start neither alone nor together, that there is no initial separation and no initial sameness, but rather that we are together as singular-plural, both separate and together. It is in the light of this that, for Nancy, the categories of same and Other – of key importance in Chapters 2 and 3 – are reworked. In place of this hierarchical dichotomy, Nancy starts from the suggestion that we are alike without hierarchy, in that we share sharing and non-identity. We do not need to look to transcendent alterity to interrupt or exceed ontology or the same, because existence itself opens up as resistance to totalisation.

This starting point means that Nancy's approach to ethics and politics is devoid of the oppositional features which might be identified in other accounts. The ethical as pre- or extra-ontological, a realm of transcendent alterity, is not cast in opposition to the realm of knowledge, calculation and commonality, which might be associated with the political. Rather, the imperatives which emerge from the indissociability of these realms are the same; the singular-plural refers to precisely the line on which both ethics and the political might emerge. It refers to the way in which we are together both as a multiplicity, where judgements and calculation are called for, and simultaneously as singularities in specific relation each time or, perhaps more accurately, to the way in which we are neither of these things, but are, in fact, both. In the terminology whereby ethics would be aligned with the singular and politics with the plural, we are always both ethical and political. The indissociability is such that we cannot think in terms of finding ourselves at one moment as singular and the next as plural, nor as caught between their competing imperatives. One thing that Nancy specifically brings out is that these imperatives are the same. Nancy's work on the political, then, is also, in this terminology, concerned with the ethical.

Nancy's reframing of the question of the political as one of keeping the question open and resisting attempts at totalisation in many ways looks similar to the ethical concerns of the other authors considered. This reframing means that to address the question of the political does not have to (in fact, cannot and should not) entail offering guidelines or prescriptions. As such, a politics which is mindful of the political on which it rests offers potential for thinking through the making of unsecured political claims.

Once the political is thus refigured as a realm of contestation and groundlessness which explicitly resists offering guidelines for decision, then ethics no longer has to serve as its ground; both are freed from foundational constraints. This allows for the conceptualisation of the political without poles or origins, and as not in opposition to ethics. The political, for Nancy, is not a tool in the service of ethics or something to be informed by ethics. Ethics here does not have to insure the decision, offer an account of a duty within it or a commitment to alterity. That is, totalisation can be resisted without a renewed appeal to transcendence.

Ethics no longer needs to occupy an outside in order to offer resistance to totalisation; being-with implicates the transcendent already within being. This means that the relationality which complicates the primacy of transcendent alterity, as drawn out in previous chapters, can itself be posited as the starting point. We can think in terms of singularity, rather than alterity. Relation, but without content, is primary here, and this lack of content resists any attempts at final or complete definitions or answers. The starting point itself is then resistance. Attempts at totalisation, the reduction to the same, are resisted already through relationality and community, which open themselves up already to an outside. Nancy provides potential for resisting totalisation in a way that does not consist of a renewed appeal to the transcendent through his concept of transimmanence – that existence itself is structured as a beyond.

The implications of this are far-reaching; we can think the starting point as ethics or ethos, but without the need to posit a pure ethical face-to-face relation as constituting that starting point. The origin as ethos or conduct opens immediately to the irreducible openness of the singular-plural. The ground from which we start is right here; there is no elsewhere to turn to. But 'right here' is constituted as being-with, so not completed or immanent. We can only start with the openness of being-with, of community as resistance to any totalisation. This is the ontology which is also ethos; an ontology of relation in which the relation itself has no content. Ethics does not need to exceed ontology, because ontology itself is displaced. Ontology is framed in terms of conduct, rather than knowledge, so is no longer the comprehension of being.

In starting with conduct, then, we start at the limits of theory, for this is where conduct emerges. Being-with resists and exceeds theory, does not have a determined mode and insists that its definition is kept open and unresolvable. The relation without content which keeps the question open then marks both the limits of theory and constitutes ethos as origin.

Nancy provides an alternative imaginary in which our ethical relations and possibilities are not grounded in individuals, community or a transcendent Other. This allows for the possibility of thinking about ethical practices without origin or foundation, abstraction or guidelines. Rather, Nancy's approach reveals the potential for thinking about 'ethics' as a series of everyday, multiple, shifting, negotiated political practices, which attempt to respond to the demand for justice to the protean modalities of being-with.

Chapter 5
The Limits of Theory: Ethics, Politics, Practice

Introduction: Displacing the Line between Ethics and Politics

The ways in which the line between ethics and politics is drawn and displaced has emerged through the preceding chapters as of central importance in any attempt to reconceptualise the political implications of a destabilisation of foundational approaches to ethics. Having examined some theoretical resources which enable an interrogation and displacement of the line, this chapter draws out their implications for reconceptualising questions of post-foundational ethics and practical politics through a focus on the assumptions and distinctions that such line drawing relies upon and reproduces.

This particular line between ethics and politics is often mirrored in discussions of the relation between the conditional and unconditional, the singular and plural, the Other and Third, the immanent and transcendent, theory and practice and so on. In turn, these relationships are integral to conceptions of ethics and responsibility and to the possibility of questioning these conceptions. There is a complex support structure surrounding any claims about ethics and politics, and it is through a reassessment of some elements of this structure which otherwise go relatively unexamined that this chapter proceeds to offer a rereading of the possibilities and limitations of poststructuralist ethics and politics.

There are three key areas drawn from the readings of Levinas, Derrida and Nancy in the previous chapters around which my rereading of the ethico-political develops. The first element is the argument that the authors I have focused on leave us not in the absence of grounds or foundations, nor with the formulation of a groundless ground, but rather at the limits of grounds and foundations. This leads to an injunction to recognise the limits of what can be theorised and the way in which conduct emerges at these limits. Our situation at the limits of grounds reformulates the questions of how we might 'do' ethics or politics with unstable foundations, because it casts us as always already engaged in the ethico-political.

This reformulation points to the second key area in my argument, which traces the implications of approaching ethics as ontology. Central to these implications is the collapse of the ontological/normative distinction, which means that ethics thus reconceptualised cannot offer normative guidance. Instead, if the origin is conduct, there is a shift in the nature of questions to which accounts of the ethico-political might be able to respond. If we start with ethos or conduct, at the limits of grounds and without an originary ethos, this entails a move away from asking how ethics might inform practical politics to an attempt at thinking practices of ethics and politics as an underivable starting point.

Underlying both of these elements is an engagement with the implications of the displacement of transcendent alterity argued for in Chapters 3 and 4, which is the third focus of my argument. It is in the light of the loss of both universal reason and transcendence to ground ethics and politics that the ethico-political needs to be repositioned as at the limits of grounds. Through the concept of transimmanence introduced by Nancy, the possibility opens up for displacing, rather than reversing, the logocentric hierarchy of same and Other. This offers an alternative to the dominant way in which the potential of poststructuralist ethics has been understood in terms of the interruption of totalisation by transcendent alterity. Here, while interruption remains important, it loses its figure or content; instead, interruption itself takes first place, returning us once again to the realm of practice.

I develop this argument through identifying some key assumptions which inform attempts to rethink politics in the light of poststructuralist ethics, and offering an analysis of the ways in which these limit possibilities for a more radical recasting of the ethico-political. I then turn to the readings of Levinas, Derrida and Nancy undertaken in previous chapters, in order to offer possible alternatives to these assumptions, first, in terms of grounds, origins and foundations and, second, in terms of transcendence and immanence. Finally, I offer an argument for approaching conduct as origin through foregrounding the 'practical'.

Grounds, Origins and Foundations

Looking for a more responsible politics

This book started with the question of how we might apply poststructuralist insights on ethics to 'practical' politics in an attempt to address the question which often confronts so-called 'poststructuralism' regarding its relevance to the 'real world'. Specifically, that is, to offer an account of the way in which, once foundational ideas have been put into question, this approach can have anything useful to say about what might be traditionally seen as 'moral' questions, such that they might inform practical political decisions.

The limitations of current accounts of poststructuralist ethics and politics are, I have argued, in part a product of the kinds of questions to which they attempt to respond and of the necessary reproduction of the assumptions underpinning those questions in any such accounts. The question is how we might conceive of a better or more ethical politics, and the task in response to this has, in large part, been approached as one of identifying a non-foundational ethical starting point and building a politics based on this. More broadly, the approach might be characterised as an attempt to reconcile the destabilising of ethics understood in terms of universal principles or reason with the desire to allow it to inform a politics. Underpinning such an approach are two interlinked assumptions: first, the continued reliance on something playing a grounding or foundational role; second, a separation between ethics and politics, such that one can inform the other. These assumptions entail a reading of the possibilities and implications of poststructuralist ethics and politics which risks reproducing the totalising approach, whose dangers a turn to poststructuralism sought to escape.

In setting up the question like this, limits are imposed on how far the implications of this destabilisation of ethics can be pursued. First, asking what politics best serves ethics or responsibility requires recourse to a ground, foundation or transcendent principle. The question diagnoses a problem with politics which can be solved at a theoretical level in terms of finding and legitimising a particular goal. Politics thus becomes a tool in the service of this goal. The question betrays disquiet with the notion of politics as ungrounded and also with the notion of politics as a practical realm. The urge is to make politics derivable from something else, something more originary, and so to make it safe and theorisable. In turn, the question tends towards an understanding of the ethical in such a way that something can be derived from it; a set of principles or origins, rather than a messy set of practices or description of how we are in the world.

Ethics then becomes positioned as something that can provide the 'answer' to political problems and questions. In asking ethics to do the job of securing politics, ethics itself must necessarily be first secured. In looking for grounds for politics, they must first be found for ethics. An approach to ethics which is content to stop, for example, at 'obligation happens', as in John Caputo's argument, is insufficient to secure politics.[1] Without an ethical starting point, we cannot answer once and for all questions such as what the best or better political system might be, whether democracy is better than other arrangements and so on. The appeal to ethics here is, then, an appeal to security, answers and origins. It is in this way that we can look for an 'ethical' politics – a politics in which decisions are insured by reference to a more originary ethics.

Second, ethics is forced to remain separate from politics in the analysis. Ethics can thus be destabilised, but this must be within the limits of it remaining a separate realm of enquiry. The question of deriving politics from ethics, when thinking in terms of separation, acts to figure politics as inherently or originally 'unethical'. It looks to something outside, a reason or rationale to encourage us to behave responsibly. The assumption is that in politics, in the realm of 'real life', we start off separate and that this needs to be rectified by recourse to ethics.

In asking what politics might best serve ethics or how we might enact an ethical politics, ethics is placed in the role of 'saving' politics. This can be seen, for example, in Critchley's notion of 'interruption', whereby politics is problematic, but can be fixed to an extent through its constant interruption by something else called ethics.[2] When ethics is used to insure a particular politics, it becomes removed from the political realm of contestation and returns us to an approach of theory and application.

The relation of ethics and politics

The readings of Levinas, Derrida and Nancy advanced in previous chapters have offered a number of resources through which a move away from these problematic assumptions is made possible. The first is the reframing of the relation between ethics and politics, whose indissociability offers an alternative to their separation in such a way that one can be derived from the other.

In arguing that ethics and politics are inseparable, I mean to suggest two things: that in the authors considered, there are key elements of each term which refer to the same things, and that one would not make sense without the other and is within the other. Both point to decision in the face of the undecidable. Both terms belong to both the realms of the general, universal or rule and of the absolute Other or the incommensurable. However, they also point towards competing hands, in that ethics refers to the Other and politics to the Third, for example, or ethics to the unconditional and politics to the conditional. Given the ways in which the Other and Third or conditional and unconditional are implicated in one another from the beginning, this also means that ethics and politics, if understood as aligned with one or other of these realms, are also immediately implicated.

The clearest illustration of this is in Derrida's argument that to respond only to the one Other, on the side of what might be thought of as the ethical, would be irresponsible. The other Others, law and generality, what might be aligned with politics all must also be taken into account. Similarly, for politics to be properly political, it must encompass concerns of the ethical. That is, to continue the illustration, if the one or absolute Other did not convey a demand to be considered as such in the face of the universalisable, then only rule following could result – there would be nothing but rules and generality, nothing to negotiate and so politics would not be political.

The two terms, then, cannot be understood without one another; they are always conjoined in the ethico-political. This is not to argue that ethics *is* politics such that one term would be redundant. Nor is it to argue that one term encompasses the other, which would be to return to the assumption that one is more originary or has first place. As Derrida demonstrates, to think of ethics and politics as either separate or conjoined would presuppose an originary separation; the relationship is rather one of both heterogeneity and indissociability.

The importance of this relation and the possibilities opened up by its interrogation is most clear in Nancy's emphasis on the need to keep the question open. For Nancy, this is the political question, which is under threat from ethics, but it can also be seen in terms of the ethical question. If either one – ethics or politics – is refused as an answer, then we open up a space for real ethico-political discussion, which cannot be closed off by recourse to ethics, on the one hand, or politics, on the other. This position of closure might be seen, for example, in an approach whereby ethics is viewed as a counterpoint to politics, thought in terms of the ways in which ethics might inform or constrain politics, as if ethics could provide the answer to politics. Conversely, it might also occur in an approach where politics is thought in terms of reality and ethics as a utopian ideal, where the 'realities' of political life must constrain ethics. The answer in this case would be given by the realities of power politics. This attempt at closure then would occur in any approach where one term is subordinated to the other or, more generally, in any approach where originary or first terms are posited. First terms sideline the critical purchase that a focus on relationality might provide, because they act to already determine the relation. Rather than the openings of Nancy's relation without content, we are left with the content of the relation determined hierarchically by the first term.

As in Nancy's discussion of community, the ethics-politics relation is not one of separate entities coming together, nor one of a pre-existing whole being subdivided. Not ethics or politics, but ethics-politics. Or, in the same way that singularity already implies plurality for Nancy, ethics, even when just used as 'ethics', already implies politics and, equally, 'politics' implies also ethics. The ethico-political operates with the same logic as the singular-plural, whereby the ethical is already political in its very concept. In this sense, while 'ethics-politics' or the 'ethico-political' might seem the most straightforward term, it should be emphasised that 'ethics' or 'politics' also already contain within themselves this hyphenation, just as singular already also means singular-plural. The ethico-political, then, points to the importance of relation within, as well as between, the concepts.

To think in terms of relation within the concepts leads to a reading of ethics that problematises, rather than relies upon, any notion of the absolute. Ethics might be understood, as shown by Derrida, in two contradictory senses. On the one hand, it refers to the realm of universal law and generality. This is the ethics of Abraham in *The Gift of Death* – one of justifying and making sense. On the other hand, it also points to absolute duty, responsibility to the one Other or to the face. The dominant readings of both Derrida and Levinas would, as shown in Chapter 1, suggest that their contribution is to bring forward this second, absolute nature of ethics. Derrida and (in particular) Levinas, it is argued, show how our thinking of ethics in terms of universal rules or reason is deeply problematic and how, in order to avoid this, we need to be attentive to the demands of absolute alterity. Ethics here remains on the side of the transcendent, the infinite or the unconditional. What opposes this realm is named politics. It is only in the light of this re-ordering that ethics can then be called on to interrupt politics.

However, if we start from the notion of the ethico-political, then such an oppositional approach provides too simple a resolution. Ethics is neither on one side nor the other, but is rather what complicates this seemingly obvious division and distinction. Ethics puts into question what both alternatives share: the ultimate recourse to one absolute law, value or origin. On the one hand, to continue with the example from *The Gift of Death*, Abraham must act and make his actions intelligible according to one universal overarching law; indeed, this is the condition of intelligibility. On the other hand, he must answer to, and before, absolute duty, in terms of ethics as a non-coded response to absolute alterity. Neither approach allows for the consideration of the multiple or singular-plural in contradistinction to the universal or generalisable where the many are subsumed under the one. Ethics understood as universal and ethics understood as absolute duty are not as different as they may initially seem. Both rely on a distinction between the many and the one in various guises, taking one side or the other of this divide as the starting point. What neither approach allows for is thinking in terms of being many-one or Nancy's singular-plural. The notion of relationality, then, problematises the idea of the absolute in either of these senses.

Immanence and Transcendence

Transimmanence and the limits of grounds

The second resource offered by my readings of Levinas, Derrida and Nancy which offers scope for displacing the dominant assumptions is a potential reframing of immanence and transcendence. Underlying the way in which the ethico-political destabilises absolutes through foregrounding relationality is a deeper move to problematise any appeal to transcendence. In a reading of ethics which prioritises the one other or absolute duty, the transcendent is positioned as the source of ethical experience.

A reading which foregrounds the role of the transcendent in these thinkers is, of course, not unsupported, particularly in the case of Levinas.[3] For example, in Levinas, the face outside presentation which resists totality is aligned with transcendence and infinity. For Levinas, this ultimate non-closure of totality is what we must look for and preserve. However, if the face is thought in terms of also including the Third, then the idea of the face as what comes from outside to interrupt totality is thrown into question. Instead, the face begins to look already interrupted and implicated in totality and generality and so highlights, instead, interruption itself as the mode of ethics.

Similarly, in Derrida, concepts such as unconditional hospitality or the pure gift are sometimes seen as being on the side of the transcendent.[4] This returns to the discussion of the pure and unconditional and their relation with transcendence. Derrida is sometimes read as aligning the transcendent with the pure or unconditional – for example, where a pure ethical realm on the side of the unconditional and transcendent is posited.[5]

However, this is not always straightforward in Derrida's work. The unconditional, for Derrida, transcends both ethics and politics: 'Unconditional hospitality is transcendent with regard to the political, the juridical, perhaps even to the ethical'.[6] However, unconditional hospitality can be thought and, through this, experienced: 'Without this thought of pure hospitality (a thought that is also, in its own way, an experience). . .'[7] Therefore, it cannot be considered completely transcendent. This is one of the places that Derrida introduces a complication in thinking about the relationship between transcendence and immanence. The two terms are implicated in one another in a 'transaction' which is not between originally completely separate terms.[8]

This aligning of democracy to come and unconditional hospitality, for example, with transcendence also sidelines the important consideration of the way in which these kinds of concepts are neither present nor non-present. The pure and unconditional would not be what they are without the conditional. They are not subjects of a corruption, nor are they something that we are – or should be – striving towards, although hindered by the real world. If the transcendent is used only to refer to that which escapes a logic of economy, then these concepts might fit there, but then so would conditional hospitality and so on. Ultimately, any positing of transcendence suggests a realm in opposition to it, in which the conditional or existing democracy and so on would reside. However, Derrida's work highlights, instead, the way that democracy, to take one example, is necessarily always informed by democracy to come and that, in fact, the aporetic structure of democracy to come is only ever played out in actual attempts at democracy. The different logic that these terms call for or rely upon is not something outside come to interrupt our logics of exchange, but rather is the (anti)logic that Derrida shows us we are enmeshed within.

If the transcendent is understood in terms of the non-present or non-presentable, then it cannot encompass concepts like the pure or unconditional. These concepts instead demonstrate precisely the way in which the present and non-present are implicated through the trace. It is for this reason that Derrida is hesitant to describe his work as negative theology;[9] this would be to offer a simple grounding in the transcendent as non-presentable. It is because of the implication of the present and non-present that Derrida offers neither a lack of ground or groundless ground as a starting point. This would return us to a reading whereby the face, the pure or the unconditional offers an originary ethics. The task at hand, then, is not to conceptualise ethics and politics in the light of a lack of foundations, but rather at the limits of foundations.

For Derrida, the ethical and political emerge only between the conditional and unconditional. However, rather than thinking in terms of a gap between the two terms, it is the indissociability that Derrida emphasises:

> . . . these two hospitalities are at once heterogeneous and indissociable. Heterogeneous because we can move from one to the other only by means of an absolute leap, a leap beyond knowledge and power, beyond norms and rules . . . But – and here is the indissociability – I cannot open the door, I cannot expose myself to the coming of the Other and offer him or her anything whatsoever without making this hospitality effective, without, in some concrete way, giving *something determinate*.[10]

This indissociability and heterogeneity, not a gap between two poles, but a relationship, a line of touching, is where ethics and politics might emerge: 'Political, juridical, and ethical responsibilities have their place, if they take place, only in this transaction . . . between these two hospitalities, the unconditional and the conditional'.[11]

So while the idea of transcendence is important in Derrida's work, it cannot be aligned with the realms of the pure or unconditional and nor can ethics be simply understood to inhabit these realms. In the same way the pure and unconditional contain already within themselves the conditional or economy of violence, Derrida finds transcendence within immanence. Or rather, it is because Derrida finds transcendence within immanence, that he thinks of concepts such as hospitality in this way. As such, Derrida's work opens the way for a rethinking of being as articulated by Nancy, in which the relationship between the immanent and transcendent is re-evaluated.

Nancy foregrounds precisely the *relationship* between the immanent and transcendent. For Nancy, both immanence and transcendence are within the field of being-with; being-with reframes ontology as transimmanent. We start not with being, but being-with. Thinking in terms of being-with makes it difficult to think of that which is immanent to it and that which transcends it, since being-with transcends itself. If immanence is associated with being within and transcendence with going beyond, then being-with makes thinking in terms of either of these difficult. Being-with is not simply immanent or transcendent. This provides a possible way out of Levinas' concern about totalising ontology, by substituting being-in-common for being – that is, by refiguring ontology itself as resistance to totalisation. If ontology is no longer what must be resisted by, or in the name of, the ethical, then we can begin to think of the ethical without having to first think of a pure ethical relation.

Nancy's work demonstrates how the displacement of the traditional assumption of original separability or separation before relation can also be seen in the treatment of immanence and transcendence. That is, rather than thinking in terms of separate terms which might then be related in various ways as the original problematic of this book was set up, even as implicated in one another or interrupting one another, the possibility emerges of thinking of the two as originally inseparable. This is not an argument regarding the difficulty of thinking about what is inside without an outside to border it or distinguish from it. Nancy's concern is not to look at oppositional relations which presuppose two already existing and clearly separable poles.

Instead, the inside itself is always structured already as outside, such that we are returned once again to the question of limits.

This move away from thinking of immanence and transcendence oppositionally means that we can move away from thinking in terms of either/or and the subsequent various 'closing off' of options that this leads to. In the context of ethics and politics, this distinction maps on to the line between the Other/Third and ethical responsibility/intelligibility, amongst other pairings. A focus on looking for or encouraging one of these over the other works to reinforce the hierarchy, hence the difficulties discussed in Chapter 1 with a politics of alterity or ethical difference. Starting with an oppositional relationship leads to calls for ethics to interrupt politics. In turn, this relies on a notion of the pure or transcendent as the source of ethics, always outside and uncontaminated.

The prioritising of alterity, otherness or transcendence, as demanded by the question of how we might go about formulating a more responsible politics associated with strands of poststructuralist thought, *reverses* rather than *deconstructs* the various hierarchies that a focus on these terms is often designed to resist. In place of recourse to rationality and universality to secure decisions, this task is shifted to the transcendent. That is, the task is seen as finding guidelines for decision in the absence of grounds or where the ground is understood in terms of that which cannot be understood, comprehended or identified – for example, alterity. The ground, then, is replaced with groundlessness or a negative ground.

However, my readings of Levinas, Derrida and Nancy suggest that the transcendent does not provide grounds or foundations, even negative ones, but is, because of its indissociability from immanence, instead aligned with the destabilisation of these grounds. Working at the limits of, rather than refusing or reformulating, grounds leads to a different kind of approach. In thinking about ethics and politics, these thinkers can also offer an approach where, rather than thinking in terms of either/or, we need instead to look for – or at – the interface, at the contact and separation of concepts not originally in opposition. That is, rather than looking for a corrective or interruption from one of the pair to the other, looking instead at how there is only the interface, interruption, transimmanence. Transimmanence does not reduce immanence and transcendence to one another, but it does reformulate the relationship in a non-oppositional way, as shown in Chapter 4. If we start from the idea of transimmanence, the interruption may remain, but the idea of a pure transcendent does not. Interruption does not come from outside, from a pure face or absolute alterity, but rather the immanent is always already opened up as transcendent. The figure and content of the interruption is lost; interruption itself has first place. This means that rather than looking to a pure outside as the source of ethics, the source can instead be refigured as the undecidable.

It is only by engaging in this reformulation of the relationship between immanence and transcendence that the hierarchy of same/ Other can be displaced, rather than reversed. Only then can we engage in the search for something outside a world where everything is already decided or answered; the pathways of either immanence or transcendence make this a difficult task. In disassociating ethics and politics from immanence or transcendence, both ethics and politics become highlighted or reformulated as practices. This is all that something wedged in the space of transimmanence can be. Attempts at theorising or grounding practices ultimately run up against a limit, and what might be considered the ethical or political can only emerge at this limit; it is only here that response is possible. Moreover, we are always running up against this limit; it is the structure of how we are together and, importantly, as will be further elaborated below, it does not absolve us of responsibility for making and defending concrete ethical or political claims, but rather suggests that this is what we are always doing and that the claims made in the name of ethics or politics can be strong, if also tentative, situated and context-bound ones without having ultimate recourse to these grounds.

Alterity without transcendence

If transcendence is no longer a pure beyond, then the notion of transcendent alterity is also put into question. A number of authors, as discussed in Chapter 4, see this as a problem in Nancy's work in terms of its utility for thinking about ethics. This is most clear in Critchley's criticism of Nancy's ontology as not allowing for absolute alterity in an asymmetric sense.[12] Critchley is correct, but this only has worrying implications for ethics if we accept its status as on the side of the absolute and transcendent or maintain the many/one distinction. In tracing the concept of alterity through the thinkers I have examined, resources can also be developed such that maintaining the otherness of the Other does not have to depend on its primary transcendent status.

The problem is clearly stated by Richard Kearney, for whom alterity and immanence are 'polar extremes'.[13] Aligned with these two extremes, he sees two possible positions with associated problems. If Others are wholly outside and 'too transcendent', we lose all contact and so become exempt from the ethical relation.[14] On the other hand, he argues, if they are too immanent, they become indistinguishable from our own totalising selves.[15] Kearney's solution is to approach the Other as neither wholly transcendent nor absolutely immanent, but somewhere between the two.[16] This is the logic on which discussion of transcendence, contact and alterity, framed in these terms, needs to rely.

There is, however, another way to approach the issue, moving away from transcendent alterity as it is usually understood, but not towards totalising immanence. The key move which enables the rethinking of ethics and politics in Levinas, Derrida and Nancy, is a shift away from the assumption of original separation, but without reverting to any simple togetherness. This is a movement which starts with Levinas. We do not lose contact with the absolutely Other as transcendent alterity in Levinas, as shown in his discussion of proximity. In fact, it is only the wholly Other that does contact us, through the face. So transcendent alterity does not imply a lack of contact for Levinas; in fact, the face is an example of the beyond opening itself up within the world – of transimmanence. The Other does not, in order to be Other, have to be transcendent in the sense of the pure beyond. Nor for there to be contact does the Other have to be subsumed within the same. As Nancy argues, separation is the condition of contact. The very idea of being-with relies on alterity, because we cannot be 'with' the same, but this is an alterity which is not transcendent in a traditional sense. We are, as discussed previously, together as singularities, one-by-one, not as same and Other, but as same-Other.[17]

For Nancy, we start off both together and separate; the Other can no longer be thought of as completely primary, but this does not mean a return to the self or the same in Levinasian terms. There is, instead, always both contact and separation – indeed, for Nancy, the law of touching is separation. This means that rather than being in an asymmetrical relation with the Other where the ethical would be irresponsible, without choice or decision (the difficulty that Derrida makes clear), for Nancy, responsibility would lie on the line of touching and separation, of the singular-plural, in which the Other is both absolute Other and one among many. Hence, the one-by-one is not a flattening of the relationship, as Critchley argues, but a rejection of the narrow choices of symmetry and asymmetry through the concept of singularity. Rather, for Nancy, the two happen together; the self and Other are, in fact, only the line of separation and contact, so neither could come first. Nancy removes the hierarchy between self and Other in insisting only on second places. There is not origin or first place, rather: 'we resemble together'.[18]

This reframing of relation and separation has far-reaching implications for how we conceptualise the role of ethics. The role of transcendent alterity takes on significance in current approaches, because it is only in the name of something which exceeds a totalising ontology that such ontology might be disrupted. However, if ontology itself is reframed not in terms of knowledge and totalisation, but as 'being-with', then this significance is displaced. If ontology *is* ethics, then the role of ethics looks rather different. Rather than offering normative guidance, it describes how we are. There is no originary ethos, rather the origin *is* ethos or, importantly, 'conduct'.[19]

It is through this rethinking that the distinction between normative and ontological claims is questioned, which refigures the answer to the question of formulating a more responsible politics or providing answers to traditionally 'moral' political questions. This is also, in part, why poststructuralism is often seen as failing to engage with normative questions. If ontology is ethics, then we are left instead with the need to think through the various ways in which this might be disavowed and the implications of these for considerations of the ethico-political. Scope also emerges for elaborating on an answer in following through Nancy's suggestion of a focus on conduct. Both of these possibilities relate to the third key assumption raised at the beginning of the chapter – that of the relation between politics and practical politics – and a reworking of this idea provides, I will argue, one answer to the original question of what poststructuralism might have to say about 'practical' politics.

Conduct as Origin: 'Practical' Politics

While the difficulties with the separation between theory and practice in asking how poststructuralism might inform practical politics are relatively well-rehearsed, there is also another distinction at play here which is instructive. This is the distinction between politics as discussed theoretically and 'practical' politics, between a discussion of what politics and the political might be and questions of how and when we make particular decisions and interventions in particular political issues. Of course, these cannot be easily separated; there is a relationship between our understanding of what politics is and how, or in virtue of what, we might make political decisions. Nonetheless, the concern with 'practical' politics remains an important and instructive one, but not necessarily in the way it has been understood or approached in the current literature. That is, the positing of a realm of practical politics offers an opening whereby we might be able to shift the focus from a concern with identifying that in virtue of which political decisions might be taken, to an attempt at thinking those decisions – 'practical' politics – as the starting point.

This is important in the context of rethinking the relation between ethics and politics, because any focus on politics that asks for general answers to political questions and then turns to ethics to inform such answers immediately places ethics, too, in the realm of theory and generality. If ethics is on the limits of theory, however, this is where politics, too, is located. Both resist any attempts at grounding; once we start with the destabilisation of ethics, we cannot ask for general or theorisable answers. Instead, the ethico-political emerges only ever on the limits of theory. At the limits of grounds and theory we can only be engaged in claims and practices: the origin is conduct.

Thinking in terms of conduct changes quite dramatically the way in which we might conceptualise the ethico-political. If we start with the origin as ethos, rather than positing an originary ethos, then the ethico-political shifts from being a potential source of normative claims or grounds to a description of how we are. That is, we are confronted by aporetic demands and offered no guarantees, security or guidelines with which to inform our responses to them. Once refigured thus, we can only ask what kinds of claims and practices are made in the name of the ethico-political and whether they affirm or deny the limits of their grounds.

This potentially leads to a focus on the points where particular decisions occur, which are always at the limits of theory. That is, on the practices of decisions at the limits of theorisation and on the practice of theorising when theory itself encounters its limits. This would be an attempt to highlight practices as such (including the practice of theory), as they exceed guarantees by rule, theory or transcendent principles, which offers one way of engaging with the various ways in which the political and ethical are constituted.[20] Of course, if we always find ourselves in the realm of the ethico-political, then while an approach in which one informs the other does not make sense, asking whether it is better if we recognise the non-sense of this does; how can we determine that a focus on limits is the better way to proceed?

Without recourse to a reading of Derrida which gives grounds for preferring openness (as opposed to one where openness is preferred, but as a political position) or a reading of Levinas where we are compelled or commanded to responsibility to the one Other, there is, in the authors I have considered, no answer to this question. That is, they provide no grounds on which to prefer openness to closure, an uncovering of the political, rather than an obscuring of it, or on which to argue that is it better to recognise the aporetic nature of ethics and responsibility. These would be normative claims, and the authors I have engaged with do not provide us with the resources to make such claims. This is precisely why, when faced with normative questions, the work of these authors is seen by many to have no answer; it does not.

The difficulty – and possibility – in the argument that I have put forward is that this question of whether it is better to recognise aporia, interruption or groundlessness cannot be answered. We cannot successfully appeal to the value of absolute alterity, the transcendent Other or anything else that might provide the answer. There is no justification, grounding or reasoning which goes all the way to providing an answer. The unconditional, the transcendent and all such similar terms which might be seen to offer a route into answering, ultimately, do not. However, as an important caveat, this is not to say that these concepts have no role to play in answering, nor is it to eschew reasons, justifications and appeals to knowledge that need to be made. It is only to say that they do not go far enough or that, rather, they stop at just the right point. The approach of theorising, understanding and generalising is necessary. As argued in previous chapters, there is no benefit to be gained from throwing out knowledge of this type. Rather than rendering poststructuralism mute regarding ethico-political questions however, it is precisely this impossibility of answering which opens up the possibility of engagement. The inability to answer the question of the better course of action itself acts as a resistance to totalisation by resisting any codification of a 'more responsible' politics.

The recognition of the limits of grounds then offers a useful strategy for resisting totalisation. This is in part because it offers one way in which we might be more sensitive to hearing and responding to demands. If called to response is how we are, then we need to think about the ethico-political in terms of what these calls or demands are and how we might respond to them. One way in which we might do this is to focus on how we encounter and respond to these demands – that is, to suggest that the origin as ethics or ethos indicates that response itself is important, without offering anything on how we might best respond.

If we do not encounter the Other as face, then we are not receptive to any demands it may make of us. While the demands may still be made (the argument that we are always already in the ethico-political realm), we are unable to respond to them in anything but a 'default' way. That is, as discussed in previous chapters, while, in one sense, subjectivity itself is structured as response such that we are always responding, limiting response to this is unsatisfying, perhaps because it is not attentive to all three modalities of response. If we cannot encounter the face as face, which would also mean being unable to encounter the Third, ethics or politics, then we cannot be responsive to the many demands and obligations that it relays to us.

In attempting to recognise the precariousness of our claims and understandings, we may become more receptive to the face and so more able to respond to it. It should be emphasised here that all this really means, given the complex nature of the idea of 'face', is having demands brought to us or being able to hear them – all sorts of demands that no theory can help us choose between. This is responsiveness in terms of Nancy's relation without content. The face, then, is not really an answer to the question. A 'politics of the face' would only mean a 'politics of politics' in the sense that politics refers to singularity, relation and non-relation, same and Other. That is, a politics of trying to recognise our situation, which cannot be done in any abstract or general way. This tells us very little about 'responsible politics'.

However, there is, as discussed in previous chapters, something positive about this 'very little' and attempts to work with, and accommodate, it, rather than bury it. By tying ethics to a theoretical or foundational approach and so doing the same to politics, a difficulty arises in any attempt to start with conduct or practice. The outcome is not an inability to talk about conduct, but rather that the inclination is to say too much, to determine the practical realm too much. There is an injunction to stop, which all work of this nature runs up against – my argument included. This is a need to stop without being pushed to offer programmatic or general answers to ethico-political questions or to try to determine out of existence the realm of conduct.[21]

What this leads to, in terms of 'practical' politics as informed by responsibility, might thus seem an unsatisfying (or even unsatisfactory) answer that does not go far enough. However, just because we cannot answer this question with any certainty does not mean we do not or that we must not. Being unable to answer is, in fact, the condition of possibility for engagement or response. We are always answering 'moral' questions, and we need to continue to do so, not least because if the relation/non-relation is how we are, then this is all we can do. Our ethical obligations are not given to us from on high or from some idea of 'community' or subject; rather, they are given to us from all of these places and more. There is no appeal to something outside to determine our adjudication between these claims, and it is because theory cannot give these answers that *we* have to, all the time, at the limits of knowledge and non-knowledge.

What is required is an attempt at answering questions, and such answers being considered legitimate, which does not rely on knowledge as the full content of the answer. We need to be able to make arguments without recourse to stable foundations (as we are always doing anyway), to outline our obligations, to make specific interventions, forcefully and persuasively. We need to find ways of making these arguments which can and do call on theory, knowledge and history, but which are not determined by them; we are not without foundations, but at their limits. These answers would, by necessity, be specific, contextual and 'practical' – always at the moment where the decision is made. As answers, they can give no guarantees, and nothing suggests that they would be aligned with more politically 'progressive', just or responsible outcomes.

Poststructuralism does not offer a set of new grounds on which to answer ethical or political questions, but an attempt to answer and show how we can, must and do answer in a firm but tentative way, without firm grounds beneath or clear direction from above. Recognising the problematic nature of grounds does not lead to relativism or conservatism or necessarily to any one outcome, but it does lead to an opening up of space for contestation, questioning and constant re-evaluation. Poststructuralist notions of responsibility or ethics tell us that nothing can secure politics and that this insecurity is the very condition of possibility for the ethico-political.

This is, emphatically, not to argue that it is any better or more ethical to act without recourse to justification in terms of foundation or principle. It is precisely this idea of the 'more ethical' which is undone by reframing in terms of the ethico-political. The terms of the debate as to what might be more or less responsible are already political, and it is the goal of the more ethical or responsible that is precisely what needs to be put into question. The 'ethical' is not a label: it does not mean 'good' or 'right', and it is not an evaluation or guide. Rather, both the ethical and the political are descriptions of the context in which we find ourselves.

This leads not to a concept of a 'politics of responsibility' or of singularity, and perhaps not a 'politics of' anything. Rather, it leads to an insistence that asking for systematic answers, which is what any 'politics of' tries to provide, will always fail and so is insufficient to the task of ethico-political engagement. If the ethico-political describes our situation, then offering answers, responses and arguments at the limits of foundations is all we can do. Our answers are always at the limits of any grounds, and this is not a weakness to be rectified. The possibility then opens of making what might traditionally be called moral claims, forcefully and persuasively, without being forced into generalising or abstracting. These are precisely the claims which cannot be given in a systematic or sustainable way and whose validity cannot be assured by appeals to any foundation or ground. These are all that there is in ethics and politics, and identification and interrogation of such singular decisions are as far as we can go in any attempt to engage with them.

Conclusion:
Ethics and Politics after Poststructuralism

In the Introduction, I argued that the ways in which we experience 'everyday' ethics as limited, fragmented and exceeding theory pointed to a problem with approaching ethics as a task of theory and application. In response to the specific ways in which this problem is manifest in poststructuralist approaches to Politics and IR, I have suggested that this approach is closely linked to the problem of foundations and that by putting ethical foundations into question, both ethics and politics are refigured as practices emerging at the limits of theory.

This makes the formulation of a 'more responsible politics', a task undertaken by the authors considered in Chapter 1, difficult if not impossible. In particular, if ethics and politics cannot be separated in the first place, then deducing one from the other becomes deeply problematic. In fact, I have argued, the force of such an attempt distorts and limits readings of key poststructuralist thinkers in such a way that the radical potential of their reformulation of the ethico-political in terms of response and relation is unrealised. The theoretical point of departure for my project, then, has been to develop a reading of these thinkers where such an attempt is resisted. Once the opposition between ethics and politics is displaced, a series of other oppositions onto which this maps are also opened up for interrogation: same/Other, conditional/unconditional, face/Third, transcendence/immanence, universal/particular and singular/plural. The approach I have taken has been to trace the ways in which these oppositions are disrupted in the work of Levinas, Derrida and Nancy.

The pivotal point in opening up such a rereading was the re-evaluation of the work of Emmanuel Levinas undertaken in Chapter

2. Once the Levinasian ethical starting point on which the dominant accounts of the possibilities of developing a poststructuralist approach to ethical politics rely is put into question, alternative ways of thinking through questions of ethics and politics open up. In particular, a consideration of the figure of the Third in Levinas, as we have seen, complicates any notion of a pure or uncontaminated ethical realm which we might oppose to politics. Once Levinasian ethics is recast, any understanding of the relationship between Levinas and Derrida as supplementary to one another is put into question. Rather than casting Levinas as the thinker of ethics and Derrida as the thinker of politics or vice versa, the work of both thinkers can be seen to offer, instead, a problematisation of the categories of ethics and politics.

The inseparability of ethics and politics traced through both Levinas and Derrida results, as I demonstrated in Chapter 3, in an approach to ethics and responsibility as im-possible. Responsibility is, for Derrida, an aporetic notion, both structurally and due to our situation amongst many Others; responsibility emerges between contradictory imperatives, and this is the very condition of its possibility. Importantly, these two imperatives are, I argued, treated equally in Derrida; ethics and responsibility are on the side both of incalculable justice and of right and law. There is no privileging of one side – for example, difference, alterity or openness. Responsibility references both alterity and generalisability, the conditional and unconditional; these cannot be separated out to provide a pure or ethical starting point.

The argument that Levinas and Derrida do not leave us with an ethical commitment to Otherness or alterity might seem, in the first instance, to return us to the debate outlined in Chapter 1 regarding the limits of poststructuralism when it comes to providing resources for affirmative ethical or political positions and, in fact, to be simply aligning itself with this criticism of the approach. Without being able to determine ethical responsibility in any systematic way, it may seem that we are unable to judge or act politically or ethically in the world. Without an ethics of the Other to guide political intervention, it is certainly more difficult to counter the accusations of relativism or inconsistency. However, as we have seen, it is not necessary to provide an ethical starting point in order that ethico-political engagement might be possible. In fact, relying on even minimal guidelines to inform an affirmative position threatens the very possibility of ethics and politics. We can only take responsible decisions (if we ever can) at the limits of the theory or criteria which might determine the 'more ethical' way forward.

This is not to turn away from the importance of responsibility to the Other in the thought of Levinas and Derrida, but to insist that such a relationship of responsibility is im-possible; there is no pure relation to Otherness which we might take as a guide, because the Other is always already also the Third. As Nancy shows us, the Other, too, is part of the singular-plural of being, and this fundamentally challenges any approach which turns to the Other to shore up the instability of grounds on which ethics might be built. It is, rather, the Other that puts the simple opposition between grounds and groundlessness into question.

By starting with the singular-plural, rather than with the opposition of same and Other, possibilities emerge for thinking about responsibility without resorting to an originary ethics. In being-with, the Other is not originary, but nor is the same; Nancy offers an alternative in which our options are broadened from the choice between everything being reduced to the same or a commitment to transcendent alterity and asymmetry. By starting with relation – the same relation we see in Levinas' discussion of the face and the Third and Derrida's exploration of the conditional and unconditional – Nancy offers a formulation whereby we can think about making affirmative claims without the need for an originary ethical ground – the prioritising of one term in the relationship – to legitimise them. Nancy, then, does not begin from the Other, because this presupposes a conflictual distinction between the same and Other. Instead, for Nancy, we begin as same-Other, inseparable, but without identity. Rather than an originary reliance on transcendent alterity in order to disrupt totalisation, Nancy turns to the concept of transimmanence, which structures existence itself as a beyond.

The idea of the transimmanent offers a way to think about the relationship between the conditional and unconditional, Other and Third and ethics and politics without having to posit originary terms, first places or grounds. This means that rather than putting forward an argument whereby ethics is understood in terms of transcendence interrupting immanence, the notion of interruption remains, but is decoupled from the problematic idea of pure transcendence. That is, rather than ethics being understood in terms of what comes to interrupt (the pure face, transcendent alterity), interruption is itself the mode of ethics. In turn, this means that the possibility emerges of thinking in terms of non-oppositional and non-hierarchical relation-ships, which place the essence in the hyphen or the relation, rather than the terms.

This movement away from an either/or approach where the imma-nent is already transcendent, the outside is already part of the inside, means that the oppositions which draw on this are also displaced: Other/Third, responsibility/knowledge, singular/universal, ethics/politics and so on. Looking for a corrective or interruption from one term in the pair to the other no longer makes sense. Instead, we are left only with the interface as the site of the ethico-political. The ethico-political then emerges as groundless practices, since this is all that something in the realm of the transimmanent can be; theorising runs up against a limit here, and it is precisely at this point that ethico-political practices or conduct might occur.

My argument that a focus on practice or conduct offers a way out of the perceived necessity to articulate an ethics from which politics can be derived should not be taken as an argument for prioritising practice over theory. The limit which theory encounters does not mark the 'end' or exhaustion of theory, but the points at which theory itself traverses the limits of its own grounds. Theorising, too, is, in this sense, conduct or practice. That is, I do not wish to argue for an inversion of the theory/practice distinction on which the criti-cisms discussed in Chapter 1 – that poststructuralist approaches 'lead nowhere' – rest. Nor do I wish to argue for a simple move outside of theory in order to encounter the ethical, which would return us to arguments starting with transcendent alterity. It is rather that theory moves outside of itself. It is at these points that we might speak in terms of conduct.

The move away from the theoretical is in terms of the theoretical identifying a ground, origin or starting point, even if that starting point is groundlessness, from which to proceed. When starting at the limits of grounds, theory potentially looks rather different: tentative, contextual, revisable and limited. In starting with ethos as origin, but without any originary ethos, it becomes impossible to offer any gen-eral answers or guidelines with which to approach ethico-political problems. This even extends to a particular way in which we might approach such questions. It is not that the better is ultimately out of reach, but available as a horizon towards which we might aim; we are being-toward, without knowing toward what.

This is not to say, however, that we are left unable to make affirmative ethico-political claims and engagements. It is, in fact, the condition for any ethico-political engagement. Even the most minimal orientation, towards alterity or a horizon of pure hospitality, as soon as that which we are oriented towards has any content, such that it could determine one route over another makes the decision immediately the application of a programme, and as Derrida explains: 'nothing could make us more irresponsible'.[1] More specifically, by positing that horizon as a relationship of responsibility to the Other when that Other is understood in terms of transcendent alterity, there is a risk of obscuring the radical potential of relationality that is the promise of the poststructuralist approach. We can only conceive of this potential in the absence of a prior determination of the content of such a relation. For, as Nancy demonstrates, that content turns us back to totalisation, and resistance to totalisation is the very impetus for the work of the authors with whom I have engaged.

If poststructuralism is concerned with ways to resist or interrupt totalisation, then to approach this task through foregrounding a relationship with transcendent alterity is problematic. This is because, at least for the authors I examined in Chapter 1, this movement is accomplished by aligning ethics with that transcendent and applying it to interrupt politics. However, once the complex interrelationship of the transcendent and immanent, Other and Third, conditional and unconditional, ethics and politics, as drawn out of the readings of Levinas, Derrida and Nancy, is taken into account, then any such account of interruption becomes problematic. Rather, we see that deconstruction is the case; that existence is structured as a beyond and is always already interrupted. We start not with a transcendent Other, but with being-together, transimmanence or the singular-plural, which means that the figure of the interruption is in the hyphen or relationship, rather than in one term in that relationship. We might also think of this starting point as the face-to-face, where the Third is already in the face of the Other or the demand for the unconditional where that demand immediately also calls for the conditional. By filling in the content of the relationship, which is done by determining in advance its constituent parts, the interruption of that undecidable relationality is covered over.

How, then, might we approach the question of affirmative ethico-political interventions, without covering over the very undecidability which is the condition for their possibility? If we can no longer posit an originary ethics with which to inform politics, the type of affirmative position we might be able to take changes. We can no longer insure or secure such positions by recourse to grounds, but nonetheless need to make affirmative gestures even in the absence or at the limits of such secure grounds. This attempt to make interventions without an ethical foundation to secure them is the task which confronts us; to remain ethico-politically engaged without an ethical starting point.

Thinking in terms of starting with the hyphen or relation can also be approached through a focus on conduct, which would enable affirmation of different positions in different times and contexts. As Nancy argues, there is no originary ethos, but rather the origin itself is ethos, being-with, relationality or conduct. It is this origin which interrupts attempts at totalisation; not through positing a non-totalising origin in opposition, but through reworking the concept of origin itself. Totalisation is disrupted through the displacement, rather than inversion, of the opposition of immanence and transcendence and the various other oppositions which rest on this. Here, the origin is itself interruption, and that interruption is without content. As such, taking conduct as the starting point potentially offers an (quasi)theoretical backdrop for the making of arguments and claims in the absence of an ethical starting point.

On this reading, we start off responsible to the Other(s) and in relation, immediately under compelling, irreconcilable demands, which happen forcefully and without foundations. But this, in fact, tells us very little; it is not a clear-cut ethical starting point. It is, rather, a relation, responsibility and demand without content and is not simply non-totalising. Responsibility is without content, because we start off with many Others in the singular-plural. This means that the demands made on us in responsibility are not (only) contradictory, such that the demands of the Other are in competition with the demands of the other Other. Rather, the demand/responsibility that comes from being in relation is to the hyphen, which distinguishes the Other from the other Other. This particular line is mobile and fleeting, which entails that we cannot ever know in a general sense what it demands. Responsibility and relation, then, are always already ethico-political.

This approach potentially offers the possibility of being able to respond to such demands, which can only be done in the absence of guidelines. Of course, it could be pointed out that response in the absence of guidelines is what we are always doing anyway, particularly if we take seriously the argument that we start in being-with or that deconstruction is the case. In this sense, we are always responding to demands without the content of that response being secured, and any such response might be thought of as an interruption of the oppositional relationships which signal totalisation. However, I am prepared to make, in Connolly's terms, a 'wager' of my own in suggesting that by not covering over the ways in which we operate only at the limits of grounds, we open up the possibility for more tentative, reversible types of claims, and that we do not open up this possibility in the same way if we prioritise alterity.[2] Demands are potentially closed off to us if we turn to either side of the oppositions and do not consider how they interpenetrate. Put another way, if we recognise the way in which we start off as responsible, but without that responsibility having a particular content, then we might be better able to be responsive to the changeable, conflicting configurations of the hyphen, the protean modalities of being-with, to which that responsibility is owed. This might better allow for the mutable structures, the refusal to answer once and for all, which track the demand for justice to the line as that line shifts in different contexts. The realm of conduct, which is necessarily contextual, might offer a point of departure for such an attentive approach.

Given that I have argued that the ethico-political is the condition in which we find ourselves, rather than a goal, horizon, project or undertaking, this attentiveness might also turn more directly to recognition of this condition. If we *are* same-Other, engaged in a negotiation of inseparability without identity, then interruption *happens*, and there may be potential for engagement in a focus on such moments of interruption; a sensitivity to the ways in which the existing order is challenged and displaced. A focus on conduct highlights the ways in which this challenge might be found in the very unsecured claims made in the name of ethics, which were the impetus for this investigation. What we do exceeds and resists any overdetermination, and recognition of these moments of conduct where theory encounters its limits offers the potential for affirmative engagement.

To engage in such a way, we might start by asking different types of questions. While, as we have seen, there is a wealth of material which engages with the questions of how a poststructuralist approach to ethics might inform politics, there is relatively little attention paid to the problem of the *type* of questions we ask about ethics and politics. In particular, given the focus on the ethico-political as 'how we are', the ways in which this is recognised or covered over, ways in which appeals to the transcendental are made and the perceived need to do this for legitimation would be a fruitful line of enquiry. These are examples of the ways in which we can and do answer, despite the limits of foundations, and are precisely the sites at which the charge that poststructuralist approaches are disengaged is most clearly refuted.

The impasse between the so-called poststructuralists and their critics, as addressed in Chapter 1, is, at least in part, a result of this lack of focus on how we pose questions. My search for a different way of thinking about the relationship between ethics and politics, which confronts the issue of the kinds of questions such concepts can and cannot be employed to answer and why it is that the answers that are desired often cannot be produced, offers one possible way out of this impasse. Recognising, but refusing, at least in any substantive sense, to answer the question posed to poststructuralist accounts of where a poststructuralist ethics might lead, what it can say about practical politics or how we can consistently and usefully apply it has been one of the key moves of the argument.

As such, my argument cannot offer resources for any general ethics or politics nor any general ethico-political commitments or guidelines. It can, however, offer an engagement with those rather neglected features of our ethico-political world gestured towards in the Introduction; the very ways in which our use, discussion, action and understanding of 'ethics' is already ethico-political, already working only at the limits of theorisation and already engaged in responding to, and negotiating, the difficult demands of relationality. We are always answering questions of how practical politics might be informed by responsibility; it is precisely because theory cannot give us these answers that we have to.

Notes

Introduction

1. This is a label which many of the authors considered within this book would hesitate to use to describe their work, but one which has come to be widely used to describe anti- or post-foundational approaches, in large part due to its usage by those criticising this body of work.
2. See, for example, Chris Brown, *International Relations Theory: New Normative Approaches* (New York, NY: Columbia University Press, 1992); Chris Brown, 'Review Article: Theories of International Justice', *British Journal of Political Science* 27: 2 (1997), 273–97; Chris Brown, '"Turtles All the Way Down": Anti-Foundationalism, Critical Theory and International Relations', *Millennium* 23: 2 (1994), 213–36; Molly Cochran, 'Postmodernism, Ethics and International Political Theory', *Review of International Studies* 21: 3 (1995), 237–50; Stephen Krasner, 'The Accomplishments of International Political Theory', in Steve Smith, Ken Booth and Marysia Zalewski (eds), *International Theory: Positivism and Beyond* (Cambridge: Cambridge University Press, 1996), pp. 108–27; Stephen K. White, 'Poststructuralism and Political Reflection', *Political Theory* 6: 2 (1988), 186–208.
3. See, for example, David Campbell, *National Deconstruction: Violence, Identity and Justice in Bosnia* (Minneapolis, MN: University of Minnesota Press, 1998); and Simon Critchley, *The Ethics of Deconstruction: Derrida and Levinas* (Edinburgh: Edinburgh University Press, 1992).

Chapter 1

1. See, for example, Chris Brown, *International Relations Theory: New Normative Approaches* (New York, NY: Columbia University Press, 1992), p. 223; Chris Brown, 'Review Article: Theories of International

Justice', *British Journal of Political Science* 27: 2 (1997), 273–97; Chris Brown, '"Turtles All the Way Down" Anti-Foundationalism, Critical Theory and International Relations', *Millennium* 23: 2 (1994), 213–36; Molly Cochran, 'Postmodernism, Ethics and International Political Theory', *Review of International Studies* 21: 3 (1995), 237–50; Stephen Krasner, 'The Accomplishments of International Political Theory', in Steve Smith, Ken Booth and Marysia Zalewski (eds), *International Theory: Positivism and Beyond* (Cambridge: Cambridge University Press, 1996), pp. 108–27; Stephen K. White, 'Poststructuralism and Political Reflection', *Political Theory* 6: 2 (1988), 186–208.

2. Many of the authors considered in the book would hesitate to subscribe to the 'poststructuralist' label, and the diversity of the work collected under this banner is huge. Only particular authors and texts can be considered, and those in the selection addressed here have in common a motivation to explicitly answer the question of applications and practical ethics and politics. See, for example, David Campbell, *National Deconstruction: Violence, Identity and Justice in Bosnia* (Minneapolis, MN: University of Minnesota Press, 1998); and Simon Critchley, *The Ethics of Deconstruction: Derrida and Levinas* (Edinburgh: Edinburgh University Press, 1992).

3. As R. B. J. Walker has argued, separating ethics and politics leads to thinking of politics in terms of application or extension; it also leads, I suggest, to thinking of ethics in terms of foundational theory. See R. B. J. Walker, *Inside/Outside: International Relations as Political Theory* (Cambridge: Cambridge University Press, 1992), pp. 50–1. Also, see Kimberley Hutchings, 'The Possibility of Judgement: Moralizing and Theorizing in International Relations', *Review of International Studies* 18: 1 (1992), 51–62, see, in particular, p. 61 for a broader discussion of the continued separation between ethics and politics in the critical literature, despite efforts to overcome it.

4. See, for example, Elizabeth Dauphinee, *The Ethics of Researching War: Looking for Bosnia* (Manchester: Manchester University Press, 2007); Jenny Edkins, *Whose Hunger: Concepts of Famine, Practices of Aid* (Minneapolis, MN: University of Minnesota Press, 2000); Véronique Pin-Fat, *Universality, Ethics and International Relations: A Grammatical Reading* (Oxon and New York, NY: Routledge, 2010); Maja Zehfuss, *Wounds of Memory: The Politics of War in Germany* (Cambridge: Cambridge University Press, 2007).

5. This is one of the moves that enable the alternative approaches taken by the authors in note 4.

6. Zygmunt Bauman, *Modernity and the Holocaust* (London: Polity, 2001).

7. See, for example, Judith Butler, *Precarious Life: The Powers of Mourning and Violence* (London: Verso, 2004), p. 150.
8. Louiza Odysseos, 'On the Way to Global Ethics? Cosmopolitanism, "Ethical" Selfhood and Otherness', *European Journal of Political Theory* 2: 2 (2003), p. 185.
9. Ibid.
10. Zygmunt Bauman, *Postmodern Ethics* (Oxford: Blackwell, 1993), p. 13.
11. Hutchings, 'The Possibility of Judgement', p. 61.
12. William E. Connolly, *The Ethos of Pluralization* (London: University of Minnesota Press, 1995), p. 36.
13. Connolly, *Ethos of Pluralization*, p. 36. See also Larry George, 'Pharmacotic War and the Ethical Dilemmas of Engagement', *International Relations* 19: 1 (2005), p. 125, who argues that the ethically responsible is aligned with resistance to totalising or closing narratives.
14. Connolly, *Ethos of Pluralization*, p. xxiv (note 7).
15. James Der Derian, 'Post-Theory: The Eternal Return of Ethics in International Relations', in Michael W. Doyle and G. John Ikenberry (eds), *New Thinking in International Relations Theory* (Boulder, CO: Westview Press, 1997), p. 55.
16. Ibid. p. 58.
17. Bauman, for example, argues that there can be a moral self, but that moral conduct cannot be guaranteed. Bauman, *Postmodern Ethics*, p. 12. See also Louiza Odysseos, 'Dangerous Ontologies: The Ethos of Survival and Ethical Theorizing in International Relations', *Review of International Studies* 28: 2 (2002), p. 414; Vivienne Jabri, 'Restyling the Subject of Responsibility in IR', *Millennium* 27: 3 (1998), 591–611; George, 'Pharmacotic War', p. 125.
18. Odysseos, 'Global Ethics', p. 194.
19. Or as Michael J. Shapiro puts it, to the Other as not simply another 'I' in a different position. Michael J. Shapiro, 'The Ethics of Encounter: Unreading, Unmapping the Imperium', in David Campbell and Michael J. Shapiro (eds), *Moral Spaces: Rethinking Ethics and World Politics* (Minneapolis, MN: University of Minnesota Press, 1999), pp. 57–90.
20. Butler, *Precarious Life*, p. 11.
21. Michael Dillon, 'Another Justice', *Political Theory* 27: 2 (1999), p. 162.
22. Although there is an argument made, for example, by Dan Bulley that this reconfiguration leads to ethics understood as hospitality and the welcoming of the Other. For Bulley, the modalities of welcome and hospitality are complex, but in his reading of Derrida, these terms are clearly associated with the ethical, while excluding is 'unethical'; Dan

Bulley, 'Negotiating Ethics: Campbell, Ontopology and Hospitality', *Review of International Studies* 32: 4 (2006), p. 652.

23. William Connolly, 'Suffering, Justice and the Politics of Becoming', in David Campbell and Michael Shapiro (eds), *Moral Spaces: Rethinking Ethics and World Politics*, (Minneapolis, London: University of Minnesota Press, 1999), p. 142.

24. As Stephen Krasner puts it: 'Post-modernism provides no methodology for adjudicating among competing claims . . . If each society has its own truth . . . what is the basis for arguing that they are wrong?' See Krasner, 'The Accomplishments of International Political Theory', p. 125.

25. Brown, 'Theories of International Justice', p. 294. See also Brown, '"Turtles All the Way Down"', p. 225 for a discussion of the need for foundations/justifications.

26. Also see Cochran, 'Postmodernism', p. 246. Cochran's critique is specifically aimed at Richard Ashley and R. B. J Walker, who discuss these types of claims in some depth in Richard K. Ashley and R. B. J. Walker, 'Reading Dissidence/Writing the Discipline: Crisis and the Question of Sovereignty in International Studies', Special Issue: Speaking the Language of Exile: Dissidence in International Studies, *International Studies Quarterly* 34: 3 (1990), p. 368. See also Marysia Zalewski, 'All These Theories Yet the Bodies Keep Piling Up', in Steve Smith, Ken Booth and Marysia Zalewski (eds), *International Theory: Positivism and Beyond* (Cambridge: Cambridge University Press, 1996), pp. 340–53 for a discussion of the problems with this type of questioning and requirements for criteria.

27. Cochran, *Normative Theory in International Relations: A Pragmatic Approach* (Cambridge: Cambridge University Press, 1999).

28. Cochran, 'Postmodernism', p. 250. See also Cochran, *Normative Theory*, especially Chapter 4; Brown, 'Theories of International Justice', p. 295; Brown, *International Relations Theory: New Normative Approaches*, p. 223.

29. Cochran, 'Postmodernism', p. 250.

30. Brown, 'Theories of International Justice', p. 295.

31. Richard K. Ashley, 'Living on Border Lines: Man, Poststructuralism and War', in James Der Derian and Michael J. Shapiro (eds), *International/Intertextual Relations: Postmodern Readings of World Politics* (Lexington, KY: Lexington Books, 1989), p. 278. Speaking more specifically about deconstruction, Morag Patrick puts forward a similar argument that: 'Demands for substance and thesis, for definitive and positive accounts, *cannot* be met by a deconstructive writing'; see Morag Patrick, *Derrida, Responsibility and Politics* (Aldershot: Ashgate, 1997), p. 121.

32. Connolly, *Ethos of Pluralization*, p. 36.
33. Ibid.
34. Richard Beardsworth, 'The Future of Critical Philosophy and World Politics', in Madeleine Fagan, Ludovic Glorieux, Indira Hašimbegović and Marie Suetsugu (eds), *Derrida: Negotiating the Legacy* (Edinburgh: Edinburgh University Press, 2007), p. 59.
35. Ibid.
36. See, for example, Campbell's argument that: 'for politics (at least for a progressive politics) one must provide an account of the decision'; Campbell, *National Deconstruction*, p. 186. Also Sergei Prozorov's concern that deconstruction does not provide an account of the decision and so, ethically speaking: 'remains suspended in irresolution and impotence'; Sergei Prozorov, 'X/XS: Toward a General Theory of the Exception', *Alternatives: Global, Local, Political* 30: 1 (2005), p. 97.
37. The desire to be able to differentiate between 'good' and 'bad' Others is evident, for example, in Richard Kearney's work. Jim George explicitly poses this question in relation to Levinas, asking 'how do we choose between competing responsibilities?', while David Hoy asks how poststructuralism might assist with normative justifications of resistance to domination. See, for example, Richard Kearney, *Strangers, Gods and Monsters: Interpreting Otherness* (London: Routledge, 2003); Jim George, 'Realist "Ethics", International Relations, and Post-modernism: Thinking Beyond the Egoism-Anarchy Thematic', *Millennium* 24: 2 (1995), p. 211; David Couzens Hoy, *Critical Resistance: From Poststructuralism to Post-Critique* (Cambridge, MA: MIT Press, 2004).
38. Connolly, *Ethos of Pluralization*, p. 36. Connolly, in *Identity\Difference*, develops a rather different vision of the ethical through drawing on Foucault and Nietzsche in the conspicuous absence of Levinas. See also Couzens Hoy, *Critical Resistance: From Poststructuralism to Post-Critique*. Poststructuralism, he argues, may need 'supplementing' if it is to be ethically and politically relevant.
39. This tendency is particularly pronounced in the work of Simon Critchley and David Campbell, which is discussed in more detail in the second part of this chapter.
40. See, for example, Butler, *Precarious Life*; Dillon, 'Another Justice', p. 164; Der Derian 'Post-Theory', p. 58 (note 11), p. 69 (note 69).
41. David Campbell, 'The Possibility of Radical Interdependence: A Rejoinder to Daniel Warner', *Millennium* 25: 1 (1996), p. 138.
42. David Campbell, *Politics without Principle: Sovereignty, Ethics, and the Narratives of the Gulf War* (London: Lynne Rienner, 1993), p. 91.
43. Campbell, 'The Possibility of Radical Interdependence', p. 138.

44. David Campbell, 'Beyond Choice: The Onto-Politics of Critique', *International Relations* 19: 1 (2005), p. 131.
45. Campbell, 'Beyond Choice', p. 128.
46. David Campbell, 'The Deterritorialization of Responsibility: Levinas, Derrida, and Ethics After the End of Philosophy', *Alternatives* 19: 4 (1994), p. 464. In *National Deconstruction*, Campbell argues that the ethical task is: 'to foster the maximum responsibility'. See Campbell, *National Deconstruction*, p. 177.
47. David Campbell, 'Why Fight: Humanitarianism, Principles and Post-Structuralism', *Millennium* 27: 3 (1998), p. 513.
48. Campbell, *Politics without Principle*, p. 93.
49. Ibid.
50. Ibid. p. 96.
51. Campbell, 'Why Fight', p. 501.
52. Ibid. p. 503.
53. Ibid.
54. David Campbell and Michael Dillon, 'Postface: The Political and the Ethical', in David Campbell and Michael Dillon (eds), *The Political Subject of Violence* (Manchester: Manchester University Press, 1993), p. 172.
55. Campbell, *National Deconstruction*, p. 181.
56. Campbell and Dillon, 'The Political and the Ethical', p. 172.
57. Campbell, *National Deconstruction*, p. 176.
58. Ibid. p. 177.
59. Ibid. p. 179.
60. Ibid. p. 177.
61. Ibid.
62. Campbell, 'Beyond Choice', p. 131.
63. Ibid.
64. Campbell, *National Deconstruction*, p. 186.
65. Ibid. pp. 5–6.
66. Ibid.
67. Ibid. p. 186.
68. Ibid. p. 187.
69. Ibid. p. 186.
70. Ibid. pp. 186–7.
71. Ibid. p. 192.
72. Campbell, 'Beyond Choice', p. 132.
73. Campbell, *National Deconstruction*, p. 192.
74. Ibid. p. 191.
75. Ibid. p. 205.
76. Campbell and Dillon, 'The Political and the Ethical', p. 174.
77. Ibid. p. 175.

78. Campbell, *National Deconstruction*, p. 203.
79. Ibid. p. 206.
80. Campbell and Dillon, 'The Political and the Ethical', p. 175.
81. Campbell, 'Beyond Choice', p. 132.
82. Campbell, *National Deconstruction*, p. 207.
83. Ibid.
84. Critchley, *The Ethics of Deconstruction*, p. xi.
85. Ibid. pp. xiv, 42.
86. Ibid. p. 5.
87. Ibid. p. 223. In his later book, *Infinitely Demanding: Ethics of Commitment, Politics of Resistance*, ethics *is*, he argues, precisely about the interruption or disturbance of the political status quo. See Simon Critchley, *Infinitely Demanding: Ethics of Commitment, Politics of Resistance* (London: Verso, 2007), p. 13.
88. Critchley, *The Ethics of Deconstruction*, p. 5.
89. Ibid.
90. The concept and understanding of the 'face' and the 'Third' in Levinas is contested and will be addressed in more detail in Chapter 2.
91. Critchley, *The Ethics of Deconstruction*, p. 5.
92. Critchley, *Infinitely Demanding*, p. 13.
93. Critchley, *The Ethics of Deconstruction*, p. 221.
94. Ibid. p. 41. This ethics, he argues, is exempt from deconstruction, because it is not part of the philosophical basis that deconstruction undermines. This means that deconstruction can, without contradiction, be understood to have an ethical grounding which itself is undeconstructable and, further, that deconstruction itself is a response to this ethics of irreducible responsibility. Critchley, *The Ethics of Deconstruction*, pp. 2, 199.
95. Critchley's account of a deconstructive reading focuses on how a text is reliant on certain presuppositions of metaphysics and how it then questions the very principles it uses. There is a space in text between what a writer intends and the text, between what the writer commands and fails to command in a language. A deconstructive reading brings the text into contradiction with itself, opening an alterity that goes against what the text wants to mean, what the consensus regarding its intelligibility is. This interruption of the dominant interpretation necessarily entails that the reader go beyond the dominant structure of intelligibility which governs the space between the intention of the writer and the text. These moments of alterity within the text are moments of ethical transcendence, where the Saying of a text overrides its Said. See Critchley, *The Ethics of Deconstruction*, pp. 7, 20–30.
96. Critchley, *The Ethics of Deconstruction*, p. xiii.

97. Ibid. p. 2.
98. Ibid.
99. Ibid. p. 30.
100. Specifically, Critchley argues that ethical transcendence occurs when a necessity other than ontology announces itself through reading. In its exposition of the alterity within a text, a deconstructive reading attains a position of exteriority to the metaphysical context governing intelligibility. It is an attempt to keep open a dimension of alterity outside of the comprehension of philosophy and resistant to incorporation into the same. By showing the impossibilities with the concepts of choice and decision, for example, this space of alterity and transcendence is opened up. See Critchley, *The Ethics of Deconstruction*, p. 192.
101. Ibid. p. 199.
102. Ibid.
103. Ibid.
104. Ibid. p. 236.
105. Ibid. p. 189.
106. Ibid. p. 99.
107. Ibid. p. xiv.
108. Ibid. p. 231.
109. Ibid. p. 220.
110. Ibid. p. 225.
111. Ibid. p. 233.
112. Ibid. p. 225.
113. Ibid. p. 236.
114. Ibid. p. 240.
115. Ibid. p. 236.
116. Ibid. p. 240.
117. Ibid. p. 227. For Critchley, as for Campbell, this democracy does not exist as anything other than a task or project to be attempted, because it is informed by an ethics characterised by infinite responsibility. Critchley is not referring to any really existing forms of government or organisation, but to the promise of democracy itself, which rests, for him, on constant interruption, reformulation and negotiation. There is, instead, a responsibility to invent and keep inventing democracy. See Critchley, *The Ethics of Deconstruction*, pp. 240–1.
118. Critchley, *Infinitely Demanding*, p. 120.
119. Jenny Edkins, 'Ethics and Practices of Engagement: Intellectuals as Experts', *International Relations* 19: 1 (2005), 64–9.
120. Campbell, *National Deconstruction*, p. 219.
121. While, for example, in 'Why Fight', Campbell acknowledges that decisions – political ones – must be made regarding who to fight,

when and how and is careful to assert that abstracted theoretical formulae cannot be found in order to do this, he precedes this with a commitment to the politics of alterity outlined above. See Campbell, 'Why Fight', p. 521.

122. Robert Bernasconi argues that this 'failure' is precisely where the political potential of deconstruction lies. Deconstruction, he argues, is politically neutral and it is this which allows for 'hyper-politicisation'; see Robert Bernasconi, 'The Crisis of Critique and the Awakening of Politicisation in Levinas and Derrida', in Martin McQuillan (ed.), *The Politics of Deconstruction: Jacques Derrida and the Other of Philosophy* (London: Pluto Press, 2007), p. 84.

123. Alex Thomson, *Deconstruction and Democracy: Derrida's Politics of Friendship*, (London: Continuum, 2005), p. 202. See also George, 'Pharmacotic War', p. 125.

124. Thomson, *Deconstruction and Democracy*, p. 101.

125. Ibid. p. 201.

126. Mark F. N. Franke, 'Refusing an Ethical Approach to World Politics in Favour of Political Ethics', *European Journal of International Relations* 6: 3 (2000), p. 327.

127. Ibid.

128. See also George, 'Pharmacotic War', p. 125.

129. R. B. J. Walker, *Inside/Outside: International Relations as Political Theory*, p. 50.

130. Critchley, *The Ethics of Deconstruction*, p. xiv.

131. Campbell, 'The Deterritorialization of Responsibility', p. 464.

132. Thomson, *Deconstruction and Democracy*, p. 118.

133. Ibid. p. 121.

134. Ibid.

135. In contrast, Elizabeth Dauphinee turns to Levinas for conceptualising both ethics and politics, which points to the possibility of a reading of Levinas which engages with politics on its own merits, rather than as a supplement. This is returned to in Chapter 2.

136. Thomson, *Deconstruction and Democracy*, p. 141.

137. See, for example, Dauphinee, *The Ethics of Researching War*; Jenny Edkins, *Poststructuralism and International Relations: Bringing the Political Back In* (Boulder, CO: Lynne Rienner, 1999); Jabri, 'Restyling the Subject of Responsibility in IR', pp. 591–611; Pin-Fat, *Universality, Ethics and International Relations*; Zehfuss, *Wounds of Memory*.

138. Edkins, 'Ethics and Practices of Engagement', p. 68.

139. See, for example, Maja Zehfuss, 'Subjectivity and Vulnerability: On the War with Iraq', *International Politics* 44: 1 (2007), pp. 58–71.

140. Dauphinee, *The Ethics of Researching War*. Dauphinee's account

is interesting in that it initially subscribes to Campbell's separation
of ethics and politics, but then goes on to focus not on overcoming
the separation, but on precisely the difficulties and interruptions that
emerge on this line.

Chapter 2

1. Simon Critchley, *The Ethics of Deconstruction: Derrida and Levinas* (Edinburgh: Edinburgh University Press, 1992), p. 225; David Campbell, 'Beyond Choice: The Onto-Politics of Critique', *International Relations* 19: 1 (2005), p. 128.
2. Even if, in the case of Thomson, this starting point is rejected. See David Campbell, *National Deconstruction: Violence, Identity and Justice in Bosnia* (Minneapolis, MN: University of Minnesota Press, 1998), p. 191; David Campbell, 'Why Fight: Humanitarianism, Principles and Post-Structuralism', *Millennium* 27: 3 (1998), p. 513; Critchley, *Ethics of Deconstruction*, p. 5.
3. See, for example, Diane Perpich, 'A Singular Justice: Ethics and Politics between Levinas and Derrida', *Philosophy Today* 42: January (1998), 59–71; Bob Plant, 'Doing Justice to the Derrida-Levinas Connection: A Response to Mark Dooley', *Philosophy and Social Criticism* 29: 4 (2003), 427–50; William Simmons, 'The Third: Levinas' Theoretical Move from An-archical Ethics to the Realm of Justice and Politics', *Journal of Philosophy and Social Criticism* 25: 6 (1999), 83–110.
4. Perpich, 'Singular Justice', pp. 62–3.
5. Plant, 'Doing Justice to the Derrida-Levinas Connection', p. 433.
6. Simon Critchley, 'Five Problems in Levinas's View of Politics and the Sketch of a Solution to Them', *Political Theory* 32: 2 (2004), p. 173.
7. Emmanuel Levinas, 'Peace and Proximity', in Adriaan Peperzak, Simon Critchley and Robert Bernasconi (eds), *Emmanuel Levinas: Basic Philosophical Writings* (Indianapolis, IN: Indiana University Press, [1984] 1996), p. 163.
8. Ibid.
9. Ibid.
10. Emmanuel Levinas, 'Substitution', in Adriaan Peperzak, Simon Critchley and Robert Bernasconi (eds), *Emmanuel Levinas: Basic Philosophical Writings* (Indianapolis, IN: Indiana University Press, [1968] 1996), p. 80.
11. Emmanuel Levinas, *Ethics and Infinity: Conversations with Phillipe Nemo*, trans. R. Cohen (Pittsburgh, PA: Duquesne University Press, 1985), p. 80.
12. Emmanuel Levinas, *Otherwise Than Being or Beyond Essence* (Pittsburgh, PA: Duquesne University Press, [1981] 2004), p. 117.

13. Emmanuel Levinas, *Totality and Infinity: An Essay on Exteriority*, trans. A. Lingis (Pittsburgh, PA: Duquesne University Press, [1961] 2005), p. 46.
14. Levinas, *Ethics and Infinity*, p. 61.
15. John Wild, 'Introduction', in *Totality and Infinity*, p. 13.
16. Ibid.
17. Levinas, *Totality and Infinity*, p. 194.
18. Levinas, *Otherwise Than Being*, p. 86.
19. Emmanuel Levinas, 'The Vocation of the Other', in Jill Robbins (ed.), *Is it Righteous to Be? Interviews with Emmanuel Levinas* (Stanford, CA: Stanford University Press, [1988] 2001), p. 106.
20. Levinas, *Totality and Infinity*, p. 35.
21. Ibid. p. 251.
22. Levinas, *Otherwise Than Being*, p. 87.
23. Levinas, *Ethics and Infinity*, p. 60.
24. Ibid. p. 77.
25. Ibid. p. 78.
26. Emmanuel Levinas 'Interview with François Poirié', in Jill Robbins (ed.), *Is it Righteous to Be? Interviews with Emmanuel Levinas* (Stanford, CA: Stanford University Press, [1986] 2001), p. 57.
27. Levinas, *Otherwise Than Being*, p. 25.
28. Emmanuel Levinas, 'Transcendence and Height', in Adriaan Peperzak, Simon Critchley and Robert Bernasconi (eds), *Emmanuel Levinas: Basic Philosophical Writings*, (Indianapolis, IN: Indiana University Press, [1962] 1996), p. 16.
29. Levinas, *Otherwise Than Being*, p. 100.
30. Levinas, *Ethics and Infinity*, p. 95.
31. Levinas, 'Transcendence and Height', p. 17.
32. Levinas, 'Interview with François Poirié', p. 66.
33. Levinas, 'Transcendence and Height', p. 18.
34. Levinas, *Otherwise Than Being*, p. 59.
35. Levinas 'Interview with François Poirié', p. 66. Levinas also expresses this in terms of the untransferable nature of the self's responsibility to the Other as the basis for the identity of the subject. He sees responsibility as untransferable because the call of the Other is addressed only to me and only I can respond to it: 'it is I who support the other and am responsible for him ... My responsibility is untransferable, no one could replace me'. See Levinas, *Ethics and Infinity*, p. 100.
36. Levinas, *Ethics and Infinity*, p. 85.
37. Ibid.
38. Ibid. p. 86.
39. Levinas, *Totality and Infinity*, p. 297.
40. Ibid.

41. Levinas, *Otherwise Than Being*, p. 86.
42. Jacques Derrida, *Writing and Difference* (London: Routledge, 1978), p. 100.
43. Levinas, *Otherwise Than Being*, p. 86.
44. Levinas, 'Substitution', p. 81.
45. Levinas, 'Interview with François Poirié', p. 48.
46. Levinas, 'The Vocation of the Other', p. 108.
47. Emmanuel Levinas, 'Being-for-the-Other', in Jill Robbins (ed.), *Is it Righteous to Be? Interviews with Emmanuel Levinas* (Stanford, CA: Stanford University Press, [1989] 2001), p. 115.
48. Levinas, *Ethics and Infinity*, p. 87.
49. Ibid. p. 120.
50. Ibid. p. 122.
51. Ibid.
52. Ibid. p. 118.
53. Levinas, 'Interview with François Poirié', p. 52.
54. Levinas, *Ethics and Infinity*, p. 97.
55. Levinas, *Otherwise Than Being*, p. 10.
56. Ibid. p. 13.
57. Ibid.
58. Ibid. p. 11.
59. Ibid. p. 112.
60. Adriaan Peperzak, 'Preface', in Adriaan Peperzak, Simon Critchley and Robert Bernasconi (eds), *Emmanuel Levinas: Basic Philosophical Writings* (Indianapolis, IN: Indiana University Press, 1996), p. xi.
61. Jill Robbins, 'Introduction', in Jill Robbins (ed.), *Is it Righteous to Be? Interviews with Emmanuel Levinas* (Stanford, CA: Stanford University Press, 2001), p. 7.
62. Levinas, 'Interview with François Poirié', p. 52.
63. Levinas, *Ethics and Infinity*, p. 95.
64. Ibid. p. 99.
65. Levinas, *Otherwise Than Being*, p. 84. Levinas also argues that responsibility: 'can and has to manifest itself also in limiting itself'. Through the requirements of justice, on the entry of the third person, the ego is called upon to concern itself with itself. See Levinas, *Otherwise Than Being*, p. 128.
66. Campbell, *National Deconstruction*, pp. 177, 191; Mark Dooley, 'The Civic Religion of Social Hope: A Reply to Simon Critchley', *Philosophy and Social Criticism* 27: 5 (2001), 35–8; Martin Hagglund, 'The Necessity of Discrimination: Disjoining Derrida and Levinas', *Diacritics* 34: 1 (2004), p. 53; Alex Thomson, *Deconstruction and Democracy: Derrida's Politics of Friendship* (London: Continuum, 2005), p. 131.

67. Critchley, 'Five Problems', p. 173.
68. Levinas, *Otherwise Than Being*, p. 159.
69. Ibid. p. 213.
70. Haggland, 'The Necessity of Discrimination', pp. 46, 50.
71. Levinas, *Otherwise Than Being*, p. 158.
72. Perpich, 'A Singular Justice', p. 60.
73. Levinas, *Totality and Infinity*, p. 212.
74. Ibid. p. 213.
75. Levinas, *Otherwise Than Being*, p. 158.
76. Levinas, 'Interview with François Poirié', p. 55.
77. Levinas, *Otherwise Than Being*, p. 157.
78. Emmanuel Levinas and Richard Kearney, 'Dialogue with Emmanuel Levinas', in Richard Cohen (ed.), *Face to Face with Levinas* (Albany, NY: State University of New York Press, 1986), p. 21.
79. Ibid.
80. Levinas, *Ethics and Infinity*, pp. 60, 85.
81. Levinas, *Totality and Infinity*, p. 305.
82. Ibid.
83. Levinas, 'The Vocation of the Other', p. 108.
84. Ibid.
85. Levinas, 'Interview with François Poirié', p. 49.
86. Levinas, *Otherwise Than Being*, p. 157.
87. Simmons, 'The Third', p. 98; Thomson, *Deconstruction and Democracy*, p. 101; Critchley, *The Ethics of Deconstruction*, p. 223; Critchley, 'Five Problems', p. 182.
88. Simmons, 'The Third', p. 96; Critchley, *The Ethics of Deconstruction*, p. xiv.
89. Levinas, *Otherwise Than Being*, p. 157.
90. Emmanuel Levinas, 'Interview with Salomon Malka', in Jill Robbins (ed.), *Is it Righteous to Be? Interviews with Emmanuel Levinas* (Stanford, CA: Stanford University Press, [1984] 2001), p. 100.
91. Levinas, *Otherwise Than Being*, p. 16.
92. Emmanuel Levinas, 'Responsibility and Substitution', in Jill Robbins (ed.), *Is it Righteous to Be? Interviews with Emmanuel Levinas* (Stanford, CA: Stanford University Press, [1988] 2001), p. 230.
93. Levinas, 'Interview with François Poirié', p. 66.
94. Ibid. p. 67.
95. Ibid.
96. Ibid.
97. Emmanuel Levinas, 'Philosophy, Justice, and Love', in Jill Robbins (ed.), *Is it Righteous to Be? Interviews with Emmanuel Levinas* (Stanford, CA: Stanford University Press, 2001 [1983]), p. 181.
98. Emmanuel Levinas, 'Who Shall Not Prophesy?', in Jill Robbins (ed.),

Is it Righteous to Be? Interviews with Emmanuel Levinas (Stanford, CA: Stanford University Press, [1985] 2001), p. 223.

99. Levinas, 'Being-for-the-Other', p. 115.
100. Levinas, Philosophy, Justice and Love', p. 169.
101. Levinas, *Otherwise Than Being*, p. 159.
102. Levinas, *Totality and Infinity*, p. 300, emphasis added.
103. Levinas, 'Interview with François Poirié', p. 69.
104. Ibid.
105. Levinas, 'Philosophy, Justice and Love', p. 167.
106. Levinas, 'Interview with François Poirié', p. 68.
107. Levinas, 'The Vocation of the Other', p. 108.
108. Levinas, *Ethics and Infinity*, p. 80.
109. Levinas, *Totality and Infinity*, p. 300.
110. Levinas, 'Being-for-the-Other', p. 116.
111. Levinas, 'Interview with François Poirié', p. 68.
112. Emmanuel Levinas, 'The Other, Utopia, and Justice', in Jill Robbins (ed.), *Is it Righteous to Be? Interviews with Emmanuel Levinas* (Stanford, CA: Stanford University Press, [1988] 2001), p. 207.
113. Levinas, 'Being-for-the-Other', p. 120.
114. Levinas, *Ethics and Infinity*, p. 80.
115. Emmanuel Levinas, 'Being-Toward-Death and "Thou Shalt Not Kill"', in Jill Robbins (ed.), *Is it Righteous to Be? Interviews with Emmanuel Levinas* (Stanford, CA: Stanford University Press, [1986] 2001), p. 132.
116. See David Campbell and Michael Shapiro, *Moral Spaces: Rethinking Ethics in World Politics* (Minneapolis, MN: University of Minnesota Press, 1999).
117. Critchley, 'Five Problems', p. 173.
118. Ibid. pp. 177–81.

Chapter 3

1. Jacques Derrida, 'Some Statements and Trusims about NeoLogisms, Newisms, Postisms, Parasitisms, and Other Small Seismisms', in D. Carroll (ed.), *The States of 'Theory': History, Art, and Critical Discourse* (New York, NY: Columbia University Press, 1990), p. 86.
2. Ibid. p. 88.
3. Ibid. p. 87.
4. Ibid. p. 87. In particular, Derrida seeks to resist a specifically 'modern' concept of theory as objectivity: 'Deconstruction resists theory then because it demonstrates the impossibility of closure, of the closure of an ensemble or totality or an organised network of theories, rules, norms, methods'. Ibid. p. 86.

5. Jacques Derrida, 'Deconstructions: The Im-Possible', in Sylvère Lotringer and Sande Cohen (eds), *French Theory in America* (London and New York, NY: Routledge, 2001), p. 22.

6. Derrida, 'Some Statements', p. 85.

7. Discourse, text and concepts here are meant very broadly. For Derrida, 'discursive meaning or content, the thematics or the semantics of a discourse' cannot be insulated. Text is 'irreducible to discourse or the book or . . . the textual' and cannot be distinguished from, or opposed to, 'reality' 'the social' or 'the historical'. See Derrida, 'Some Statements', pp. 86–7.

8. Derrida, 'Deconstructions', p. 22.

9. Jacques Derrida, 'Hospitality, Justice and Responsibility: A Dialogue with Jacques Derrida', in Richard Kearney and Mark Dooley (eds), *Questioning Ethics: Contemporary Debates in Philosophy* (London: Routledge, 1999), p. 66; Jacques Derrida, 'Villanova Roundtable' , in John D. Caputo (ed.), *Deconstruction in a Nutshell: A Conversation with Jacques Derrida* (New York, NY: Fordham University Press, 1997), p. 17; Jacques Derrida, 'Autoimmunity: Real and Symbolic Suicides – A Dialogue with Jacques Derrida', in Giovanna Borradori (ed.), *Philosophy in a Time of Terror: Dialogues with Jürgen Habermas and Jacques Derrida* (London: University of Chicago Press, 2003), p. 129.

10. Thomas Keenan, *Fables of Responsibility: Aberrations and Predicaments in Ethics and Politics* (Stanford, CA: Stanford University Press, 1997), p. 1.

11. Jacques Derrida, *The Gift of Death*, trans. David Wills (London: University of Chicago Press, 1995), p. 1.

12. Jacques Derrida, *Rogues: Two Essays on Reason* (Stanford, CA: Stanford University Press, 2005), p. 83.

13. Jacques Derrida, 'Force of Law', in Drucilla Cornell, Michel Rosenfield and David Gray Carlson (eds), *Deconstruction and the Possibility of Justice* (London: Routledge, 1992), p. 26.

14. Jacques Derrida, *The Politics of Friendship*, trans. George Collins (London: Verso, [1994] 2005), p. 79.

15. Derrida, 'Force of Law', p. 26.

16. Derrida, *Rogues*, p. 145.

17. Derrida, *The Gift of Death*, p. 24.

18. Derrida, 'Force of Law', p. 23.

19. Jacques Derrida, 'Perhaps or Maybe', in Jonathan Dronsfield and Nick Midgley (eds), Special Issue: Responsibilities of Deconstruction, *PLI: Warwick Journal of Philosophy* 6 (1997), p. 7.

20. Derrida, 'Force of Law', p. 26.

21. Keenan, *Fables*, p. 12.

22. Derrida, 'Force of Law', p. 26.
23. Derrida, 'Force of Law', p. 23.
24. Derrida, *Politics of Friendship*, p. xi.
25. Jacques Derrida, 'Remarks on Deconstruction and Pragmatism', in Chantal Mouffe (ed.), *Deconstruction and Pragmatism: Simon Critchley, Jacques Derrida, Ernesto Laclau and Richard Rorty* (London: Routledge, 1996), p. 84.
26. Jacques Derrida, *Adieu to Emmanuel Levinas* (Stanford, CA: Stanford University Press, 1999), p. 24.
27. Jacques Derrida, *Deconstruction Engaged: The Sydney Seminars*, Paul Patton and Terry Smith (eds) (Sydney: Power Publications, 2001), p. 103.
28. Derrida, 'Perhaps or Maybe', p. 14.
29. Derrida, *Deconstruction Engaged*, p. 64.
30. Derrida, *Adieu: To Emmanuel Levinas*, p. 23.
31. Derrida, *Deconstruction Engaged*, p. 64.
32. Derrida, 'Remarks on Deconstruction and Pragmatism', p. 84.
33. Derrida, 'Deconstructions', p. 27.
34. Derrida, 'Perhaps or Maybe', p. 14.
35. Derrida, *Deconstruction Engaged*, p. 103.
36. Derrida, 'Villanova Roundtable', p. 13.
37. Derrida, 'Perhaps or Maybe', p. 13.
38. Jacques Derrida, '"Eating well" or the Calculation of the Subject: An Interview with Jacques Derrida', in Eduardo Cadava, Peter Connor and Jean-Luc Nancy (eds), *Who Comes After the Subject* (London: Routledge, 1991), p. 103.
39. Derrida, '"Eating well"', p. 100. The centrality of alterity as allowing for relation and the approach to subjectivity as fragmented and in relation resonates clearly with the themes explored in the previous chapter. The approaches of Levinas and Derrida, at this point, are very close. As Derrida states: 'everything I have said here implies something I share with Levinas, that is the absolute irreducibility of the otherness of the Other . . . infinitely other'. See Derrida, 'Perhaps or Maybe', p. 13.
40. Derrida, 'Villanova Roundtable', p. 14.
41. Ibid.
42. Ibid.
43. Ibid.
44. Ibid. This approach to the Other as absolutely other goes so far as to throw into doubt the meaning of the Other as another human subject, and it is here that Derrida may be seen to go further than or diverge from Levinas. For Levinas, responsibility and response are always linked explicitly to the Other as the other person, the other

human being. Derrida, on the other hand, is concerned about this certainty regarding subjectivity: 'If I am absolutely sure, no matter how undetermined he or she may be, that the Other is a subject, then their surprise is under control . . . if a human subject their surprise will be under control to some extent' (See Derrida, 'Perhaps or Maybe', p. 4). It is this move that allows for the argument, which is made, for example, by Michael Shapiro, that an understanding of the Other as completely other demands an approach towards the Other of absolute openness (See Michael J. Shapiro, 'The Ethics of Encounter: Unreading, Unmapping the Imperium', in David Campbell and Michael J. Shapiro (eds), *Moral Spaces: Rethinking Ethics and World Politics* (Minneapolis, MN: University of Minnesota Press, 1999), p. 64).

45. Jacques Derrida, 'On Responsibility: Interview with Jonathan Dronsfield, Nick Midgley, Adrian Wilding', in Jonathan Dronsfield and Nick Midgley (eds), Special Issue: Responsibilities of Deconstruction, *PLI: Warwick Journal of Philosophy* 6 ([1993] 1997), p. 25.

46. Jacques Derrida and Bernard Stiegler, *Echographies of Television* (Cambridge: Polity Press, 2002), p. 21.

47. Christina Howells, *Derrida: Deconstruction from Phenomenology to Ethics* (Cambridge: Polity Press, 1999), p. 135.

48. Caroline Williams, *Contemporary French Philosophy: Modernity and the Persistence of the Subject* (London: Athlone Press, 2001), p. 116.

49. Derrida, *Adieu*, p. 23.

50. Howells, *Derrida*, p. 135.

51. Derrida, 'Force of Law', p. 16.

52. Derrida, 'Force of Law', p. 16.

53. Jacques Derrida, *The Other Heading: Reflections on Today's Europe*, trans. Pascale-Anne Brault and Michael B. Naas (Bloomington, IN: Indiana University Press, 1992), p. 41.

54. Derrida, *Politics of Friendship*, p. 250.

55. Ibid.

56. Derrida, *The Gift of Death*, p. 64.

57. Derrida, *Deconstruction Engaged*, p. 86.

58. Derrida, *The Gift of Death*, p. 67.

59. Ibid. p. 74.

60. Ibid. p. 68.

61. Ibid.

62. Ibid. p. 71.

63. Ibid. p. 78.

64. Ibid. p. 87.

65. Alex Thomson, *Deconstruction and Democracy: Derrida's Politics of Friendship* (London: Continuum, 2005), p. 23.

66. Derrida, *Politics of Friendship*, p. 276.

67. Derrida, 'Hospitality, Justice and Responsibility', p. 69.
68. Derrida, *The Gift of Death*, p. 61.
69. Ibid.
70. Derrida, *The Other Heading*, p. 44.
71. Derrida, 'Hospitality, Justice and Responsibility', p. 73.
72. Jacques Derrida, 'Politics and Friendship: A Discussion with Jacques Derrida' (University of Sussex: Centre for Modern French Thought, 1997), available at http://www.sussex.ac.uk/Units/frenchthought/derrida.htm (accessed 7 October 2006), p. 6.
73. Ibid. p. 8.
74. Derrida, *Adieu*, p. 68.
75. Derrida, 'Autoimmunity', p. 128.
76. Ibid.
77. Derrida, 'On Responsibility', p. 25.
78. Derrida, *Echographies of Television*, p. 21.
79. Derrida, 'Autoimmunity', p. 129.
80. Ibid.
81. Ibid.
82. Ibid. pp. 127–8.
83. Ibid. p. 127.
84. Ibid. p. 129.
85. Derrida, 'Politics and Friendship', p. 6.
86. Derrida, 'Autoimmunity', p. 129.
87. Jacques Derrida, *On Cosmopolitanism and Forgiveness*, trans. Mark Dooley and Michael Hughes (London: Routledge, 2001), p. 17.
88. Derrida, 'On Responsibility', p. 27.
89. Ibid.
90. Derrida, 'Hospitality, Justice and Responsibility', p. 73.
91. Derrida, *On Cosmopolitanism and Forgiveness*, p. 45.
92. Ibid.
93. John Caputo (ed.), *Deconstruction in a Nutshell: A Conversation with Jacques Derrida* (New York, NY: Fordham University Press, 1997), p. 128.
94. Ibid. p. 131.
95. Derrida, *Adieu*, p. 33.
96. Derrida, *On Cosmopolitanism and Forgiveness*, p. 44.
97. Derrida, *Adieu*, p. 33.
98. Derrida, 'Hospitality, Justice and Responsibility', p. 79.
99. Jacques Derrida, *Limited Inc* (Evanston, IL: Northwestern University Press, 1988), p. 148.
100. Ibid.
101. Ibid.
102. Keenan, *Fables*, p. 12.

103. Derrida, 'Remarks on Deconstruction and Pragmatism', p. 86.
104. Derrida, *Limited Inc*, p. 116.
105. Derrida, 'Hospitality, Justice and Responsibility', p. 69.
106. Derrida, *Limited Inc*, p. 116.
107. Derrida, 'Force of Law', p. 24.
108. Derrida, *Rogues*, p. 35.
109. Derrida, 'On Responsibility', p. 23.
110. Derrida, 'Hospitality, Justice and Responsibility', p. 66.
111. Derrida, *Politics of Friendship*, p. 219.
112. Derrida, *Rogues*, p. 82. Occasionally, Derrida names 'the bad', for example, as: 'the worst violences, those we recognise all too well without having thought them through, the crimes of xenophobia, racism, anti-Semitism, religious or nationalist fanaticism' (See Derrida, *The Other Heading*, p. 6). This may seem to be already determining the distinction between good and evil, as Campbell, for example, reads it, which enables him to extend these statements into political guidelines. However, given the context of Derrida's work, which suggests that we cannot legislate against the bad or even know what it might be in any systematic sense, it should, I suggest, be read as a particular political intervention on his part, as a particular decision made and unsecured, an attempt at responsibility. Further, even if Derrida can be seen as defining evil or the worst, he does not legislate against it. Rather, it is used as an example of the magnitude of the threats one may run when confronting the aporia of responsibility. These possibilities, of xenophobia and so on, are the risks which must be run.
113. Derrida, 'Remarks on Deconstruction and Pragmatism', p. 87.
114. Derrida, *Politics of Friendship*, p. 219.
115. Derrida, *Limited Inc*, p. 116.
116. Thomson, *Deconstruction and Democracy*, p. 141.
117. Derrida, *Rogues*, p. 60.
118. Derrida, 'Hospitality, Justice and Responsibility', p. 72.
119. Derrida, *Adieu*, p. 99.
120. Ibid. p. 115.
121. Ibid. p. 112.
122. Ibid. p. 115.
123. Ibid. p. 20.
124. Ibid. p. 115.
125. Ibid. p. 114.
126. Ibid. p. 117.
127. Ibid. p. 21.
128. See Chapter 1 for a discussion of some of the criticisms of poststructuralism which take this position, as well as my argument that those poststructuralist authors concerned with developing a politics from

ethics ultimately also rely on an account of ethics to make deconstruction politically engaged.

129. Simon Critchley, *The Ethics of Deconstruction: Derrida and Levinas* (Edinburgh: Edinburgh University Press, 1992), p. xiv.
130. Chantal Mouffe, 'Deconstruction, Pragmatism and the Politics of Democracy', in Chantal Mouffe (ed.), *Deconstruction and Pragmatism* (London: Routledge, 1996), p. 4.
131. Derrida, 'Some Statements', p. 94
132. Thomson, *Deconstruction and Democracy*, p. 3.
133. Derrida, 'Politics and Friendship', p. 2.
134. Derrida, 'Remarks on Deconstruction and Pragmatism', p. 85.
135. David Campbell, *National Deconstruction: Violence, Identity and Justice in Bosnia* (Minneapolis, MN: University of Minnesota Press, 1998).
136. Derrida, 'Some Statements', p. 85.
137. Derrida, 'Deconstructions', p. 20.
138. Derrida, 'Villanova Roundtable', p. 13.
139. Derrida, 'Hospitality, Justice and Responsibility', p. 65.
140. Derrida, 'On Responsibility', p. 34.
141. Derrida, 'Perhaps or Maybe', p. 6.
142. Ibid.
143. Derrida, 'Politics and Friendship', p. 6.
144. Derrida, 'On Responsibility', p. 34.
145. Derrida, *Adieu*, p. 115.
146. Derrida, *Rogues*, p. xv.
147. Derrida, 'On Responsibility', p. 26.
148. Derrida, *Limited Inc*, p. 152.

Chapter 4

1. Jean-Luc Nancy, *Being Singular Plural* (Stanford, CA: Stanford University Press, 2000), p. 29.
2. Ibid. p. 30.
3. Ibid. p. 34.
4. Ibid. p. 60.
5. Ibid.
6. Jean-Luc Nancy, 'The Insufficiency of "Values" and the Necessity of "Sense"', *Journal for Cultural Research* 9: 4 (2005), p. 440.
7. Nancy, *Being Singular Plural*, p. 35.
8. Ibid. p. 96.
9. Ibid. p. xv.
10. Ibid. p. 37.
11. Ibid.

12. Ibid.
13. Jean-Luc Nancy, *The Sense of the World* (Minneapolis, MN: Minnesota University Press, 1997), p. 71.
14. Nancy, *Being Singular Plural*, p. 32.
15. Ibid.
16. Ibid.
17. Ibid.
18. Ibid. p. 5.
19. Ibid.
20. Jean-Luc Nancy, *The Inoperative Community* (London: University of Minnesota Press, 1991), p. 29.
21. Ibid. p. 30.
22. Jean-Luc Nancy, 'Of Being-in-Common', in Miami Theory Collective (ed.), *Community at Loose Ends* (Minneapolis, MN: University of Minnesota Press, 1991), p. 6.
23. Ibid.
24. Ibid.
25. Nancy, *Being Singular Plural*, p. 60.
26. Ibid. p. 65.
27. Ibid.
28. Ibid.
29. Nancy, 'Of Being-in-Common', p. 6.
30. Nancy, *Being Singular Plural*, p. 186.
31. Ibid.
32. Jean-Luc Nancy, *The Creation of the World or Globalization* (Albany, NY: The State University of New York Press, 2007), p. 110.
33. Nancy, *The Inoperative Community*, p. 6.
34. Nancy, *Being Singular Plural*, p. 33.
35. Ibid.
36. Jenny Edkins, 'What it is to be Many: Subjecthood, Responsibility and Sacrifice in Derrida and Nancy', in Madeleine Fagan, Ludovic Glorieux, Indira Hašimbegović and Marie Suetsugu (eds), *Derrida: Negotiating the Legacy* (Edinburgh: Edinburgh University Press, 2007), p. 180.
37. Nancy, 'Of Being-in-Common', p. 7.
38. Ibid. p. 1.
39. Nancy, *Inoperative Community*, p. 64.
40. Jean-Luc Nancy, *Philosophical Chronicles*, trans. Franson Manjali (New York, NY: Fordham University Press, 2008), p. 5.
41. Nancy, *Inoperative Community*, p. 66.
42. Nancy, *Being Singular Plural*, p. 155.
43. Nancy, *Inoperative Community*, p. 66.
44. Ibid. p. 34.

45. Ibid. p. 33.
46. Ibid.
47. Nancy, *Being Singular Plural*, p. 93.
48. Nancy, *Inoperative Community*, p. xl.
49. Ibid. p. 29.
50. Ibid.
51. Ibid.
52. Ibid. p. 76.
53. Ibid. p. 29.
54. Christopher Watkin, 'A Different Alterity: Jean-Luc Nancy's "Singular Plural"', *Paragraph* 30: 2 (2007), p. 59.
55. Ibid.
56. Jean-Luc Nancy, *The Ground of the Image* (New York, NY: Fordham University Press, 2005), p. 4.
57. Ibid.
58. Ibid.
59. Ibid. p. 12.
60. Ibid. p. 7.
61. Martin Coward, 'Editor's Introduction', Special Issue: Jean-Luc Nancy, *Journal for Cultural Research* 9: 4 (2005), p. 325.
62. Ibid.
63. Nancy, *Inoperative Community*, p. 40.
64. Ibid. p. 75.
65. Ibid.
66. Nancy, 'Of Being-in-Common', p. 7.
67. Jean-Luc Nancy, *The Birth to Presence*, trans. Brian Holmes and others (Stanford, CA: Stanford University Press, 1993), p. 318.
68. Nancy, *Inoperative Community*, p. x.
69. Ibid. p. 35.
70. Ibid. p. 58.
71. Ibid. p. 35.
72. Ibid. p. xxxix.
73. Ibid. p. x.
74. Ibid.
75. Ibid. p. 40.
76. Nancy, *The Birth to Presence*, p. 53.
77. Nancy, *Philosophical Chronicles*, p. 24.
78. Ibid.
79. Phillipe Lacoue-Labarthe and Jean-Luc Nancy, *Retreating the Political* (London: Routledge, 1997), p. 111.
80. Ibid.
81. Nancy, *Philosophical Chronicles*, p. 24.
82. Lacoue-Labarthe and Nancy, *Retreating the Political*, p. 126.

83. Ibid. p. 112.
84. Nancy, *Inoperative Community*, p. xxxviii.
85. Lacoue-Labarthe and Nancy, *Retreating the Political*, p. 129.
86. Ibid.
87. Ibid. p. 112.
88. Ibid. p. 133.
89. Nancy, *The Birth to Presence*, p. 52.
90. Lacoue-Labarthe and Nancy, *Retreating the Political*, p. 129.
91. Nancy, *Philosophical Chronicles*, pp. 9–10.
92. Ibid.
93. Lacoue-Labarthe and Nancy, *Retreating the Political*, p. 129.
94. Nancy, *Inoperative Community*, p. 35.
95. Ibid.
96. Jean-Luc Nancy, *A Finite Thinking* (Stanford, CA: Stanford University Press, 2003), p. 187.
97. Nancy, *The Sense of the World*, p. 55.
98. Ibid. p. 17.
99. See, for example, Andrew Norris, 'Jean-Luc Nancy and The Myth of the Common', *Constellations* 7: 2 (2000), 272–95; Todd May, *Reconsidering Difference: Nancy, Derrida, Levinas and Deleuze* (Pennsylvania, PA: Pennsylvania University Press, 1997).
100. Norris, 'Jean-Luc Nancy and The Myth of the Common', p. 274.
101. Ibid.
102. Ian James, *The Fragmentary Demand: An Introduction to the Philosophy of Jean-Luc Nancy* (Stanford, CA: Stanford University Press, 2006), p. 192. See also May, *Reconsidering Difference*, for a similar critique.
103. Ian James, 'On Interrupted Myth', *Journal of Cultural Research* 9: 4 (2005), p. 340.
104. Ibid. p. 347.
105. Lacoue-Labarthe and Nancy, *Retreating the Political*, p. 158.
106. Nancy, *The Sense of the World*, p. 90.
107. Lacoue-Labarthe and Nancy, *Retreating the Political*, p. 157.
108. Ibid.
109. Ibid.
110. Ibid. p. 158.
111. Nancy occasionally approaches ethics in the sense of moral doctrine (Lacoue-Labarthe and Nancy, *Retreating the Political*, p. 2), and he is (unsurprisingly) critical of this. A privileging of the ethical, he argues in this context, cuts short the question of the essence of the political, which is the essence of relation, and leaves no space for political choice. Ethics, in these terms, is a closing or totalising discourse (Ibid. p. 146).

112. Nancy, 'Of Being-in-Common', p. 7.
113. Simon Critchley, *Ethics, Politics, Subjectivity: Essays on Derrida, Levinas and Contemporary French Thought* (London: Verso, 1999), p. 257.
114. Ibid.
115. Ibid. p. 255.
116. Ibid. p. 250.
117. Nancy, *Being Singular Plural*, p. xiii. See also James, *The Fragmentary Demand*, p. 191.
118. Nancy, *Being Singular Plural*, p. 69.
119. Critchley, *Ethics, Politics, Subjectivity*, p. 245.
120. Nancy, *A Finite Thinking*, p. 187.
121. Coward, 'Editor's Introduction', p. 326.
122. Nancy, *A Finite Thinking*, p. 184.
123. Ibid. p. 187.
124. Nancy, *Being Singular Plural*, p. 34.
125. Ibid. p. 77.
126. Nancy, *The Creation of the World*, p. 61.
127. Ibid. p. 61.
128. Ibid. p. 110.
129. Ibid.
130. Ibid.
131. Ibid. pp. 110–11.
132. Ibid. p. 111.
133. Ibid. p. 112.
134. Nancy, *Inoperative Community*, p. 81.
135. Jean-Luc Nancy, 'The Insufficiency of "Values"', p. 440.
136. Ibid.
137. Nancy, *The Creation of the World*, p. 59.
138. Nancy, 'The Insufficiency of "Values"', p. 441.

Chapter 5

1. See John Caputo, *Against Ethics: Contributions to a Poetics of Obligation with Constant Reference to Deconstruction* (Bloomington, IN: Indiana University Press, 1993).
2. Simon Critchley, *The Ethics of Deconstruction: Derrida and Levinas* (Edinburgh: Edinburgh University Press, 1992), p. 233.
3. Giorgio Agamben, for example, classifies the work of both Levinas and Derrida as concerned with transcendence. See Giorgio Agamben, *Potentialities: Collected Essays in Philosophy* (Stanford, CA: Stanford University Press, 1999), p. 239.
4. Daniel Smith, 'Deleuze and Derrida, Immanence and Transcendence:

Two Directions in Recent French Thought', in Paul Patton and John Protevi (eds), *Between Deleuze and Derrida* (London: Continuum, 2003), p. 56.

5. Connolly, for example, sees the pure, absolute and infinite in Derrida's work as the transcendent, which is sought, but never attained. William E. Connolly, 'Immanence, Abundance, Democracy', in Lars Tonder and Lasse Thomassen (eds), *Radical Democracy: Politics Between Abundance and Lack* (Manchester: Manchester University Press, 2005), p. 239.

6. Jacques Derrida, 'Autoimmunity: Real and Symbolic Suicides – A Dialogue with Jacques Derrida', in Giovanna Borradori (ed.), *Philosophy in a Time of Terror: Dialogues with Jürgen Habermas and Jacques Derrida* (London: University of Chicago Press, 2003), p. 129.

7. Ibid.

8. Ibid. p. 130.

9. John Caputo, *The Prayers and Tears of Jacques Derrida* (Bloomington, IN: Indiana University Press, 1997), p. 2.

10. Derrida, 'Autoimmunity', p. 129.

11. Ibid. p. 130.

12. Simon Critchley, *Ethics, Politics, Subjectivity: Essays on Derrida, Levinas and Contemporary French Thought* (London: Verso, 1999), p. 257.

13. Richard Kearney, *Strangers, Gods and Monsters: Interpreting Otherness* (London: Routledge, 2003), p. 77.

14. Ibid. p. 35.

15. Ibid.

16. Ibid. p. 77.

17. One useful way of conceptualising this repositioning of the Other is through John Caputo's argument that the Other is not an infinity, but a 'partiality' – a part that defies the totality, whilst being strictly earthbound (see Caputo, *Against Ethics*, p. 19). Obligation happens, for Caputo, and that is all that can be said; it is a strictly 'earthbound' communication. Obligations, he argues: 'do not come from some central source of power. Obligations are strictly local events, sublunary affairs, between us. They are matters of flesh and blood, without cosmic import or support' (see Caputo, *Against Ethics*, p. 227).

18. Jean-Luc Nancy, *The Inoperative Community* (London: University of Minnesota Press, 1991), p. 33.

19. Jean-Luc Nancy, *A Finite Thinking* (Stanford, CA: Stanford University Press, 2003), p. 184.

20. See, for example, Jenny Edkins, *Poststructuralism and International Relations: Bringing the Political Back In* (Boulder, CO: Lynne Rienner, 1999), p. 2.

21. Being attentive to this limit is something which Caputo deftly argues for in the ethical realm, but which must also, I suggest, be taken into account in the traditionally political realm. See Caputo, *Against Ethics*.

Chapter 6

1. Jacques Derrida, *Adieu: to Emmanuel Levinas* (Stanford, CA: Stanford University Press, 1999), p. 117.
2. William E. Connolly, *Identity\Difference: Democratic Negotiations of Political Paradox* (London: Cornell University Press, 1991), p. 13.

Bibliography

Agamben, Giorgio, *Potentialities: Collected Essays in Philosophy* (Stanford, CA: Stanford University Press, 1999).

Ashley, Richard K., 'Living on Border Lines: Man, Poststructuralism, and War', in James Der Derian and Michael J. Shapiro (eds), *International/Intertextual Relations: Postmodern Readings of World Politics* (Lexington, KY: Lexington Books, 1989), pp. 259–320.

Ashley, Richard K. and R. B. J. Walker, 'Reading Dissidence/Writing the Discipline: Crisis and the Question of Sovereignty in International Studies', Special Issue: Speaking the Language of Exile: Dissidence in International Studies, *International Studies Quarterly* 34: 3 (1990), 367–416.

Bauman, Zygmunt, *Postmodern Ethics* (Oxford: Blackwell, 1993).

Bauman, Zygmunt, *Modernity and the Holocaust* (London: Polity, 2001).

Beardsworth, Richard, 'The Future of Critical Philosophy and World Politics', in Madeleine Fagan, Ludovic Glorieux, Indira Hašimbegović and Marie Suetsugu (eds), *Derrida: Negotiating the Legacy* (Edinburgh: Edinburgh University Press, 2007), pp. 45–66.

Bernasconi, Robert, 'The Crisis of Critique and the Awakening of Politicisation in Levinas and Derrida', in Martin McQuillan (ed.), *The Politics of Deconstruction: Jacques Derrida and the Other of Philosophy* (London: Pluto Press, 2007), pp. 81–97.

Brown, Chris, *International Relations Theory: New Normative Approaches* (New York, NY: Columbia University Press, 1992).

Brown, Chris, '"Turtles All the Way Down": Anti-Foundationalism, Critical Theory and International Relations', *Millennium* 23: 2 (1994), 213–36.

Brown, Chris, 'Review Article: Theories of International Justice', *British Journal of Political Science* 27: 2 (1997), 273–97.

Bulley, Dan, 'Negotiating Ethics: Campbell, Ontopology and Hospitality', *Review of International Studies* 32: 4 (2006), 645–63.

Butler, Judith, *Precarious Life: The Powers of Mourning and Violence* (London: Verso, 2004).

Campbell, David, *Politics without Principle: Sovereignty, Ethics, and the Narratives of the Gulf War* (London: Lynne Rienner, 1993).

Campbell, David, 'The Deterritorialization of Responsibility: Levinas, Derrida, and Ethics After the End of Philosophy', *Alternatives* 19: 4 (1994), 455–84.

Campbell, David, 'The Possibility of Radical Interdependence: A Rejoinder to Daniel Warner', *Millennium* 25: 1 (1996), 129–41.

Campbell, David, *National Deconstruction: Violence, Identity and Justice in Bosnia* (Minneapolis, MN: University of Minnesota Press, 1998).

Campbell, David, 'Why Fight: Humanitarianism, Principles and Post-Structuralism', *Millennium* 27: 3 (1998), 497–521.

Campbell, David, *Writing Security: United States Foreign Policy and the Politics of Identity* (Manchester: Manchester University Press, 1998).

Campbell, David, 'Beyond Choice: The Onto-Politics of Critique', *International Relations* 19: 1 (2005), 127–34.

Campbell, David and Michael Dillon, 'Postface: The Political and the Ethical', in David Campbell and Michael Dillon (eds), *The Political Subject of Violence* (Manchester: Manchester University Press, 1993), pp. 161–79.

Campbell, David and Michael J. Shapiro, 'Introduction: From Ethical Theory to the Ethical Relation', in David Campbell and Michael J. Shapiro (eds), *Moral Spaces: Rethinking Ethics and World Politics* (Minneapolis, MN: University of Minnesota Press, 1999), pp. vii–xx.

Campbell, David and Michael J. Shapiro (eds), *Moral Spaces: Rethinking Ethics and World Politics* (Minneapolis, MN: University of Minnesota Press, 1999).

Caputo, John, *Against Ethics: Contributions to a Poetics of Obligation with Constant Reference to Deconstruction* (Bloomington, IN: Indiana University Press, 1993).

Caputo, John (ed.), *Deconstruction in a Nutshell: A Conversation with Jacques Derrida* (New York, NY: Fordham University Press, 1997).

Caputo, John, *The Prayers and Tears of Jacques Derrida* (Bloomington, IN: Indiana University Press, 1997).

Cochran, Molly, 'Postmodernism, Ethics and International Political Theory', *Review of International Studies* 21: 3 (1995), 237–50.

Cochran, Molly, *Normative Theory in International Relations: A Pragmatic Approach* (Cambridge: Cambridge University Press, 1999).

Connolly, William E., *Identity\Difference: Democratic Negotiations of Political Paradox* (London: Cornell University Press, 1991).

Connolly, William E., *The Ethos of Pluralization* (London: University of Minnesota Press, 1995).

Connolly, William E., 'Suffering, Justice and the Politics of Becoming', in David Campbell and Michael Shapiro (eds), *Moral Spaces: Rethinking*

Ethics and World Politics (London and Minneapolis, MN: University of Minnesota Press, 1999), pp. 125–54.

Connolly, William E., 'Immanence, Abundance, Democracy', in Lars Tonder and Lasse Thomassen (eds), *Radical Democracy: Politics Between Abundance and Lack* (Manchester: Manchester University Press, 2005), pp. 239–56.

Couzens Hoy, David, *Critical Resistance: From Poststructuralism to Post-Critique* (Cambridge, MA: MIT Press, 2004).

Coward, Martin, 'Editor's Introduction', Special Issue: Jean-Luc Nancy, *Journal for Cultural Research* 9: 4 (2005), 323–9.

Critchley, Simon, *The Ethics of Deconstruction: Derrida and Levinas* (Edinburgh: Edinburgh University Press, 1992).

Critchley, Simon, *Ethics, Politics, Subjectivity: Essays on Derrida, Levinas and Contemporary French Thought* (London: Verso, 1999).

Critchley, Simon, 'Five Problems in Levinas's View of Politics and the Sketch of a Solution to Them', *Political Theory* 32: 2 (2004), 172–85.

Critchley, Simon, *Infinitely Demanding: Ethics of Commitment, Politics of Resistance* (London: Verso, 2007).

Dauphinee, Elizabeth, *Finding the Other in Time: On Ethics, Responsibility and Representation*, Doctoral Thesis (Toronto: York University, 2005).

Dauphinee, Elizabeth, *The Ethics of Researching War: Looking for Bosnia* (Manchester: Manchester University Press, 2007).

Der Derian, James, 'Post-Theory: The Eternal Return of Ethics in International Relations', in Michael W. Doyle and G. John Ikenberry (eds), *New Thinking in International Relations Theory* (Boulder, CO: Westview Press, 1997), pp. 54–76.

Derrida, Jacques, *Writing and Difference* (London: Routledge, 1978).

Derrida, Jacques, *Limited Inc* (Evanston, IL: Northwestern University Press, 1988).

Derrida, Jacques, 'Some Statements and Truisms about Neologisms, Newisms, Postisms, Parasitisms, and Other Small Seismisms', in D. Carroll (ed.), *The States of 'Theory': History, Art, and Critical Discourse* (New York, NY: Columbia University Press, 1990), pp. 63–94.

Derrida, Jacques, '"Eating well" or the Calculation of the Subject: An Interview with Jacques Derrida', in Eduardo Cadava, Peter Connor and Jean-Luc Nancy (eds), *Who Comes After the Subject* (London: Routledge, 1991), pp. 96–119.

Derrida, Jacques, 'Force of Law', in Drucilla Cornell, Michel Rosenfield and David Gray Carlson (eds), *Deconstruction and the Possibility of Justice* (London: Routledge, 1992), pp. 3–67.

Derrida, Jacques, *The Other Heading: Reflections on Today's Europe*, trans. Pascale-Anne Brault and Michael B. Naas (Bloomington, IN: Indiana University Press, 1992).

Derrida, Jacques, *The Gift of Death*, trans. David Wills (London: University of Chicago Press, 1995).

Derrida, Jacques, 'Remarks on Deconstruction and Pragmatism', in Chantal Mouffe (ed.), *Deconstruction and Pragmatism: Simon Critchley, Jacques Derrida, Ernesto Laclau and Richard Rorty* (London: Routledge, 1996), pp. 77–90.

Derrida, Jacques, 'On Responsibility: Interview with Jonathan Dronsfield, Nick Midgley, Adrian Wilding', in Jonathan Dronsfield and Nick Midgley (eds), Special Issue: Responsibilities of Deconstruction, *PLI: Warwick Journal of Philosophy* 6 ([1993] 1997), 19–35.

Derrida, Jacques, 'Perhaps or Maybe', in Jonathan Dronsfield and Nick Midgley (eds), Special Issue: Responsibilities of Deconstruction, *PLI: Warwick Journal of Philosophy* 6 (1997), 1–18.

Derrida, Jacques, 'Politics and Friendship: A Discussion with Jacques Derrida' (University of Sussex: Centre for Modern French Thought, 1997), available at http://www.sussex.ac.uk/Units/frenchthought/derrida.htm (accessed 7 October 2006).

Derrida, Jacques, 'Villanova Roundtable', in John D. Caputo (ed.), *Deconstruction in a Nutshell: A Conversation with Jacques Derrida* (New York, NY: Fordham University Press, 1997), pp. 1–30.

Derrida, Jacques, *Adieu: to Emmanuel Levinas* (Stanford, CA: Stanford University Press, 1999).

Derrida, Jacques, 'Hospitality, Justice and Responsibility: A Dialogue with Jacques Derrida', in Richard Kearney and Mark Dooley (eds), *Questioning Ethics: Contemporary Debates in Philosophy* (London: Routledge, 1999), pp. 65–83.

Derrida, Jacques, *Deconstruction Engaged: The Sydney Seminars*, Paul Patton and Terry Smith (eds) (Sydney: Power Publications, 2001).

Derrida, Jacques, 'Deconstructions: The Im-Possible', in Sylvère Lotringer and Sande Cohen (eds), *French Theory in America* (London and New York, NY: Routledge, 2001) pp. 13–33.

Derrida, Jacques, *On Cosmopolitanism and Forgiveness*, trans. Mark Dooley and Michael Hughes (London: Routledge, 2001).

Derrida, Jacques, 'Autoimmunity: Real and Symbolic Suicides – A Dialogue with Jacques Derrida', in Giovanna Borradori (ed.), *Philosophy in a Time of Terror: Dialogues with Jürgen Habermas and Jacques Derrida* (London: University of Chicago Press, 2003), pp. 85–136.

Derrida, Jacques, *Paper Machine* (Stanford, CA: Stanford University Press, 2005).

Derrida, Jacques, *Rogues: Two Essays on Reason* (Stanford, CA: Stanford University Press, 2005).

Derrida, Jacques, *The Politics of Friendship*, trans. George Collins (London: Verso, [1994] 2005).

Derrida, Jacques and Bernard Stiegler, *Echographies of Television* (Cambridge: Polity Press, 2002).

Dillon, Michael, 'Another Justice', *Political Theory* 27: 2 (1999), 155–75.

Dooley, Mark, 'The Civic Religion of Social Hope: A Reply to Simon Critchley', *Philosophy and Social Criticism* 27: 5 (2001), 35–58.

Edkins, Jenny, *Poststructuralism and International Relations: Bringing the Political Back In* (Boulder, CO: Lynne Rienner, 1999).

Edkins, Jenny, *Whose Hunger: Concepts of Famine, Practices of Aid* (Minneapolis, MN: University of Minnesota Press, 2000).

Edkins, Jenny, 'Ethics and Practices of Engagement: Intellectuals as Experts', *International Relations* 19: 1 (2005), 64–9.

Edkins, Jenny, 'What it is to be Many: Subjecthood, Responsibility and Sacrifice in Derrida and Nancy', in Madeleine Fagan, Ludovic Glorieux, Indira Hašimbegović and Marie Suetsugu (eds), *Derrida: Negotiating the Legacy* (Edinburgh: Edinburgh University Press, 2007), pp. 172–92.

Franke, Mark F. N., 'Refusing an Ethical Approach to World Politics in Favour of Political Ethics', *European Journal of International Relations* 6: 3 (2000), 307–33.

George, Jim, 'Realist "Ethics", International Relations, and Post-Modernism: Thinking Beyond the Egoism-Anarchy Thematic', *Millennium* 24: 2 (1995), 195–223.

George, Larry, 'Pharmacotic War and the Ethical Dilemmas of Engagement', *International Relations* 19: 1 (2005), 115–25.

Hagglund, Martin, 'The Necessity of Discrimination: Disjoining Derrida and Levinas', *Diacritics* 34: 1 (2004), 40–71.

Howells, Christina, *Derrida: Deconstruction from Phenomenology to Ethics* (Cambridge: Polity Press, 1999).

Hutchings, Kimberley, 'The Possibility of Judgement: Moralizing and Theorizing in International Relations', *Review of International Studies* 18: 1 (1992), 51–62.

Jabri, Vivienne, 'Restyling the Subject of Responsibility in IR', *Millennium* 27: 3 (1998), 591–611.

James, Ian, 'On Interrupted Myth', *Journal of Cultural Research* 9: 4 (2005), 331–49.

James, Ian, *The Fragmentary Demand: An Introduction to the Philosophy of Jean-Luc Nancy* (Stanford, CA: Stanford University Press, 2006).

Kearney, Richard, *Strangers, Gods and Monsters: Interpreting Otherness* (London: Routledge, 2003).

Keenan, Thomas, *Fables of Responsibility: Aberrations and Predicaments in Ethics and Politics* (Stanford, CA: Stanford University Press, 1997).

Krasner, Stephen, 'The Accomplishments of International Political Theory', in Steve Smith, Ken Booth and Marysia Zalewski (eds), *International*

Theory: Positivism and Beyond (Cambridge: Cambridge University Press, 1996), pp. 108–27.

Lacoue-Labarthe, Phillipe and Jean-Luc Nancy, *Retreating the Political* (London: Routledge, 1997).

Levinas, Emmanuel, *Ethics and Infinity: Conversations with Phillipe Nemo*, trans. R. Cohen (Pittsburgh, PA: Duquesne University Press, 1985).

Levinas, Emmanuel, 'Peace and Proximity', in Adriaan Peperzak, Simon Critchley and Robert Bernasconi (eds), *Emmanuel Levinas: Basic Philosophical Writings* (Indianapolis, IN: Indiana University Press, [1984] 1996), pp. 161–71.

Levinas, Emmanuel, 'Substitution', in Adriaan Peperzak, Simon Critchley and Robert Bernasconi (eds), *Emmanuel Levinas: Basic Philosophical Writings* (Indianapolis, IN: Indiana University Press, [1968] 1996), pp. 79–97.

Levinas, Emmanuel, 'Transcendence and Height', in Adriaan Peperzak, Simon Critchley and Robert Bernasconi (eds), *Emmanuel Levinas: Basic Philosophical Writings* (Indianapolis, IN: Indiana University Press, [1962] 1996), pp. 11–32.

Levinas, Emmanuel, 'Being-For-The-Other', in Jill Robbins (ed.), *Is it Righteous to Be? Interviews with Emmanuel Levinas* (Stanford, CA: Stanford University Press, [1989] 2001), pp. 114–20.

Levinas, Emmanuel, 'Being-Toward-Death and "Thou Shalt Not Kill"', in Jill Robbins (ed.), *Is it Righteous to Be? Interviews with Emmanuel Levinas* (Stanford, CA: Stanford University Press, [1986] 2001), pp. 130–9.

Levinas, Emmanuel, 'Interview with François Poirié', in Jill Robbins (ed.), *Is it Righteous to Be? Interviews with Emmanuel Levinas* (Stanford, CA: Stanford University Press, [1986] 2001), pp. 23–84.

Levinas, Emmanuel, 'Interview with Salomon Malka', in Jill Robbins (ed.), *Is it Righteous to Be? Interviews with Emmanuel Levinas* (Stanford, CA: Stanford University Press, [1984] 2001), pp. 93–105.

Levinas, Emmanuel, 'Philosophy, Justice, and Love', in Jill Robbins (ed.), *Is it Righteous to Be? Interviews with Emmanuel Levinas* (Stanford, CA: Stanford University Press, [1983] 2001), pp. 165–81.

Levinas, Emmanuel, 'Responsibility and Substitution', in Jill Robbins (ed.), *Is it Righteous to Be? Interviews with Emmanuel Levinas* (Stanford, CA: Stanford University Press, [1988] 2001), pp. 228–33.

Levinas, Emmanuel, 'The Other, Utopia, and Justice', in Jill Robbins (ed.), *Is it Righteous to Be? Interviews with Emmanuel Levinas* (Stanford, CA: Stanford University Press, [1988] 2001), pp. 200–10.

Levinas, Emmanuel, 'The Proximity of the Other', in Jill Robbins (ed.), *Is it Righteous to Be? Interviews with Emmanuel Levinas* (Stanford, CA: Stanford University Press, [1986] 2001), pp. 211–18.

Levinas, Emmanuel, 'The Vocation of the Other', in Jill Robbins (ed.), *Is it Righteous to Be? Interviews with Emmanuel Levinas* (Stanford, CA: Stanford University Press, [1988] 2001), pp. 105–13.

Levinas, Emmanuel, 'Who Shall Not Prophesy?', in Jill Robbins (ed.), *Is it Righteous to Be? Interviews with Emmanuel Levinas* (Stanford, CA: Stanford University Press, [1985] 2001), pp. 219–27.

Levinas, Emmanuel, *Otherwise Than Being or Beyond Essence* (Pittsburgh, PA: Duquesne University Press, [1981] 2004).

Levinas, Emmanuel, *Totality and Infinity: An Essay on Exteriority*, trans. A. Lingis (Pittsburgh, PA: Duquesne University Press, [1961] 2005).

Levinas, Emmanuel and Richard Kearney, 'Dialogue with Emmanuel Levinas', in Richard Cohen (ed.), *Face to Face with Levinas* (Albany, NY: State University of New York Press, 1986), pp. 13–34.

May, Todd, *Reconsidering Difference: Nancy, Derrida, Levinas and Deleuze* (Pennsylvania, PA: Pennsylvania University Press, 1997).

Mouffe, Chantal, 'Deconstruction, Pragmatism and the Politics of Democracy', in Chantal Mouffe (ed.), *Deconstruction and Pragmatism* (London: Routledge, 1996), pp. 1–12.

Nancy, Jean-Luc, 'Of Being-in-Common', in Miami Theory Collective (ed.), *Community at Loose Ends* (Minneapolis, MN: University of Minnesota Press, 1991), pp. 1–12.

Nancy, Jean-Luc, *The Inoperative Community* (London: University of Minnesota Press, 1991).

Nancy, Jean-Luc, *The Birth to Presence*, trans. Brian Holmes and others (Stanford, CA: Stanford University Press, 1993).

Nancy, Jean-Luc, *The Sense of the World* (Minneapolis, MN: Minnesota University Press, 1997).

Nancy, Jean-Luc, *Being Singular Plural* (Stanford, CA: Stanford University Press, 2000).

Nancy, Jean-Luc, *A Finite Thinking* (Stanford, CA: Stanford University Press, 2003).

Nancy, Jean-Luc, *The Ground of the Image* (New York, NY: Fordham University Press, 2005).

Nancy, Jean-Luc, 'The Insufficiency of "Values" and the Necessity of "Sense"', *Journal for Cultural Research* 9: 4 (2005), 437–41.

Nancy, Jean-Luc, *The Creation of the World or Globalization* (Albany, NY: The State University of New York Press, 2007).

Nancy, Jean-Luc, *Philosophical Chronicles*, trans. Franson Manjali (New York, NY: Fordham University Press, 2008).

Norris, Andrew, 'Jean-Luc Nancy and the Myth of the Common', *Constellations* 7: 2 (2000), 272–95.

Odysseos, Louiza, 'Dangerous Ontologies: The Ethos of Survival and Ethical Theorizing in International Relations', *Review of International Studies* 28: 2 (2002), 403–18.

Odysseos, Louiza, 'On the Way to Global Ethics? Cosmopolitanism, "Ethical" Selfhood and Otherness', *European Journal of Political Theory* 2: 2 (2003), 183–207.

Patrick, Morag, *Derrida, Responsibility and Politics* (Aldershot: Ashgate, 1997).

Peperzak, Adriaan, 'Preface', in Adriaan Peperzak, Simon Critchley and Robert Bernasconi (eds), *Emmanuel Levinas: Basic Philosophical Writings* (Indianapolis, IN: Indiana University Press, 1996), pp. vii–xv.

Perpich, Diane, 'A Singular Justice: Ethics and Politics between Levinas and Derrida', *Philosophy Today* 42 (January 1998), 59–71.

Pin-Fat, Véronique, *Universality, Ethics and International Relations: A Grammatical Reading* (Oxon and New York, NY: Routledge, 2010).

Plant, Bob, 'Doing Justice to the Derrida-Levinas Connection: A Response to Mark Dooley', *Philosophy and Social Criticism* 29: 4 (2003), 427–50.

Prozorov, Sergei, 'X/Xs: Toward a General Theory of the Exception', *Alternatives: Global, Local, Political* 30: 1 (2005), 81–112.

Robbins, Jill, 'Introduction', in Jill Robbins (ed.), *Is it Righteous to Be? Interviews with Emmanuel Levinas* (Stanford, CA: Stanford University Press, 2001), pp. 1–20.

Shapiro, Michael J., 'The Ethics of Encounter: Unreading, Unmapping the Imperium', in David Campbell and Michael J. Shapiro (eds), *Moral Spaces: Rethinking Ethics and World Politics* (Minneapolis, MN: University of Minnesota Press, 1999), pp. 57–90.

Simmons, William, 'The Third: Levinas' Theoretical Move from An-Archical Ethics to the Realm of Justice and Politics', *Journal of Philosophy and Social Criticism* 25: 6 (1999), 83–10.

Smith, Daniel, 'Deleuze and Derrida, Immanence and Transcendence: Two Directions in Recent French Thought', in Paul Patton and John Protevi (eds), *Between Deleuze and Derrida* (London: Continuum, 2003), pp. 46–67.

Thomson, Alex, *Deconstruction and Democracy: Derrida's Politics of Friendship* (London: Continuum, 2005).

Walker, R. B. J., *Inside/Outside: International Relations as Political Theory* (Cambridge: Cambridge University Press, 1992).

Watkin, Christopher, 'A Different Alterity: Jean-Luc Nancy's "Singular Plural"', *Paragraph* 30: 2 (2007), 50–64.

White, Stephen K., 'Poststructuralism and Political Reflection', *Political Theory* 6: 2 (1988), 186–208.

Williams, Caroline, *Contemporary French Philosophy: Modernity and the Persistence of the Subject* (London: Athlone Press, 2001).

Zalewski, Marysia, 'All These Theories Yet the Bodies Keep Piling Up', in Steve Smith, Ken Booth and Marysia Zalewski (eds), *International*

Theory: Positivism and Beyond (Cambridge: Cambridge University Press, 1996), pp. 340–53.

Zehfuss, Maja, 'Subjectivity and Vulnerability: On the War with Iraq', *International Politics* 44: 1 (2007), 58–71.

Zehfuss, Maja, *Wounds of Memory: The Politics of War in Germany* (Cambridge: Cambridge University Press, 2007).

Index